SPIRITS OF THE BORDER IV:

THE HISTORY AND MYSTERY OF NEW MEXICO

BY

KEN HUDNALL
&
SHARON HUDNALL

Omega Press
El Paso, Texas

2\SPIRITS OF THE BORDER

Spirits of the Border IV: The History and Mystery of New Mexico

Copyright © 2005 Ken Hudnall

OMEGA PRESS
An Imprint of Omega Communications Group, Inc.

For Information address:

Omega Press
5823 N. Mesa, #823
El Paso, Texas 79912

Or

http://www.kenhudnall.com

First Edition

Printed in the United States of America

OTHER WORKS BY THE SAME AUTHOR
UNDER THE NAME KEN HUDNALL

SERIES

MANHATTAN CONSPIRACY
Blood on the Apple
Capital Crimes
Angel of Death
Confrontation

THE OCCULT CONNECTION
U.F.O.S, Secret Societies and Ancient Gods
The Hidden Race

DARKNESS
When Darkness Falls
Fear The Darkness

SPIRITS OF THE BORDER
The History and Mystery of El Paso Del Norte
The History and Mystery of Fort Bliss, Texas
The History and Mystery of The Rio Grande

THE ESTATE SALE MURDERS
Dead Man's Diary

As ROBERT K. HUDNALL

No Safe Haven: Homeland Insecurity

The Northwood Conspiracy

DEDICATION

As with all of my books, the one whose support has been most important to the completion of the project has been my lovely wife, Sharon. Without her assistance, all of my ideas would remain just ideas.

6\SPIRITS OF THE BORDER

TABLE OF CONTENTS

PREFACE

The state of New Mexico is called the Land of Enchantment and for very good reason. There is more mystery surrounding certain potions of this state than canbe recorded in one single book. Many events certainly support the idea that nothing short of enchantment and magic plays a part in what happens in this area.

Though I have recorded over one hundred hauntings in these pages, this listing is certainly not exhautive. There are a large number of events that I just did not have sufficient information about to make it worth recording. However, research continues and there will certainly be another installment in the story of the spirits that haunt this border state.

Ken Hudnall
El Paso, Texas
2005

14\SPIRITS OF THE BORDER

PART I

A MOST UNUSUAL PLACE

16\SPIRITS OF THE BORDER

CHAPTER ONE

THE LAND OF ENCHANTMENT

New Mexico has long been called a timeless land of ancient cultural traditions and striking environmental diversity. For thousands of years, man has traveled through this unusually beautiful land leaving footprints and clues to a rich and colorful past. Some of the earliest known inhabitants included the Paleo-Indians of the Folsom Period who wandered into the area hunting the animals upon which their very survival depended. Some of which have now been extinct for more than 10,000 years.

The earliest settlers of this land of mystery are believed to be tribes of Indians that farmed the fertile land along the Rio Grande, producing corn, beans and squash. One of these early civilizations that settled in this region was the mysterious race that is today called the Anasazi. We do not know what this early civilization called itself, as the word "Anasazi" is a Navajo word meaning "Ancient Ones." They are thought to be ancestors of the modern Pueblo Indians, inhabited the Four Corners country of southern Utah, southwestern Colorado, northwestern New Mexico, and northern Arizona from about A.D. 200 to A.D. 1300, leaving a heavy accumulation of house remains and debris.

Recent research has traced the Anasazi to the "archaic" peoples who practiced a wandering, hunting, and food-gathering life-style from about 6000 B.C. until some of them began to develop into the distinctive Anasazi culture in the last millennium B.C. During the last two centuries B.C., this historically wandering people began to supplement their food gathering with maize horticulture. By A.D. 1200 horticulture had assumed a significant role in the economy[1].

Because their culture changed continually (and not always gradually), researchers have divided the occupation into periods, each with its characteristic complex of settlement and artifact styles. Since 1927 the most widely accepted nomenclature has been the "Pecos Classification," which is generally applicable to the whole Anasazi Southwest. Although originally intended to represent a series of developmental stages, rather than periods, the Pecos Classification has come to be used as a period sequence:

- Basket maker I: pre-1000 B.C. (an obsolete synonym for Archaic)
- Basket maker II: c. 1000 B.C. to A.D. 450
- Basket maker III: c. A.D. 450 to 750
- Pueblo I: c. A.D. 750 to 900
- Pueblo II: c. A.D. 900 to 1150
- Pueblo III: c. A.D. 1150 to 1300
- Pueblo IV: c. A.D. 1300 to 1600
- Pueblo V: c. A.D. 1600 to present (historic Pueblo)

The last two periods are not important to this discussion, as the Pueblo peoples had left Utah by the end of the Pueblo III period.

As the Anasazi settled into their village/farming lifestyle, recognizable regional variants or subcultures emerged, which can be usefully combined into two larger groups. The eastern branches of the Anasazi culture include the Mesa Verde Anasazi of southeastern Utah and southwestern Colorado, and the Chaco Anasazi of northwestern New Mexico. The western Anasazi include the Kayenta Anasazi of northeastern Arizona and the Virgin Anasazi of southwestern Utah and northwestern Arizona. To the north of the Anasazi peoples - north of the Colorado and Escalante rivers - Utah was the home of a heterogeneous group of small-village dwellers known collectively as the Fremont.

Although they continued to move around in pursuit of seasonally available foods, the earliest Anasazi concentrated increasing amounts of effort on the growing of crops and the storage of surpluses. They made exquisite baskets and sandals, for which reason they have come to be known as "Basket makers."

They stored their goods (and often their dead) in deep pits and circular cists - small pits often lined with upright stone slabs and roofed over with a platform of poles, twigs, grass, slabs or rocks, and mud. Basket maker II houses were somewhat more sturdy than those of their Archaic predecessors, being rather like a Paiute winter wickiup or a Navajo hogan. Very few have been excavated.

---

[1] This research was conducted by Nicole Torres and Steven Stuart and reported at http://www.crystalinks.com/anasazi.html

By A.D. 500 the early Anasazi peoples had settled into the well-developed farming village cultural stage that we know as Basket maker III. Although they probably practiced some seasonal traveling and continued to make considerable use of wild resources, they primarily had become farmers living in small villages.

Their houses were well-constructed pit structures, consisting of a hogan-like superstructure built over a knee-or waist-deep pit, often with a small second room or antechamber on the south or southeast side.

Settlements of this time period are scattered widely over the canyons and mesas of southern Utah; they consist of small hamlets of one to three houses and occasionally villages of a dozen or more structures.

By about A.D. 700 evidence of the development of politico-religious mechanisms of village organization and integration appears in the form of large, communal pit structures. One such structure, with a diameter of forty feet, has been excavated next to the old highway in Recapture Creek by archaeologists from Brigham Young University.

Three important changes took place before A.D. 750: the old atlatl (spear thrower) that had been used to propel darts (small spears) from time immemorial was replaced by the bow and arrow; the bean was added to corn and squash to form a major supplement to the diet; and the people began to make pottery. By A.D. 600 the Anasazi were producing quantities of two types of pottery - gray utility ware and black-on-white painted ware.

By A.D. 750 these farming and pottery-making people in their stable villages were on the threshold of the lifestyle that we think of as being typically Puebloan, and from this time on we call them Pueblos.

Perhaps the most significant developments in Pueblo I times (A.D. 750 to 900) were:

- the replacement of pit house habitations with large living rooms on the surface
- 2) the development of a sophisticated ventilator-deflector system for ventilating pit rooms
- 3) the growth of the San Juan red ware pottery complex (red-on-orange, then black-on-orange, pottery manufactured in southeastern Utah)
- 4) some major shifts in settlement distribution, with populations concentrating in certain areas while abandoning others.

The two-hundred-fifty-year period subsequent to A.D. 900 is known as Pueblo II. The tendency toward aggregation evidenced in Pueblo I sites reversed itself in this period, as the people dispersed themselves widely over the land in thousands of small stone houses.

During Pueblo II, good stone masonry replaced the pole-and-adobe architecture of Pueblo I, the surface rooms became year-round habitations, and the pit houses (now completely subterranean) probably assumed the largely ceremonial role of the pueblo kiva. It was during this period that small cliff granaries became popular.

The house style known as the unit pueblo, which had its beginning during the previous period, became the universal settlement form during this period. In the unit pueblo the main house is a block of rectangular living and storage rooms located on the surface immediately north or northwest of an underground kiva; immediately southeast of this is a trash and ash dump or midden.

The red ware pottery industry continued to flourish, as a fine, red-slipped ware with black designs was traded throughout much of the Colorado Plateau. During the middle-to-late Pueblo II period, however, the red ware tradition ended in the country north of the San Juan River, although it blossomed in the area south of the river.

Virtually all of the red or orange pottery found in San Juan County sites postdating A.D. 1000 was made south of the San Juan River around Navajo Mountain in the Kayenta Anasazi country. The reasons for this shift are unknown, and the problem is a fascinating one. Production and refinement of the black-on-white and the gray (now decorated by indented corrugation) wares continued uninterrupted in both areas, but the red ware tradition migrated across what appears to have been an ethnic boundary.

The styles of stone artifacts also changed somewhat during Pueblo II. The beautiful barbed and tanged "Christmas tree" style point that had been popular since late Basket maker III times was replaced first by a corner-notched style with flaring stem and rounded base, then by a triangular style with side notches.

Also, by the end of the period, the old trough-shaped metate that had been popular for half a millennium was replaced by a flat slab form with no raised sides. The change in grinding technology appears to have accompanied a change from a hard, shattering, flint type of corn to a soft, non-shattering flour corn. This permitted use of smaller metates, and thus also increased the efficient use of the floor space.

During the 1100s and 1200s the Anasazi population began once again to aggregate into large villages. This period is known as Pueblo III, and it lasted until the final abandonment of the Four Corners country by the Anasazi during the late 1200s. Numerous small unit pueblos continued to be occupied during this period, but there was a tendency for them to become more massive and to enclose the kivas within the room block.

A number of very large villages developed. It was during this period that most of the cliff villages such as the famous examples at Mesa Verde National Park and Navajo National Monument were built.

During Pueblo III times the Mesa Verde Anasazi developed the thick-walled, highly polished, incredibly beautiful pottery known as Mesa Verde Black-on-White.

They also continued to make corrugated gray pottery. Red wares, often with two- or three-color designs continued to be imported north of the river from the Kayenta country. Arrowheads continued in the triangular, side-notched form, but were often smaller than those of the previous period.

Starting sometime after A.D. 1250 the Anasazi moved out of San Juan County, often walking away from their settlements as though they intended to return shortly. However, they never returned. Why did they leave behind their beautiful cooking pots and baskets? Perhaps because they had no means to transport them. When forced to migrate a long distance, it was more efficient to leave the bulky items and replace them after they reached their destination.

We do know that they moved south. Classic late Mesa Verde-style settlements can still be recognized in New Mexico and Arizona, in high, defensible locations in areas where the local Anasazi sites look quite different. By A.D. 1400 almost all the Anasazi from throughout the Southwest had aggregated into large pueblos scattered through the drainages of the Little Colorado and Rio Grande rivers in Arizona and New Mexico. Their descendants are still there in the few surviving pueblos.

By the end of the 13th century, the Anasazi had completely abandoned their high-walled cities in northwestern New Mexico and the rest of the Four Corners area and drifted south where, along with the farmers from the Rio Grande, they developed the sophisticated Pueblo communities.

Shortly before the arrival of the Spanish, the Athapascan tribes entered the Southwest. Divided into two related groups, the Apache and the Navajo, the Athapascans established permanent villages only in the last 200 years.

Explorer Vasquez de Coronado trekked through New Mexico in 1540. In search of treasure, and convinced that the adobe pueblos were the legendary Seven Cities of Cibola, Coronado had orders to conquer the Indians and claim their riches. Failing to find the fabled gold, however, he and his men returned to New Spain without any newly won wealth.

Don Juan de Oñate made the first successful exploration of Mexico del Norte's wilderness. In 1598 he marched up the Rio Grande claiming land for Spain, accompanied by troops, colonists and cattle.

Santa Fe was founded as the capital in 1609 by New Mexico's third governor, Don Pedro de Peralta. For the next 70 years the Spanish pushed on with sword and cross, building missions and converting Indians to the Catholic religion.

The first church in North America was constructed in 1598 at San Juan Pueblo, 30 miles north of Santa Fe. Within the first quarter of the 17th century, 50 churches had been built in New Mexico. These churches, which predate the great missions along the coast of California by a century and a half, are beautiful examples of Spanish Colonial architecture and provide a glimpse of the earliest history of American culture.

Some Indians accepted Christianity, others found it oppressive. By the middle of the 17th century, there was growing discontent among the Pueblo people. On Aug. 10, 1680, after years of careful planning, the tribes rose up and drove the Spanish out of Santa Fe in the great Pueblo Revolt. By 1692, however, the Spanish had returned. Don Diego De Vargas, the newly appointed governor and captain-general of New Mexico, began to reconquer the northern pueblos, a task that took four years.

New Mexico remained under Spanish rule for another 125 years until 1821 when Mexico won its independence from Spain. Soon after, another passage in New Mexico history was born, the Santa Fe Trail. Running from Missouri to Santa Fe, the trail opened trade with the U.S. and brought new lifestyles, money and settlers to New Mexico.

The United States declared war on Mexico in 1846. Shortly thereafter, U.S. General Stephen Watts Kearny maneuvered his troops down the Santa Fe Trail and declared New Mexico an American territory Due to the help of former Consul to Mexico Magoffin, Mexican forces surrendered New Mexico without a short being fired.

During the U.S. Civil War, federal troops, aided by the New Mexico Volunteers, foiled a Confederate invasion at Apache Pass near present-day Glorrietta.

In the late 1880s, railroad companies laid their tracks across New Mexico, bringing with them improved commerce and access to new markets. The beef industry boomed, and cattle barons like John Chisum trailed longhorns in from Texas, creating vast cattle kingdoms on the southeastern plains.

Chisum was also associated with events leading to the Lincoln County War, a bloody merchant conflict that sparked the brief outlaw career of Billy the Kid and involved even territorial Gov. Lew Wallace, author of the novel Ben Hur.

Although New Mexico was colonized nearly 25 years before the Pilgrims' arrival at Plymouth Rock, it did not achieve statehood until Jan. 6, 1912, when it was admitted to the Union as the 47th state. Since that time, New Mexico has experienced a whirlwind of growth and change.

Two regiments from New Mexico endured the Bataan Death March during World War II, while Navajo "code talkers" used their native language to send military messages that were incomprehensible to the Japanese. On July 16, 1945, the first atomic bomb was detonated at Trinity Site near Alamogordo, a dramatic opening to the nuclear age.

In the decades between 1940 and 1980, New Mexico's population tripled. The state now boasts more than a million and a half inhabitants, a third of whom live in Albuquerque, New Mexico's largest city.

Centuries-old agricultural and ranching traditions exist alongside a rapidly developing electronics industry. Los Alamos National Laboratory and Sandia National Laboratory in Albuquerque are leaders in the defense industry, taking giant steps forward in energy-related and high-tech computer research.

Today, New Mexico continues to lure people with its clear skies and abundance of sunshine. The limitless landscapes encourage people both to retrace the paths of New Mexico's rich heritage and to leave their own footprints on the pages of the state's rich history.

CHAPTER TWO

NEW MEXICO'S HIDDEN HISTORY

As if New Mexico's known history is not fascinating enough, there is also the hidden history that is normally the fodder for conspiracy theories of one type of another. There have been stories coming out of this state about everything from crashed UFOs and recovered alien bodies to vast treasures being hidden in remote parts of the state. No matter which brand of conspiracy theory someone may adhere to, there is something related that can be found in the state of New Mexico

UNDERGROUND ALIEN BASES?

Certainly no book on New Mexico would be complete without at least touching on all of the many stories about secret underground alien bases that are supposed to be hidden around the state.

Buried deep in the desert near Dulce, New Mexico are caverns allegedly populated by aliens. Numerous abductees have reported being taken to the base to be examined, and most have seen members of various branches of our military, primarily United States Air Force personnel interacting with these mysterious aliens. According to some reports, the aliens are carrying on genetic experimentations, in secret agreement with our government.

In 1969, according to ex-Naval Intelligence Officer Milton Cooper, a confrontation took place between the aliens and our own scientist in which 60 humans were killed. This site is said to be connected to the installations at Los Alamos by an underground shuttle.

However, let me stress that the U.S. government, especially the United States Air Force, denies any knowledge of any alien base, joint genetic experiments, or any deaths of either civilian and/or military personnel connected to this perhaps, non-existent base.

However, and with that being said, consider the following which came from a website called ABOVE TOP SECRET.COM[2]. On the home page of this very interesting website is an expose' regarding the alleged underground alien base located at Dulce, New Mexico.

EXTRA-TERRESTRIAL INSTALLATION
IN DULCE, NEW MEXICO

THE FOLLOWING MATERIAL COMES FROM PEOPLE WHO KNOW THE DULCE (UNDERGROUND) BASE EXISTS. THEY ARE PEOPLE WHO WORKED IN THE LABS; ABDUCTEES TAKEN TO THE BASE; PEOPLE WHO ASSISTED IN THE CONSTRUCTION; INTELLIGENCE PERSONAL (NSA, CIA ,FBI etc.) AND UFO / INNER-EARTH RESEARCHERS.

Located almost two miles beneath Archuleta Mesa on the Jicarrilla Apache Indian Reservation near Dulce, New Mexico is an installation classified so secret, its existence is one of the least known in the world. Here is Earth's first and main joint United States Government/alien biogenetics laboratory. Others exist in Colorado, Nevada, and Arizona.

The multi-level facility at Dulce goes down for at least seven known levels, and is reported to have a central HUB which is controlled by base security. The level of security required to access different sections rises as one goes further down the facility. There are over 3000 real-time video cameras throughout the complex at high-security locations (entrances and exits). There are over 100 secret exits near and around Dulce. Many of the secret entrances are around Archuleta Mesa, while others to the south around Dulce Lake and some are even as far east as Lindrith. Deep sections of the complex also connect into natural cavern systems that underlie this region.

The Grey Species

Most of the aliens reside on sub-levels 5, 6, and 7 with alien housing on level 5. The alien species which control the majority of the complex are the Greys, a devious race, now considered an enemy of the New World Order. In the Fifties, the Greys began taking large numbers of humans for experiments. By the Sixties, the rate was speeded up and they began getting careless and self-involved. By the Seventies, their true intentions became very obvious, but the "Special Group" of the Government still kept covering up for them. By the Eighties, the Government realized there was no defense against the Greys. So,

---

[2] http://www.abovetopsecret.com/pages/dulce.html.

programs were enacted to prepare the public for open contact with non-human ET beings.

Perhaps there is a possible ally, the Reptoids are an enemy species of the Greys and as a result their relationship is in a constant state of tension. The Greys only known enemy is the Reptillian Race, and they are on their way to Earth.

A man named Thomas C., famous for stealing the so-called "Dulce Papers", says that there are over 18,000 short "greys" at the Dulce facility. He also has stated how a colleague of his had come face-to-face with a 6-foot tall Reptoid which had materialized in his house. The Reptoid showed a great interest in research maps of New Mexico and Colorado which were on the wall. The maps were full of colored push-pins and markers to indicate sites of animal mutilations, caverns, locations of high UFO activity, repeated flight paths, abduction sites, ancient ruins, and suspected alien underground bases.

Some forces in the Government want the public to be aware of what is happening. Other forces (The Collaborators) want to continue making "whatever deals are necessary" for an Elite few to survive the conflicts.

Cloning Humans (by Humans) for Slave Hybrids

The Secret Government cloned humans by a process perfected in the world's largest and most advanced bio-genetic research facility, Los Alamos. The elite humans now have their own disposable slave-race. Like the alien Greys, the US Government secretly impregnated females, and then removed the hybrid fetus after a three month time period, before accelerating their growth in laboratories. Biogenetic (DNA Manipulation) programming is then instilled - they are implanted and controlled at a distance through RF (Radio Frequency) transmissions.

Many Humans are also being implanted with brain transceivers. These act as telepathic communication "channels" and telemetric brain manipulation devices. This network was developed and initiated by DARPA. Two of the procedures were RHIC (Radio-Hypnotic Intercerebral Control) and EDOM (Electronic Dissolution of Memory).

They also developed ELF and EM wave propagation equipment which affect the nerves and can cause nausea, fatigue, irritability, even death. This research into biodynamic relationships within organisms has produced a technology that can change the genetic structure and heal.

Overt and Covert Research

U.S. Energy Secretary John Herrington named the Lawrence Berkeley Laboratory and New Mexico's Los Alamos National Laboratory to house new advanced genetic research centers as part of a project to decipher the human genome. The genome holds the genetically coded instructions that guide the transformation of a single cell, a fertilized egg, into a biological organism.

"The Human Genome Project may well have the greatest direct impact on humanity of any scientific initiative before us today", said David Shirley, Director of the Berkeley Laboratory.

Covertly, this research has been going on for years at the Dulce bio-genetics labs. Level 6 is hauntingly known by employees as "Nightmare Hall". It holds the genetic labs at Dulce. Reports from workers, who have seen bizarre experimentation, are as follows:

"I have seen multi-legged 'humans' that look like half-human/half-octopus. Also reptilian-humans, and furry creatures that have hands like humans and cries like a baby, it mimics human words... also huge mixture of lizard-humans in cages. There are fish, seals, birds and mice that can barely be considered those species. There are several cages (and vats) of winged-humanoids, grotesque bat-like creatures...but 3 1/2 to 7 feet tall. I have also seen Gargoyle-like beings and Draco-Reptoids."

"Level 7 is worse, row after row of thousands of humans and human mixtures in cold storage. Here too are embryo storage vats of humanoids in various stages of development. I frequently encountered humans in cages, usually dazed or drugged, but sometimes they cried and begged for help. We were told they were hopelessly insane, and involved in high risk drug tests to cure insanity. We were told to never try to speak to them at all. At the beginning we believed that story. Finally in 1978 a small group of workers discovered the truth. It began the Dulce Wars".

When the truth was evident that humans were being produced from abducted females, impregnated against there will, a secret resistance group formed. This did little though, over time they were assassinated or "died under mysterious circumstances".

As previously stated, there are over 18,000 "aliens" at the Dulce complex. In late 1979, there was a confrontation, primarily over weaponry and the majority of human scientists and military personnel were killed. The facility was closed for a while, but is currently active.

Human and animal abductions slowed in the mid-1980s, when the Livermore Berkeley Labs began production of artificial blood for Dulce. William Cooper states: "A clash occurred where in 66 people, of our people, from the National Recon Group, the DELTA group, which is responsible for security of all alien connected projects, were killed."

Members of the DELTA Group (within Intelligence Support Activity) have been seen with badges which have a black Triangle on a red background. DELTA is the fourth letter of the Greek alphabet. It has the form of a triangle, and figures prominently in certain Masonic Signs. EACH BASE HAS ITS OWN SYMBOL. The Dulce Base symbol is a triangle with the Greek letter "Tau" (T) within it and then the symbol is inverted, so the triangle points down.

The Insignia of "a triangle and 3 lateral lines" has been seen on "Saucer (transport) Craft", The Tri-Lateral Symbol. Other symbols mark landing sights and alien craft.

Inside the Dulce Complex

Security Officers wear jumpsuits, with the Dulce Symbol on the front upper left side. The standard hand weapon at Dulce is a "Flash Gun", which is good against humans and aliens. The ID card (used in card slots, for the doors and elevators) has the Dulce Symbol above the ID photo. "Government Honchos" use cards with the Great Seal of the U.S. on it, stating the words New World Order in Latin.

After the second Level, everyone is weighed in the nude, and then given a uniform. Visitors are given an 'off white' uniform. In front of ALL sensitive areas are scales built under the doorway, by the door control. The person's card must match with the weight and code or the door won't open. Any discrepancy in weight (any change over three pounds) will summon security. No one is allowed to carry anything into or out of sensitive areas. All supplies are put through a security conveyor system. The Alien Symbol language appears a lot at the Facility.

During the construction of the facility (which was done in stages, over many years) the aliens assisted in the design and construction materials. Many of the things assembled by the workers were of a technology they could not understand, yet it would function when fully put together. Example: The elevators have no cables. They are controlled magnetically. The magnetic system is inside the walls.

There are no conventional electrical controls. All is controlled by advanced magnetism. That includes a magnetically induced (phosphorescent) illumination system. There are no regular light bulbs. All exits are magnetically controlled. It has been reported that, "If you place a large magnet on an entrance, it will affect an immediate interruption. They will have to come out and reset the system."

Mind Manipulation Experiments

Dulce has studied mind control implants, Bio-Psi Units, ELF devices capable of mood, sleep and heartbeat control.

DARPA is using these technologies to manipulate people. They establish 'The Projects', set priorities, coordinate efforts and guide the many participants in these undertakings. Related projects are studied at Sandia Base by "The Jason Group" (of 55 scientists). They have secretly harnessed the dark side of technology and hidden the beneficial technology from the public.

Other projects take place at the Groom Lake installation in Nevada, also known as Area 51. These projects include studies in: ELMINT (Electro-Magnetic

Intelligence), Code Empire, Code Eva, Program His (Hybrid Intelligence System), BW/CW, IRIS (Infrared Intruder System), BI-PASS, REP-TILES.

The studies on Level 4 at Dulce include Human-Aura research, as well as all aspects of dreams, hypnosis and telepathy. They know how to manipulate the bioplasmic body of humans. They can lower your heart beat, with deep sleep-inducing delta waves, induce a static shock, and then re-program via a neurological-computer link. They can introduce data and programmed reactions into your mind (information impregnation - the "Dream Library").

We are entering an era of the technologicalization of psychic powers. The development of techniques to enhance man/machine communications, nanotechnology, bio-technological micro-machines, PSI-War, E.D.O.M. (Electronic Dissolution of Memory), R.H.I.C. (Radio-Hypnotic Intra-Cerebral Control) and various forms of behavior control (by chemical agents, ultra-sonics, optical and other forms of EM radiation).

Is there a secret underground base in or around Dulce, New Mexico? I do not have an answer to that question, at least as of yet. This would certainly be an exciting topic for a new book about some of the mysteries of New Mexico. However, in the interim, let us look at another fascinating aspect of New Mexico's hidden history. This topic would be the very famous, or infamous crash of a UFO at Roswell, New Mexico.

THE CRASH AT ROSWELL, NEW MEXICO

According to all reports, in 1947 something crashed or was shot down just outside of Roswell, New Mexico. This incident has caused more controversy as to what really happened than most other UFO events in current history. According to many researchers, agents of the United States government came in and removed a mysterious craft and perhaps some alien bodies.

Rancher Mac Brazel reported finding portions of a crashed UFO on his ranch. The sheriff of Chaves County passed this information along to officials at Roswell Army Air Field (RAAF) and an investigation was begun by Maj. Jesse Marcel, an intelligence officer.

A press release was issued by RAAF about the flying saucer on July 8, 1947. The following day, the official story was changed by Army Air Force officials. (Both stories were reported in front page articles in the Roswell Daily Record.) This Roswell Daily Record web site lets you explore the various reports on what has been termed the "Roswell Incident," a subject that has generated many news reports, books and motion pictures[3].

Roswell Daily Record for July 8, 1947

---

[3] http://www.crystalinks.com/newmexico.html

The intelligence office of the 509th Bombardment group at Roswell Army Air Field announced at noon today, that the field has come into possession of a flying saucer.

According to information released by the department, over authority of Maj. J. A. Marcel, intelligence officer, the disk was recovered on a ranch in the Roswell vicinity, after an unidentified rancher had notified Sheriff Geo. Wilcox, here, that he had found the instrument on his premises.

Major Marcel and a detail from his department went to the ranch and recovered the disk, it was stated.

After the intelligence officer here had inspected the instrument it was flown to higher headquarters. The intelligence office stated that no details of the saucer's construction or its appearance had been revealed.

Mr. and Mrs. Dan Wilmot apparently were the only persons in Roswell who saw what they thought was a flying disk.

They were sitting on their porch at 105 South Penn. last Wednesday night at about ten o'clock when a large glowing object zoomed out of the sky from the southeast, going in a northwesterly direction at a high rate of speed.

Wilmot called Mrs. Wilmot's attention to it and both ran down into the yard to watch. It was in sight less then a minute, perhaps 40 or 50 seconds, Wilmot estimated.

Wilmot said that it appeared to him to be about 1,500 feet high and going fast. He estimated between 400 and 500 miles per hour.

In appearance it looked oval in shape like two inverted saucers, faced mouth to mouth, or like two old type washbowls placed, together in the same fashion. The entire body glowed as though light were showing through from inside, though not like it would inside, though not like it would be if a light were merely underneath.

From where he stood Wilmot said that the object looked to be about 5 feet in size, and making allowance for the distance it was from town he figured that it must have been 15 to 20 feet in diameter, though this was just a guess.

Wilmot said that he heard no sound but that Mrs. Wilmot said she heard a swishing sound for a very short time.

The object came into view from the southeast and disappeared over the treetops in the general vicinity of six mile hill.

Wilmot, who is one of the most respected and reliable citizens in town, kept the story to himself hoping that someone else would come out and tell about having seen one, but finally today decided that he would go ahead and tell about it. The announcement that the RAAF was in possession of one came only a few minutes after he decided to release the details of what he had seen.

Roswell Daily Record for July 9, 1947 - AP

An examination by the army revealed last night that mysterious objects found on a lonely New Mexico ranch was a harmless high-altitude weather balloon - not a grounded flying disk. Excitement was high until Brig. Gen. Roger M. Ramey, commander of the Eighth air forces with headquarters here cleared up the mystery.

The bundle of tinfoil, broken wood beams and rubber remnants of a balloon were sent here yesterday by army air transport in the wake of reports that it was a flying disk.

But the general said the objects were the crushed remains of a ray wind target used to determine the direction and velocity of winds at high altitudes.

Warrant Officer Irving Newton, forecaster at the army air forces weather station here said, "We use them because they go much higher than the eye can see."

The weather balloon was found several days ago near the center of New Mexico by Rancher W. W. Brazel. He said he didn't think much about it until he went into Corona, N. M. last Saturday and heard the flying disk reports.

He returned to his ranch, 85 miles northwest of Roswell, and recovered the wreckage of the balloon, which he had placed under some brush.

Then Brazel hurried back to Roswell, where he reported his find to the sheriff's office.

The sheriff called the Roswell air field and Maj. Jesse A. Marcel, 509th bomb group intelligence officer was assigned to the case.

Col. William H. Blanchard, commanding officer of the bomb group, reported the find to General Ramey and the object was flown immediately to the army air field here.

Ramey went on the air here last night to announce the New Mexico discovery was not a flying disk.

Newton said that when rigged up, the instrument "looks like a six-pointed star, is silvery in appearance and rises in the air like a kite."

In Roswell, the discovery set off a flurry of excitement.

Sheriff George Wilcox's telephone lines were jammed. Three calls came from England, one of them from The London Daily Mail, he said.

A public relations officer here said the balloon was in his office "and it'll probably stay right there."

Newton, who made the examination, said some 80 weather stations in the U. S. were using that type of balloon and that it could have come from any of them.

He said he had sent up identical balloons during the invasion of Okinawa to determine ballistics information for heavy guns.

Story 2

W. W. Brazel, 48, Lincoln county rancher living 30 miles south of Corona, today told his story of finding what the army at first described as a flying disk, but the publicity which attended his find caused him to add that if he ever found anything else short of a bomb, he sure wasn't going to say anything about it.

Brazel was brought here late yesterday by W. E. Whitmore, of radio station KGFL, had his picture taken and gave an interview to the Record and Jason Kellahin, sent here from the Albuquerque bureau of the Associated Press to cover the story. The picture he posed for was sent out over AP telephoto wire sending machine specially set up in the Record office by R. D. Adair, AP wire chief sent here from Albuquerque for the sole purpose of getting out his picture and that of sheriff George Wilcox, to whom Brazel originally gave the information of his find.

Brazel related that on June 14 he and an 8-year old son, Vernon, were about 7 or 8 miles from the ranch house of the J. B. Foster ranch, which he operates, when they came upon a large area of bright wreckage made up on rubber strips, tinfoil, a rather tough paper and sticks.

At the time Brazel was in a hurry to get his round made and he did not pay much attention to it. But he did remark about what he had seen and on July 4 he, his wife, Vernon and a daughter, Betty, age 14, went back to the spot and gathered up quite a bit of the debris.

The next day he first heard about the flying disks, and he wondered if what he had found might be the remnants of one of these.

Monday he came to town to sell some wool and while here he went to see Sheriff George Wilcox and "whispered kinda confidential like" that he might have found a flying disk.

Wilcox got in touch with the Roswell Army Air Field and Maj. Jesse A. Marcel and a man in plain clothes accompanied him home, where they picked up the rest of the pieces of the "disk" and went to his home to try to reconstruct it.

According to Brazel they simply could not reconstruct it at all. They tried to make a kite out of it, but could not do that and could not find any way to put it back together so that it could fit.

Then Major Marcel brought it to Roswell and that was the last he heard of it until the story broke that he had found a flying disk.

Brazel said that he did not see it fall from the sky and did not see it before it was torn up, so he did not know the size or shape it might have been, but he thought it might have been about as large as a table top. The balloon which held it up, if that was how it worked, must have been about 12 feet long, he felt, measuring the distance by the size of the room in which he sat. The rubber was smoky gray in color and scattered over an area about 200 yards in diameter.

When the debris was gathered up the tinfoil, paper, tape, and sticks made a bundle about three feet long and 7 or 8 inches thick, while the rubber made a bundle about 18 or 20 inches long and about 8 inches thick. In all, he estimated, the entire lot would have weighed maybe five pounds.

There was no sign of any metal in the area which might have been used for an engine and no sign of any propellers of any kind, although at least one paper fin had been glued onto some of the tinfoil.

There were no words to be found anywhere on the instrument, although there were letters on some of the parts. Considerable scotch tape and some tape with flowers printed upon it had been used in the construction.

No strings or wire were to be found but there were some eyelets in the paper to indicate that some sort of attachment may have been used.

Brazel said that he had previously found two weather observation balloons on the ranch; but that what he found this time did not in any way resemble either of these.

"I am sure that what I found was not any weather observation balloon," he said. "But if I find anything else besides a bomb they are going to have a hard time getting me to say anything about it."

OTHER UFOS SPOTTED IN SOUTHWEST

I do not know if a UFO crashed at Roswell in 1947, but I do know that UFOs and their activities continue to be an area of major concern to both the United States government as well as that of Mexico. Consider if you will the following news story that made major headlines in 2004[4].

Mexican Air Force Films UFOs

Associated Press
11:17 AM May. 12, 2004 PT

Mexican Air Force pilots filmed 11 unidentified flying objects in the skies over southern Campeche State, a spokesman for Mexico's Defense Department confirmed Tuesday.

A videotape made widely available to the news media on Tuesday shows the bright objects, some sharp points of light and others like large headlights, moving rapidly in what appears to be a late-evening sky.

The lights were filmed on March 5 by pilots using infrared equipment. They appeared to be flying at an altitude of about 11,500 feet, and reportedly surrounded the jet as it conducted routine anti-drug trafficking vigilance in Campeche. Only three of the objects showed up on the plane's radar.

"Was I afraid? Yes. A little afraid because we were facing something that had never happened before," said radar operator Lt. German Marin in a taped interview made public Tuesday.

---

[4]http://www.wired.com/news/technology/0%2C1282%2C63433%2C00.html?tw=wn_top head_9

"I couldn't say what it was ... but I think they're completely real," added Lt. Mario Adrian Vazquez, the infrared equipment operator. Vazquez insisted that there was no way to alter the recorded images.

The plane's captain, Maj. Magdaleno Castanon, said the military jets chased the lights "and I believe they could feel we were pursuing them."

When the jets stopped following the objects, they disappeared, he said.

A Defense Department spokesman confirmed Tuesday that the videotape

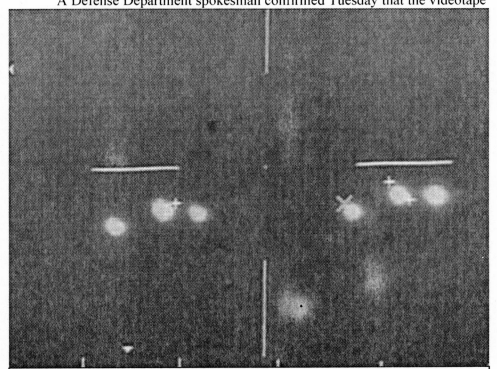

Figure 1: This is a photo taken by one of the planes.

was filmed by members of the Mexican Air Force. The spokesman, who spoke on the condition of anonymity, declined to comment further.

The video was first aired on national television Monday night then again at a news conference Tuesday by Jaime Maussan, a Mexican investigator who has dedicated the past 10 years to studying UFOs.

"This is historic news," Maussan told reporters. "Hundreds of videos (of UFOs) exist, but none had the backing of the armed forces of any country.... The armed forces don't perpetuate frauds."

Maussan said he obtained the video from Secretary of Defense Gen. Ricardo Vega Garcia.

THE "OTHER" UFO CRASH IN NEW MEXICO

Much less well known than the famous Roswell UFO crash incident, there was said to be a crash of a UFO at the little town of Aztec, New Mexico.

According to the reports, on March 25, 1948, radar at Muroc Air Force Base in California and at two installations in Colorado tracked an object over the state of New Mexico as it came down and apparently crashed. By using triangulation, the military was able to narrow the site where it came to earth to an area 12 miles east of Aztec, New Mexico.

The military alerted local authorities, who secured the area. General George C. Marshall, Secretary of State, ordered a search party sent in from Camp Hale in Colorado. The helicopter team located the crash site on a rocky plateau. The object was a saucer about thirty feet in diameter, and it was undamaged except for a small hole in one of its portholes.

Scientists, including Dr. Carl Heiland of the Colorado School of Mines, Dr. Horace van Valkenberg of The University of Colorado, and Dr. Detlev Bronk, met at Durango, Colorado and were flown to the crash site.

Through the hole, the assembled group of scientists, led by a mysterious Dr. Gee, could see sixteen small but perfectly formed humanoids. All were dead, their skin brown as if having been burned. Since the only damage to the craft was the hole, it was theorized that a meteorite had hit the craft, making the hole, and "burning" the occupants by rapid decompression.

After trying to open hatches, and failing to cut or burn through the hull, the military stuck a long pole through the hole in the porthole and, while probing around with it, accidentally hit a control that opened a door.

The scientists entered the ship and brought out the sixteen bodies and laid them on the ground near the ship. Dr. Gee studied the bodies and found that every one had perfect teeth, that they were between thirty-five and forty, and that they probably came from Venus. They were all between thirty-six and forty-two inches tall, and they ate small wafers and drank water that was twice as heavy as Earth water. They wore clothing that was almost indestructible.

Measurements of the craft showed that it was 99.99 feet in diameter, 18 feet across, and 72 inches high. Several booklets filled with pictograms were found in the ship. Dr. Gee determined that the craft flew by jumping from one magnetic line of force to the next, there being 1,257 of these lines per square centimeter.

The ship and occupants were taken to Muroc Air Force Base, where President Eisenhower flew in to see them. After that, they were taken to Wright-Patterson Air Force Base near Dayton, Ohio.

Dr. Gee was privileged to examine another craft that landed in an Arizona desert near a proving ground, also 72 feet across and containing 16 dead aliens. The occupants had died when they opened the door and were exposed to Earth's atmosphere.

Finally, he had examined another craft that had landed in Paradise Valley, near Phoenix, Arizona. This craft was only 36 feet across and contained only two aliens. One had died sitting at the controls and the other was halfway out the hatch. Apparently they, too, had died when exposed to the air of this planet.

Dr. Gee told his friend Silas M. Newton about the crashes and gave him some small metallic discs taken from one of the ships. Newton, a millionaire oilman who had rediscovered the Rangely oil field by using microwaves, promptly scheduled a lecture on the crashes on March 8, 1950 at the University of Denver. Newton also talked to Variety columnist Frank Scully, who wrote about the crashes in his book Behind the Flying Saucers, published in September of 1950.

This was the basic story, but then it really gets mysterious. In 1952, a reporter named J.P. Cahn, on assignment for True magazine, investigated the story. He tracked down Newton and found that there was no evidence of his claim to having discovered oil fields using microwaves. Cahn was able to obtain one of the small metal discs that Newton claimed had come from one of the crashed UFOs and which he claimed would resist heat of 10,000 degrees. On analysis it turned out to be ordinary aluminum that would melt at 650 degrees. Cahn also located the mysterious "Dr. Gee", who turned out to be Leo Gebauer, an electrician who lived in Arizona. It was then believed that Newton and Gebauer were a couple of con men who had conned Frank Scully.

In October, 1974, Robert S. Carr, the southern director of NICAP (National Investigation Committee on Aerial Phenomenon) and also a former teacher at the University of South Florida resurrected the Aztec crash story.

In 1978, Flying Saucer Review published a paper by Leonard H. Stringfield that claimed Carr had eyewitness testimony to substantiate the Aztec crash. One was from a surgical nurse, now deceased (sound familiar?), who was said to have assisted in the autopsy of a dead alien. Carr would not give names, so none of his claims could be verified.

In 1986, William S. Steinman and Wendelle C Stevens reopened the case yet again with a book called UFO Crash at Aztec. The book was mostly speculation, but one of its sources was Dr. Robert Sarbacher, onetime consultant to the Research and Development Board, who said Scully's version of the Aztec crash was "substantially correct." However, Sarbacher admitted that his information was secondhand.

In the early 1980s, William Moore investigated Silas M. Newton and Leo Gebauer and found that Newton was in trouble with the law as early as 1928, was charged in 1959 with selling worthless securities, was under indictment in 1970 for grand theft, and when he died in 1972, he had been charged with salting mines and oil wells to deceive investors. Gebauer had been investigated for violation of the White Slave Traffic Act, had been a Nazi sympathizer, and had at least a dozen aliases. He certainly wasn't a doctor.

Interviews with former (circa 1948) Aztec deputy sheriffs, newspaper editors, and townspeople, have found no evidence that a crash occurred there[5].

Of course, if as everyone maintains, the United States Government has a program of covering up such things as UFO crashes and alien bodies, then it is to be expected that a disinformation program would be instituted to discredit the story of a crash landing of a UFO at Aztec, New Mexico.

The most confusing aspect of trying to find out what happened is that when you begin to deal with UFOs and the "secret" government and the so called MJ-12 group, nothing is as it seems.

The most bizarre part of this entire situation is that there is no absolute proof that a UFO crashed in either Roswell or in Aztec, but then again there is no proof that there were no crashes either. I guess the big question is how do you prove that something "Didn't" happen?

OTHER MYSTERIES

The question of whether or not UFOs crashed in New Mexico and the purported recovery of strange alien bodies is not the only mystery coming out of New Mexico. Alamogordo, New Mexico also has gone on record with sightings of some very strange aerial objects.

According to this story, strange green fire-balls that darted through the sky have been observed from the 1950's through the 1970's. A 'flap' of spectacular sightings occurred in 1957. Several of these unexplained sightings were reported over the Mescalero Apache Reservation in October of that year.

At 1:00 P.M. on November 4, a 'glowing oval object' flew over Highway 54 and caused automobiles to stall. The automobiles' lights, radios, and engines, all failed at the same time. An electronics engineer in one of the cars reported he felt 'waves of heat' as the object passed overhead. The exposed portions of his skin later became reddened and itchy.

At the same location, at 9:20 A.M. on November 7, a couple spotted an identical object and reported that their speedometer appeared to malfunction. All of the UFO reports led famous meteor researcher Dr. Lincoln La Paz to set up a research project to study them. Although the sightings of the 'fire-balls' or the 'objects' were never explained, the United States Air Force took an extreme interest in the project and treated 'them' very seriously.

Then the area of White Sands is also bothered with these pesky mystery lights. The White Sands area of New Mexico was a hotbed of missile testing in the 40s through the 60s. It was also a focal point of high UFO activity, particularly early on.

During a balloon launch on April 24, 1949, a General Mills engineer named Charles B. Moore Jr., along with four Navy personnel, witnessed a white spherical object in the sky. Moore had been looking for the balloon using a

---

[5] Story by Roy Lawhon, http://ufos.about.com/od/ufocrashes/a/aa110704.htm.

theodilite when he saw the UFO. He soon saw that it was more elliptical than round and that it seemed to be pursuing his balloon. This sighting later became a Blue Book "Unknown."

On June 10th, two more circular UFOs were sighted in the area. During a missile launch, the two objects were seen circling and passing through the weapon's exhaust, though the rocket was moving at 1430 mph. 5 tracking posts also confirmed having seen the objects.

In 1950, UFOs were finally caught on film, two times. On April 27, filming of a fallen missile also caught a UFO hovering nearby. Then, on May 29, two more UFOs were filmed moving at a speed of over 2000 mph.

More film was taken on July 14, 1951. During a test of the F-86 jet, several UFOs were seen and caught on film. The objects also appeared on radar.

UFO activity in the area still continued for years to follow and in fact there are a number of sightings almost every year.

Even the United States Air Force is not immune to these mysterious forces. At Kirtland Air Force in August through September of 1980 saw a series of alarming UFO incidents taking place near an active Air Force Base. Among the incidents were:

A UFO flying over a weapons storage area maneuvering in ways a helicopter could not.

A disk-shaped object near the ground behind an "alarmed structure," viewed by a former helicopter mechanic.

A craft landing in a restricted test range.

Air Force Radar Approach Control equipment and scanner radar were rendered inoperative by "high frequency jamming from an unknown cause." A thorough check in the area resulted in no answers.

According to the government document related to the incidents acquired through the Freedom of Information Act, the conclusion of the case, especially the latter jamming, included the terse comment: "The presence of hostile intelligence jamming cannot be ruled out."

So who would have the power and ability to jam the Untied States Air Force?

CHAPTER THREE

LOST TREASURES IN NEW MEXICO

For the lucky treasure hunter, New Mexico can be one of the biggest bank vaults in history. Like the Spanish did in every region that they conquered, they searched for treasures, both of nature and of man. The search for the fabled wealth was inevitable. Coronado's quest of these treasures and lost cities led to the eventual discovery, exploration, and the naming of New Mexico. Although the Franciscan friars were searching for new converts, the rest of the exploration parties were really searching for the wealth that might be in the region of New Mexico.

Francisco Vasquez de Coronado was an ambitious adventurer who desired great wealth. He searched for fabled cities with vast treasure, but these places were not to be found. Instead, his quest for increased wealth left him with huge financial losses and a tarnished reputation.

Coronado was the governor of Nueva Galicia when Fray Marcos de Niza returned from Cibola. He heard Fray Marcos' tales of seeing one of the seven cities and went with him to meet with Viceroy Antonio de Mendoza. Mendoza selected Coronado to lead the expedition which was funded by themselves and other investors.

As they crossed southeastern Arizona, supplies began to run out. After six months on the trail, the ragged expedition entered Cibola for rest and food supplies. Many future expeditions into New Mexico would also arrive low on provisions and would continue the trend of expecting the Indians to supply their needs. Leaving Cibola in pursuit of riches, they entered Hawikuh and the group immediately saw that Fray Marcos' stories were lies. A detachment under Pedro de Tovar was sent to Tusayan in northern Arizona, but this village inhabited by the Hopi Indians was in poor condition too. Another group, led by Captain Garcia Lopez de Cardenas, went west and found the Grand Canyon. Melchor Diaz located the lower Colorado River and then crossed into the desert area of California.

An Indian chief named Bigotes led them to a new province called Tiguex where Tiwa pueblos were built next to the Rio Grande River. Coronado, needing shelter for his army, made the Indians vacate the village of Alconfor. He then ordered the Tiwa villagers to provide them with grain and blankets. The Indians rebelled and two villages were demolished by the Spanish. Coronado's diplomatic blunder set the pattern for other explorations for exploitation of the Indians and led to the growing mistrust of the Spanish by the Indian tribes.

While wintering in the village, an Indian named Turk told Coronado tales of riches in the east. The following spring, the expedition left for the fabled Quivara, but they only discovered the grass houses of the Wichita Indians. Due to his fabrications, Turk was killed by Spaniards frustrated by the failure of their expedition.

By the expedition's completion, Coronado suffered from financial loss and a broken spirit. Charges were brought against him alleging his abuse of the Tiguex Indians and his failure to enlarge Spanish holdings by not establishing a settlement near the Rio Grande River. Coronado was acquitted on these charges, but his reputation was ruined.

However, this expedition was a success in other ways. The adventurer expanded the world's geographical knowledge of North America. His men were the first Europeans to see the Grand Canyon and the Colorado River, to explore the pueblo interior, to reach the Continental Divide, to associate with the Hopi Indians, and to cross the plains of North America. Historically, he is remembered more for these successes then he is for his failure to find the seven lost cities.

The three sub-expeditions that were off-shoots of Coronado's "Big Search" were attempts by the leader to locate hidden wealth that might be in the Southwest. After Coronado failed to find any riches in New Mexico, he sent smaller groups from the expedition in other directions. Every time a new story or rumor was told by local and visiting Indians, he sent his troops in search of the fabled city or treasure. Sub-expeditions were sent westward with the hope that something was out there to be found. Garcia Lopez de Cardenas discovered the Grand Canyon of Colorado. Pedro de Tovar encountered the Hopi Villages. Melchor Diaz located the Colorado River and searched into the desert region of California. Each sub-expedition returned without any financial success.

Coronado is an important historical figure because of his travels and the discoveries of his sub-expeditions. Although none of the sub-expeditions found any wealth, they are historically important because these sub-adventures expanded the world's geographical knowledge of North America.

The Spanish attitude toward the Indians was that they saw themselves as guardians of the Indian's basic rights. The Spanish goal was for the peaceful submission of the Indians. The laws of Spain controlled the conduct of soldiers during wars, even when the tribes were hostile. The missionary's role was to convert the Indians to Christianity. This would be followed by the Indians being accepted as members of the Spanish civilization. However, the exploitation of the Indian occurred constantly.

The Anglo attitude, however, was one of total removal of the natives from their lands or total inhalation. The Indian was continually pushed aside or killed.

The colonial Spaniards put great faith in the legends and myths which were being told throughout Spain. These beliefs led Fernando Cortez to discover Mexico. Spanish soldiers conquered the Aztec Indians, and discovered precious metals. Astonishing tales concerning great treasures in the North were being told by local and visiting Indians.

The Spanish, believing the tales of the Indians, began searching for the Seven Cities of Gold, the Gran Quivira, the Seven Cities of the Seven Bishops, and the Seven Caves of Origin of the Aztecs. During 1536, four survivors of the Narvaez Expedition arrived in Caliacan. Alvar Nunez Cabeza de Vaca claimed to have seen only small supplies of cotton shawls, beads, and turquoise among the Indians during his trip. He also saw five arrowheads made out of emeralds. However, he reported hearing stories of people who lived in large houses in the North who traded in turquoise and other goods.

In 1539, a Spanish Franciscan friar named Father Marcos de Niza set out with friendly Indians and Estevanico, the black slave from the Narvaez Expedition party, to learn the secrets of the North. When the friar returned to Mexico City from the journey he falsely claimed to have seen one of the fabled cities from a distance. The friar's news led to the expedition of Francisco Vasquez de Coronado. Coronado's expedition and all other Spanish expeditions to follow were centered around the search for the fabled riches and lost cities.

The search for the fabled wealth was inevitable. Coronado's quest of these treasures and lost cities led to the eventual discovery, exploration, and the naming of New Mexico. Although the Franciscan friars were allegedly searching for new converts, the rest of the exploration parties were really searching for the wealth that might be in the region of New Mexico.

THE LOST DUTCHMAN MINE

For more than 120 years, the legend of the Lost Dutchman Mine has haunted the minds and souls of treasure seekers throughout the world. It is said to be the most famous lost mine of all time, and to this day it continues to draw prospectors to the Superstition Mountains of Arizona in search of its rich gold.

There are a large number of stories about the Dutchman's wealth. Some say he found an incredibly wealth gold mine and others say that he found a lost treasure stored in a cavern in the mountains. Whatever the truth might be, there is no doubt that he had access to a vast fortune in gold.

Most stories about the Lost Dutchman Mine make a great deal out of a so-called curse by the Apache's who considered the Superstition Mountains to be sacred and the home of their gods. The curse also protects the treasure of the Superstitions, whose secret location the Apache are said to know, which may include the Lost Dutchman Mine.

The actually origin of the curse can be traced back the early 1500s, when Jesuit priests from Spain began to build missions in the area now known as Arizona and New Mexico. It was during this period that the Jesuits established relations with Native Americans, who helped them mine gold, some of which was sent back to the King of Spain.

However, in the late 1700s, after a falling out, the King of Spain ordered the Jesuits out of Mexico. The Jesuits had no choice but to obey the royal order, but they had no desire to let the King have all of the treasure that they had accumulated over the years.

Some believe the Jesuits hid away their records of mines, treasures and ore deposits before leaving the country. Others believe that the Jesuits convinced Native Americans that bad things would happen if they ever revealed the location of these riches to outsiders. Whatever may have been the truth, for centuries, the Indians who are native to this part of the country have kept the location and in some cases the very knowledge of the existence of these treasures a secret and to this day many are reluctant to provide any related information.

There is, however, another side to this story. Before the Lost Dutchman Mine was discovered by Jacob Waltz (the Dutchman) in the early 1870s, there was a legend of another rich mine which was discovered in the same area and mined by the Peralta family from Sonora, Mexico. It is believed by many that the Lost Dutchman Mine is only one of the rich mines discovered by the Peraltas.

Historians say there is no hard evidence establishing that the Peralta family actually mined in the area, but they have become a significant part of the legend. According to this legend, the Peralta family made a number of gold mining expeditions to the Superstitions. Their last is said to have occurred between 1847 and 1852. Before this expedition could return to Sonora with gold, it was attacked by a band of Apache Indians.

Different versions of the story portray a variety of outcomes. One version says the Peralta expedition consisted of two groups, the Gonzales group and the Peralta group. It was the Gonzales group that was massacred by the Apaches while the Peralta s made a safe return to Sonora loaded with gold. Another version of the massacre left only one survivor of the Peralta expedition, who escaped to Sonora to tell the story of what happened. Which, if either version is correct, is left to the reader's imagination.

There is evidence of a skirmish between the Spanish and the Apaches at the area of the said massacre. Since the turn of the century, remnants of mining equipment, high-grade gold ore, old guns, weapons, gear and a pack train have been discovered at the site of the massacre.

The legend includes details on how the Peraltas buried the rich mines with rocks to hide their discovery. Some also believe that after the Spanish miners left the area, the Apache removed up all evidence of mining by filling holes, mines, tunnels, etc. with dirt and rocks.

Peirpont C. Bicknell, a free-lance writer and seeker of lost mines, was the first person to link the Peraltas and Weaver's Needle (a pinnacle landmark) with Jacob Waltz and the Lost Dutchman Mine in written documentation dating January, 1895.

In 1952, the infamous "Peralta" stone tablet maps were discovered in the foothills of the Superstition Mountains by a man on vacation with his family. These stone maps have been authenticated by more than one authority as being more than 100 years old. One of the most famous lost treasures in the state of New Mexico is called the Lost Dutchman Mine. For over a hundred years men have searched for this supposed vast hidden treasure. Searching had died down for a time until the finding of the mysterious Peralta Stones.

About once a year someone discovers the Peralta Stones and immediately jumps to the conclusion that they have at long last found the key to the whereabouts of the Lost Dutchman Gold Mine. And without further ado, not even a flake of gold, or any serious research, these would be treasure hunters immediately want to tell everybody about it.

There is no question that Jacob Waltz, the so called Dutchman of the Lost Dutchman legend found a fortune in gold; however, there are a large number of possible explanations for the source of his wealth.

The stone tablets are now in possession of the Arizona Museum of Mines and Minerals in Phoenix. They're not on display, but the folks at the museum will be happy to show them to anyone who is interested. They'll also be happy to tell you what they know about them, which is plenty. No one at the museum believes that they are anything but a hoax.

The stones have been examined by a number of experts in various related fields over the years, but the most careful and pains-taking examination was by Father Charles Polzer, a Jesuit priest and a well-known ethno historian associated with the Southwestern Mission Research Center at the Arizona State Museum. Father Polzer's work is highly regarded, and he can easily be described as eminent in his field. He reportedly laughed when he was told that the drawings were purported to be more than a hundred years old. Father Polzer also believes that the stones are fakes.

In spite of this, many people have been convinced of the authenticity of the Peralta Stones because the Peralta family name is mentioned so often in the history books. It's true that the Peraltas were many and that some of them were quite prominent in business and in politics in their time. Don Pedro de Peralta was installed in 1609 as the first governor of the Spanish Territory of New Mexico. The territory actually had a more elaborate Spanish name suggesting a kingdom, and it included almost the whole southwestern quarter of the United States, but it's usually referred to as the Spanish territory, so I'll leave it at that.

Don Pedro was so far from Spain that he did pretty much as he pleased in the name of the king, and he appointed his relatives to all of the important government posts in the territory. He also had the power to make land grants in the name of the king, and he did so for several of his friends and relatives. One of the largest Spanish land grants in the New World was the famous Peralta holding in California, which was held intact until the late 19th century by Don Luis Peralta and his heirs.

Peraltas multiplied at an astonishing rate in the New Mexico territory, as well as in Chihuahua and Sonora. Peralta became a common family name, and there were thousands of them by the middle of the 19th century. Today Peralta is still a common surname in Mexico and the U.S. Southwest. The Phoenix telephone directory lists dozens, and every city in California and New Mexico has its fair share of Peraltas.

So who are these particular Peraltas who figure so prominently in the Lost Dutchman legend? The two blamed most often are Pablo Peralta and his youngest son, Miguel. They were real people, prospectors and miners..

Pablo Peralta owned a silver mine in Ures, Sonora, for many years, but by the middle of the 19th century the silver was about exhausted and corruption in the local government forced him to abandon the mine. He moved his family to the Mother Lode country in Central California. There is substantial documentary evidence of their presence in Tuolumne County during the Gold Rush years.

It was probably about 1863 when Pablo and Miguel left California and went to Arizona. They held a registered mining claim on the Agua Fria River a few miles from present day Black Canyon City, and they called their mine the Valenciana, the same name as the abandoned silver mine in Mexico. The existence and location of that mine is well documented, and prospectors today occasionally rework the tailings that the Peraltas left behind.

In all probability, the Valenciana produced a fair amount of gold, but Indian raids were always a problem, and Pablo and Miguel were attacked several times. During one of the battles an Indian with a lance seriously wounded Pablo. Miguel then sold the mine to a group of investors from California, and they moved to the new town of Wickenburg, about a hundred miles to the southwest, which was booming after the discovery of the Vulture mine.

Shortly after they arrived in Wickenburg, Pablo died of his wounds. Miguel then opened a dry goods store, married, and prospered. He opened a second store in Seymour when the Central Arizona Mining Company constructed its stamp mill there in 1879. Later on, he moved to Phoenix where he opened a larger general merchandise store at the corner of Washington Street and Center Street – now Central Avenue – the geographical center of the modern Phoenix.

It is certainly reasonable to assume that Jacob Waltz and Miguel Peralta they knew each other at least casually. They were in the same places in California and Arizona at the same times, and they were doing much the same thing, looking for gold. Miguel was well-known in Phoenix, and Phoenix was a small community in the 1880s.

Although there were several authentic Spanish land grants in what is now the State of Arizona, none of them involved anyone with the surname Peralta. However, there is reason to believe that Miguel was involved with Doc Willing and James Addison Reavis in the infamous Peralta-Reavis Spanish Land Grant affair, which was a complete fabrication and a fraud. Doctor Willing died of natural causes in 1872 before the fraud was discovered; James Addison Reavis ultimately went to prison for his part in the scheme, and Miguel fled to Mexico. He later took his own life in a Nogales, Sonora, hotel room. But that's another story.

All of this, of course, does not preclude the possibility that some of the other Peraltas may have mined gold and/or silver in the Superstition Mountains during some period of time. There is evidence of early Spanish and Mexican mining activity in the general area, and it's reasonable to assume that some of the Peraltas would have had a hand in it, given their numbers and the prominence of the family.

Getting back to the Peralta Stones, one writer assures us that Professor Dana, a geologist at the University of Redlands in California, examined the stones and issued a letter attesting to the fact that they were more than one hundred years old. If such a letter ever existed, no one can find a copy of it.

The University of Redlands was founded as a liberal arts college in 1907. The university has since covered a broad field of studies over the years and currently offers more than forty majors in thirty departments. Professor Dana is not presently on the faculty, investigators can find no record that a Professor Dana ever taught at the College.

There many mysteries involved with the so-called Lost Dutchman Mine. However, there is one fact that no one can dispute. Jacob Waltz did have a lot of gold when he was living in Phoenix, and its source has never been satisfactorily explained. Let's keep in mind, though, that he was a prospector and a gold miner all of his life, and he was pretty good at it. The Southwest desert is full of gold; you just have to know where to look, how to recognize it when you find it, and how to get it out of the ground and into your pocket. None of that would have been much of a problem for Jacob Waltz.

Whether his gold came from a real mine or he found a cache of gold hidden by the Jesuits or some other group, there is no doubt that Jacob Waltz really did find a fortune. The only question now is where it the rest?

THE FOUR CORNERS TREASURE STORY[6]

As wild as this story will sound, there is a great deal of solid evidence that this particular treasure story is true. The lucky finder would never have to work again. There are several versions of this story in existence today and the searching for the buried gold continues even today.

---

[6] http://www.ancienttreasurehunter.com/fourcorners.htm

The story begins on April 15, 1934 in Cuernavaca, Mexico. On this day there was a fateful meeting called by investment banker Rafael Borega. In attendance were Leon Trabuco: Rancher and large scale miner from Chihuahua, Mexico, Ricardo Artega: Wealthy rancher from Torreon, Mexico, Carlos Sepulvedo: Wealthy rancher from Coahuila, Mexico, Professor Guzman Morada: Economical specialist called in by investment bankers from Spain, and Rafael Borega: International banker for Spain and Mexico.

Professor Morada had developed a plan to profit from President Roosevelt's April 5, 1933 executive order forbidding the hoarding of gold by Untied States citizens. President Roosevelt also urged Congress to pass a United States Gold Act, in effect, taking the Untied States off of the Gold Standard.

. The Committees went to work on the wording of the Act, and had the Act prepared by late 1933, passed on January 13, of 1934. Due to this change in monetary policy, Professor Morada was positive that the United States Government would be forced to devalue the as a result, gold and other metals will gain in price.

In 1929 the stock market crashed and that cost investors $60 million dollars and from 1929 to 1933, 4,376 United States banks had collapsed."

Professor Morada was absolutely certain that the price of gold on the western world market would go from 20.67 per ounce to at least $40.00 per ounce. He predicted that a wise group could reap millions in profits by accumulating the bullion at the present price and holding it in the United States for the anticipated increase in value.

Only two among the group inquired as to the problems that might arise on crossing the international borders with the gold. Morada assured all that no problems would come up at the border. A plan was adopted by the group. Trabuco, being the wealthiest and with mining operation knowledge, would lead the group. Trabuco would supply much of the gold that he was personally hoarding estimated at 12 tons or 300,000 troy ounces. This would be combined with some of Ricardo Artega's gold. The two wealthy ranchers, Ricardo Artega and Carlos Sepulvedo, supplied millions of pesos in Dollar form to Rafael Borega so that he could purchase more gold from miners. Borega canvassed the mining communities and amassed five tons of gold, an estimated $3,500,000.00 worth.

The gold was stored at a rented rancho near Pueblo, Mexico. Trabuco supplied trusted guards at Puebla, and when the tonnage was accumulated and ready to be moved, the gold, in ingot form, was moved north to Trabuco's mine in northern Chihuahua, Mexico. All summer long and into the winter 17 tons was accumulated. In December Trabuco was elated to locate a United Sates safe property to move the gold to. Trabuco talked to a pilot, William C. Elliot, and wanted him to fly in search of a suitable stash area.

Elliot ran a charter service and was more than happy to fly to Kirtland, New Mexico to discuss the project. Trabuco and Elliot met in Kirtland and struck a deal where they would fly and locate a good area and Elliot would receive

$2,500.00 per flight to move the gold from Mexico to a site in New Mexico. Trabuco wanted Elliot to locate and lease a secluded mesa top, out of the view of civilization. The Mexican partners approved the deal with the exception that Trabuco would never allow anyone, including Elliot, to know what the gold was buried once it had been flown in.

From Torreon to the United States Border is about 400 air miles and then it is an additional 400 miles to the Four Corners area. Approximately 400 total air miles with the flights being planned as night runs.

Kirtland is half way between Shiprock City (not the rock) and Farmington, New Mexico. It is stated that Elliot's plane could fly 1500 pounds with a safety factor. Elliot would need to make at least 23 trips from Mexico to the mesa. It is presumed that the trips were completed by mid January to the end of February 1934.

Trabuco had two trusted and well armed guards stay with the gold and cover it with tarps. Trabuco then released Elliot with his $57,500.00 Flight pay. Trabuco had traveled to Bloomfield, New Mexico to acquire tools for digging and he had his one-ton truck from his mining operations in Mexico. When everything seemed clear, Trabuco had his guards load the gold, one ton at a time, and alone he moved it to a hole that he had dug himself on top of a wind swept mesa. After the entire 17 tons were laid in the hole, he covered it up with dirt, tarps and waxed paper, returned to pick up his guards and returned to Mexico.

On January 17, 1934 the president signed and passed the United States Gold Act. There was an immediate order for banks, storage houses and metal brokers to turn in their gold for paper dollars at an exchange rate of $35.00 per ounce. As some had predicted, the dollar devaluation did occur, and gold did rise to $35.00 per ounce. However tied to the Act, was the fact that all citizens of the United States must have all their gold traded in within five years.

34,000 pounds of gold would not require a very great area to store only about, plus or minus, 27 cubic feet. One cubic yard equals 440,000 troy ounces.

Trabuco's gold was worth $20.67 per ounce in 1933. Borega had purchased tons of gold at $25.00 per ounce and the cost of moving the gold by plane had already peen paid. At $35.00 per ounce, there would have been approximately six and three quarters of a million dollars profit if the gold had been moved in 1934, but greed ruled the group and they wanted more.

By 1939 the United States had held the gold price at $35.00 per ounce. Borega had died in his Mexico office in 1939 leaving three members of the group still alive. In 1940 Carlos Sepulvedo was killed in a car crash just outside of Monterrey, Mexico. Now Trabuco was the only survivor.

Trabuco was never aware that the pilot, Elliot, had doubled back on one his flights and discovered the hiding place of the gold. When Elliot learned of the death of most of the group of investors, he planned to go back and dig up the gold for himself. However, before he could put his plan into operation, the Japanese attacked Pearl Harbor on December 7th 1941 and the United States had declared war.

As a pilot, Elliot's skills were in great demand so in 1942 William C. Elliot enlisted in the United States Army Air Corps. Unfortunately, he was killed in action in 1944 while flying over Germany[7]. After World War ll, Trabuco tried to sell the gold to private buyers, but all sales fell through because the buyers were leery of the old Gold Act and did not wish to enter into any illegal or gray area with the United States Government. Trabuco tried a sale with a German immigrant, but when the German learned that the gold was stored in the United States, he backed out of the deal.

PROFESSOR MORADA'S MISTAKE

Everything that Professor Morada had predicted had come to pass. However, he had not counted on the United States Government getting deeply involved in the buried gold.

It was suspected that one of the possible United States buyers leaked information to the Treasury Department about the hidden gold and in late 1945 an investigation was opened. In 1946 Trabuco hired an attorney to represent him with the Treasury Department. President Truman himself was consulted and the Treasury Department called in the Justice Department. A determination was made that the Mexicans had direct knowledge of the Gold Act and chose to violate this U.S. Law. Trabuco could come forward and divulge the hiding place of the gold, allow the United States Government to recover it and then sue for rightful ownership and take his chances with the Federal court system. Trabuco turned down this offer and did not travel within the United States boundaries.

In 1952 a second attempt by a lawyer was made to the Treasury Department. The Justice Department then turned the case over to the Federal Grand Jury, Los Angeles, California District. The Federal Grand Jury issued an indictment, naming Trabuco as violating both United States smuggling laws and cited other open laws that may be named at a later date.

It is alleged that Trabuco did maintain some guards near his leased treasure site on the mesa. Most searchers have concentrated their search on an old Spanish Land Grant Property southwest of the landmark (Shiprock, New Mexico). This theory is based on the fact that other properties surrounding the area are part of the sovereign Navajo Indian reservation and in 1933 the land available to the group had to be semi-private property. During the post world war ll era, the land grant became part of the vast Navajo Nation. This is speculation at best and some other areas in the 1933-45 eras were so remote that there could be several candidate sites.

In 1958 Trabuco sold his mines and ranch properties in Chihuahua, Mexico and departed to Europe. In 1962 Trabuco visited Mexico City and made some calls to his lawyer in Los Angeles, California. Trabuco returned to Spain that year with no action having been taken in the United States. In 1974 there

---

[7] Jameson, W.C., New Mexico Treasure Tales, Caxton Press, Caldwell, Idaho. 2003.

were some inquiries by the Trabuco Los Angeles law firm to the United States Treasury and Justice Departments. The outcome of these inquires was not revealed but no one has seen Trabuco since that time. The law firm must have made some kind of deal because they hired agencies to locate Trabuco in Europe with no results.

Trabuco was thought to be around 45 years of age in 1933 which would make him 74 when he visited Mexico in 1962. When the search began in 1974 he would have been 86 years old.

The truck Trabuco had in New Mexico could haul one ton easily. This would mean that 17 trips were made in one day with five miles to his secret site and five miles back to the guarded taped site. 170 miles in one day with handling and burying, could all fit into one long day time frame. No map was made and the only statement that anyone can remember Trabuco saying was "The gold is only a few miles from a major New Mexico land mark."

Earlier in this story it was mentioned that one of the private United States buyers may have leaked the information to the Fed's and from later documents we find the names and the players.

In 1950 a prominent Los Angeles cattleman named E. George Lucky reported to the United States Secret Service that he had been asked to serve as an intermediary in arranging a large-scale bullion sale. 35,000 pounds of gold at $35.00 an ounce making this a $20,000,000.00 deal. Mr. Lucky stated that the deal had been brought to him by a man named Bruce Clews, a Los Angeles public relations man. An attorney named Prentiss Moore sat in on the meeting. Clews stated that the deal had been brought to him by a metal imports dealer named Isadore M. Nobel and an international mining consultant named Martin Hougan. Hougan, the mining consultant, had power of attorney to represent the foreign seller.

The sale of the gold was to be handled through as escrow system located at the First National Bank of Ontario, California. B.J. Klepper was the escrow office of this bank. The attorney, Prentiss Moore advised the group to tell the story to the Secret Service and to get advice from both the Treasury Department and the Justice Department prior to violating any United States Laws. This advice was taken and the Secret Service handed the file to the Federal Justice Department in Los Angeles. The Prosecuting Attorneys took the entire file to the Federal Grand Jury in order to seek indictments. All known participants were brought before the Grant Jury. This included the escrow files and an affidavit from Martin Hougan, the mining consultant who had stated that he had seen the gold with his own eyes and could guarantee that the gold did exist. Hougan did not appear at the hearings and when a warrant was issued in his name, he avoided being served by seeking foreign employment. Mr. Hougan never did surface and his whereabouts are unknown.

Angus D. McEachen, the United States Prosecuting Attorney, entered the file in the Federal court system in 1952 and again in 1960 so that the stature of limitations would not run out. The United States Government renewed the claim in 1974.

The Hougan affidavit stated that the gold was buried somewhere in the far extreme northwest corner of the state of New Mexico in San Juan County.

Shiprock has been the center of several searches for this horde. Both legally permitted Navajo searches and trespassers on reservation lands. As recent as 1990 an air infrared search was done by a California company in the Shiprock area. They covered a 20-mile circle around the rock. A potential landing field east of the rock was found and could easily be reached by truck to haul the bullion away to its hiding place.

The filming was done with 35MM color and infrared black and white film. The films have been studied and determined that the filming and the developing was not up to the state of the art that was available. It is also noted that the alleged landing site was in an open plain where passers by could see the field for miles. The truck carrying the gold would have to cross over the highway which was between the supposed landing site and Shiprock. The facts and the stores do not go together. Another researcher from Farmington, New Mexico states that there was an old Spanish/Mexican Land Grant 20 miles south of Shiprock and he suspects that this area is now part of the Navajo Indian Reservation and could have been available to Trabuco in 1933. This area was also filmed by the California Company and nothing was found by infrared filming. However, once again, the filming and developing was below par.

Ed Foster, a long time researcher for this treasure, found some interesting evidence six miles east of Aztec, New Mexico. He stated that there were some major Landmarks north of this area listed on several old Mexican maps. These landmarks were "Way-Points". He also found a rock, which has the inscription 1033/16 tons. When Mr. Foster's story is pieced together, it seems to further confuse the story. He alleges that the plane landed at Conger Mesa, which is in the center of the village of Old La Plata, New Mexico. He states that he interviewed an old Indian woman who saw a plane land on Conger Mesa near 1933. Fosters complete story covers an area of thirty miles when all of his research is placed together.

The shed that Trabuco supposedly used as a guard shack and to hold the gold for transport is far from the Conger Mesa Strip. During the 1920's and 1930's La Plata was a major smelting district for several active mines which operated north of La Plata and into Colorado. Several mines would bring their ore to these lower elevation smelters for final refining. Most of the ore was then sold to eastern buyers or shipped by road to Denver, Colorado. It was not uncommon for officials to fly onto these rough landing strips in those days. This may be the reason that some planes were seen flying into the area.

The area of interest was isolated in the 1930's. It was considered by the Indians to be part of the old people's cave dwelling grounds prior to it's being established as the Navajo Indian reservation. All of this area was what the Indians called "Ancestors Grounds". The old people built adobes on protective ledges and caves, mostly on the south facing slopes of the high mesa. They did this for protection from the weather and hostile nomadic non working tribes who often took the hard eared stores from the working Indians. These cave dwellings were often built away from watering holes and required that potable water be hauled up to their homes. Other food items were also hauled up to their adobe homes for grinding and storage. The protected dwellings were most likely used only occasionally in the good weather months while small clans grew their crops and hunted for game that could be dried for winter use. By the winter months, the clans moved into their winter dwellings with pre-stored foods and water.

In June of 1933, Trabuco traveled north by truck and made a decision on what mesa was out of sight of roads, and settlements. The mesa needed to be in an unclaimed area with no mines, ranching, and no interest by the smaller Navajo Nation. Trabuco rented mules from a farmer in the old La Plata area and entered the mesa from the east and graded a landing strip. He later brought three horses for his men to use to get on and off the mesa with camp supplies. He used the mules to grade the landing site and made a camp by using flat stones from several of the old Indian rock Hogans that were on the mesa.

There were six stripped hogans where only the foundations remained near the pantry. One Hogan was located near the makeshift landing strip and had a two foot base where the bullion could have been kept with a tarp over it until it was moved to its hiding place.

The gold was all flown in by February 1934 and he and his guards could ride to town and take turns guarding the horde. Sometime in early 1934 Trabuco learned that the gold had indeed jumped to $35.00 per ounce but as the leader of the group, he decided to wait to see if the price would jump even more and that is when he decided to bury the gold. This is when he traveled to Bloomfield to purchase hard ground digging tools (factual). In February 1934 Trabuco had his guards help him tow his truck to the mesa and then sent the guards to town. He took his time and loaded one or two tons at a time and moved the gold to his pre-dug hiding place.

When the gold was all buried, he could easily drive the truck down the east side to Kirkland and pick up his men and deliver them back to Mexico to await the possible rise in the gold market.

By late 1934 his partners were disturbed because their time and money were tied up. The United States Gold Act laws were just beginning to be defined and the project started to look bleak for hoarders of gold. By 1935 the partnership wanted guards posted at the mesa to further insure the safety of the gold. Trabuco took new help to an out post area near the gold site.

Trabuco hauled building blocks onto the mesa and had the team construct a year around type adobe to keep trespassers away from the area. This house is next to the original pantry that the Indians had built. A small herd of sheep was brought in to make the homestead look more like a working ranch. An attempt to sell some gold to private buyers in Denver was made in 1941 but the illegal sale scared the buyers away. Soon after the war broke out, the partners tried to sell some of the gold to the treasury department at a low rate but Roosevelt's representatives turned the deal down.

During the War it was almost impossible for the partners to do any moving around in the United States without raising suspicions and all interstate traffic had to have office of price administration permits (O.P.S.) to buy gas stamps and a letter of approval to do long range private driving.

After World War II, new attempts were made with both the United States Government and private buyers but the gold act was still in effect. All of Trabuco's partners were now dead, including the pilot who had originally flown the gold to New Mexico. Trabuco could afford to be patient because he was already very wealthy from Mexican mines and ranching. He was also heir to lands and resources which dated back to the times of the Conquistadors. By moving to Spain he avoided any United States or Mexican legal problems.

However, it would appear that Trabuco also died before anything could be done with this king's ransom of gold. As far as anyone knows, the gold is still buried on the mesa. There have been one or two groups who claim to know the whereabouts of this massive treasure, but the Federal Government has taken them to court in order to lodge a claim for the gold if and when it is found. The claim is that the very presence of the gold in the United States constituted a crime and thus the gold will be confiscated of the finding is made public.

This chapter discusses two major treasure stories that have come from the State of New Mexico. Of course, there are hundreds more that have every possibility of being valid. There is a fortune waiting to be found by the lucky person who journeys into the desert on the road to wealth.

PART II

THE GHOSTS OF

NEW MEXICO

CHAPTER FOUR

ALAMOGORDO, NEW MEXICO

The city of Alamogordo, which is the county seat of Otero County, New Mexico, is the micropolitan center of the Tularosa Basin. The city is the commercial and governmental center for the county with a population of roughly 35,000+ residents. The city's mild climate and pristine scenery offer its people an ambiance that enriches their quality of life. The Tularosa Basin is surrounded by the majestic Organ, San Andres and Sacramento Mountain ranges.

Alamogordo was founded in 1898 as a terminal for the railroad. The community's activities promoted the growth of logging, tourism and health related enterprises. A national survey rated Alamogordo as one of the 50 healthiest places to live in the U.S. The basic beginnings are still in place. Many of the early buildings are still occupied by businesses. Tourism related activity and light manufacturing contribute to the economy. White Sands National Monument is a major attraction as are the New Mexico Museum of Space History and the Lincoln National Forest.

Holloman Air Force Base, the area's largest employer, is located near Alamogordo, and is the home of the F-117 Stealth Fighter Wing, the German Air Force in the U.S., and the High Speed Test Track. The U.S. Army installation near Alamogordo is the second largest overland testing range in the world. As the birthplace of the U.S. rocket program in the 1940s, today White Sands Missile Range is the testing site for the reusable rocket and numerous Department of Defense research and evaluation programs. The City of Alamogordo is closely linked to both Holloman and White Sands, both of whom represent a combined impact of military civilian annual payroll of more than $200 million and an economic impact of more than $450 million to the local economy[8].

---

[8] http://www.alamogordo.com/profile/index.html

THE DWI OFFICES
Alamogordo, New Mexico

The DWI offices are located in the oldest part of the city of Alamogordo. A number of people who have worked in the DWI offices are adamant in their belief that there is a ghost haunting this location. The DWI Offices is comprised of the former sheriff's office and cell block. A number of former workers and visitors to the facility claim that they see and hear doors open, footsteps, and occasionally see a young man dressed in an old style suit from the early nineteen hundreds.

Most of those who have had experiences in these offices say that they do not feel threatened by the ghosts and the spirits generally keep to themselves unless someone makes a lot of noises such as running or moving the furniture about the room. The noises seem to disturb the spirits than this is when they are the most active. Those in the building at the time feel cold drafts and heard doors open and then slam shut.

CHAPTER FIVE

ALBUQUERQUE, NEW MEXICO

Albuquerque, New Mexico's largest city was named to honor a Spanish Duke, the 10th Duke of Albuquerque. Colonial Governor Don Francisco Cuervo y Valdez elected the name but over the centuries, the first "r" has been dropped.

In 1706, Albuquerque was founded by a group of colonists who had been granted permission by King Philip of Spain to establish a new villa (city) on the banks of the Rio Grande (which means big or great river). The colonists chose a place along the river where it made a wide curve providing good irrigation for crops, a source of wood from the bosque (cottonwoods, willows and olive trees) and nearby mountains. The site also provided protection and trade with the Indians from the pueblos in the area.

The early Spanish settlers were religious people, and the first building erected was a small adobe chapel. Its plaza was surrounded by small adobe homes, clustered close together for mutual protection against any threats posed by hostile forces in this vast and dangerous country. The church, San Felipe de Neri, still stands on the spot. The building itself has been enlarged several times and remodeled, but its original thick adobe walls are still intact. The church is the hub of Old Town, the historic and sentimental heart of Albuquerque, with activity revolving around shopping and dining. To this day, special holidays and feast days are still commemorated as part of the year-round attractions of this "original" Albuquerque.

Whether due to its age or its location, or the open mindedness of its citizens, but the City of Albuquerque is also one with a number of haunted locations that we shall explore in this volume.

ALBUQUERQUE PRESS CLUB
201 Highland Park Circle, SW,
Albuquerque, NM 87102

Figure 2: The Albuquerque Press Club.

The Albuquerque Press Club is an organization that was founded in order to promote fellowship and understanding among men and women engaged in journalism and its allied fields. It also sponsors such cultural, educational and social activities as may promote good fellowship and professional growth among members; and to extend reciprocity to similar clubs in other parts of the nation and world. The Albuquerque Press Club is over a hundred years old at the time of this writing.

After a long search, the Albuquerque Press Club purchased the Whittlesey House in the seventies as its permanent quarters. This historic old home was designed by architect Charles F. Whittlesey and built on the Highland east of Albuquerque to be his family home in 1903[9]. It is a three-story frame structure designed after a Norwegian villa. Low-pitch roofs with exposed log fronting, rough log-cut facades and a wide porch, which surrounds its eastern rooms, characterize the house.

In 1908 the Whittleseys sold to Theodore S. Woolsey, Jr., Assistant District Forest Ranger U.S.F.S, who owned the house for the next twelve years. Early photos suggest that he added the addition to the south side of the house and framed out the northwest corner of the main porch. Records show that in 1916 he leased the house to Mr. Andros, President of Whitney Hardware, and in 1917 to Mr. Raynolds, President of the First National Bank.

In 1920, Arthur Hall purchased the home from Theodore Woolsey for his new bride. IN fact, according to the history of this historic old home, she refused to marry him unless he purchased this particular house as their home. Also, this was not to be a happy home for the couple, as Clifford Hall, the woman who would wed Arthur Hall only if this particular house was her home, divorced her

---

[9] http://www.albuquerquepressclub.org.

husband in 1930. In the property settlement, she was adamant that she wanted ownership of the house that she had come to love. In fact, she lived in her house for the next forty yeas. It was 'home' to her more than to any family prior to or after her ownership. She brought the house through periods of extensive remodeling and interior style changes.

By 1935, the former Mrs. Hall was remarried to Herbert McCallum, but this too would end in divorce in 1938. During the periods of time that she was single, Clifford supplemented her income as a nurse by renting portions of the house. The south porch was framed out and part of the first level was sealed off to make a separate apartment The original stable was renovated and added to, making it an apartment complex. An additional apartment was built adjacent to it. As new building materials were introduced, Clifford resurfaced the interior walls of the house. 'Whittlesey's rough wood and burlap surfaces were covered by celutex, plaster and wood planking.

Clifford McCallun loved this old home and put her heart and sole into making it into a showplace. However, there comes a time when the frailty of the human form becomes an added factor that must be considered. So too did this happen to he indomitable Clifford McCallum.

Though it was as hard as selling one of her children, in 1960 Clifford McCallum sold the house. Her increasing age, the extensive upkeep on the structure and numerous other reasons contributed to her decision. Zeta Mu Zeta House Corp. of Lambda Chi Alpha Fraternity purchased the house to be a fraternity house. The structure with it many rooms and apartment-like situation suited the fraternity well. Little information was available about the fraternity's activities, their members having moved elsewhere, inadequate fraternity records, etc. The fraternity sold the house in 1966 to John T. Roberson, who leased the structure.

A BIT OF HISTORY ABOUT CHARLES F. WHITTLESEY

Charles Frederick Whittlesey was born on March 10, 1867 in Alton, Illinois. He studied architecture in Chicago under Louis Sullivan, whose influences can be seen in Whittlesey's later concrete structures in California. The extent of friendship between Whittlesey and Frank Lloyd Wright, who also worked in Sullivan's office during this time period, is unknown. But, the expertise that Whittlesey was to later gain in reinforced concrete in California, prior to its extensive use by Wright, suggests that the two friends shared information when their paths again crossed in California.

In 1891 (age 24) Whittlesey began his own practice. Within this decade, he married his first wife, Edith May, and began to raise his family -- two sons, Harold and Austin and two daughters, Enid and Beatrice. He made his home in Riverside, a suburb of Chicago.

By 1900 (age 33) the Santa Fe Railroad, in recognizing Whittlesey's originality and talent, appointed him chief architect in charge of hotels and stations. Thus, in 1901 he came to Albuquerque, New Mexico to supervise the construction of the Alvarado Hotel. This hotel was one of his most noted works, with its mission style and pueblo Indian motif, characteristic of railroad structures extending to and through California. During these early years of the century, Whittlesey conducted his business from Albuquerque, as might be noted by a classified ad appearing in the Albuquerque Journal Democrat during the first half of May 1902:

"Architect, Charles F. Whittlesey, Main off. Albuquerque, Branch off. Chicago, El Paso, Los Angeles, Patronage solicited all over the southwest. Wide experience to all kinds of building."

Whittlesey's family arrived in Albuquerque on May 8, 1902, just three days prior to the opening of the Alvarado Hotel.

"Architect Whittlesey is happy for another reason besides the opening of the new hotel. His wife and children arrived yesterday from Coronado Beach."

The family residence, it seems, would always be a distance from Charles Whittlesey's active concerns. While the family resided in Albuquerque, 1902 to 1905 and possible as late as 1908, he was active supervising the construction of Harvey Hotels at Merced, Bakersfield, and Cochran, California; Trinidad, Colorado; Raton, New Mexico, and Shawnee. It was in 1902, in Albuquerque, that he designed tow structures in log and stone. The first of these was the El Tovar hotel at the Grand Canyon, a design still recognized today. The other was his Albuquerque residence, the structure covered by this survey.

By 1905 Charles Whittlesey was spending most of his time in Los Angeles. During these years, he observed, studied and tested the principles of reinforced concrete until he became convinced of its value as a building material. In Los Angeles, he designed and directed the construction of the Philharmonic Auditorium (1905) and soon afterwards, the Hunington Hotel in Pasadena (originally Hotel Wentworth). The Philharmonic Auditorium was designed with cantilevered concrete balconies (max. cantilever 28' and concrete bowed beams (max. span 112'). The Hunington Hotel used cellular concrete construction consisting of 6" bearing walls at each room partition, continuous floor slabs and no furred ceiling space. For their day, they were hold and innovative uses of reinforced concrete.

In 1906 Whittlesey went to San Francisco to assist in its reconstruction after the earthquake. The Pacific Building (still standing today at 421 Market, the southwest corner of Market and 4th SL), a ten-story concrete structure, is an example of his work there. His expertise in reinforced concrete was well noted by 1908, both in the many buildings that bore his name and in the various writings and expositions he wrote.

The Whittlesey family followed Charles from Albuquerque to Los Angeles and San Francisco. They lived there through 1920. Charles conducted his practice from the Pacific Building through 1912 and then from his residence. In 1912 his first wife Edith divorced him. He later married Mabel. His son Austin studied under him and later became an architect; Harold became a structural engineer, both collaborating on many designs built on the West Coast. Of Whittlesey's life and work beyond this date, little information was available at the time of this writing.

For the record, the following four buildings designed by Whittlesey are listed:

In Los Angeles:
- The Mayflower Hotel (1926-27);
- The residence of Mrs. Bartlett;
- The Whittlesey Residence (corner of Pico Blvd. and St. Andrews Place (unknown if still existent); and
- The Green Hotel in Pasadena.

THE GHOSTS

Clifford Ball McCallum loved this house more than anything else in the world. So is it any wonder that she would want to keep an eye on the house where she had spent so much of her life? The spirit of "Mrs. M", as she has become known, has been known to appear in the bar area. Some bartenders even go so far as to leave a drink on the bar in case she should want a drink.

The sound of high heeled shoes has been heard by several witnesses walking across the floors of the bar and lobby area. Noises have also been associated with the pool table in a room downstairs. Voices and balls moving about on the pool table of their own accord comprise a few of these accounts. The piano in the lobby has also been played (3 notes) by an unseen presence.

The apparition of a woman in a black shawl has been reported on several occasions in various locations throughout the building. Cats at the club have been observed watching and hissing at an unseen presence.

THE ARROYRO
Albuquerque, New Mexico

The Arroyro is believed to be haunted by Albuquerque's version of La Llorona. This particular spirit is called "el Yorone" the crier is the ghost of a mother whose child was drowned in the drainage ditch. It s said at night she wanders the ditch crying and searching for her lost child"

CARRIE TINGLY CHILDREN'S HOSPITAL
1113 University Boulevard
Albuquerque, New Mexico

Until the 1930s, a child with polio was most likely to be kept home and very little said. However, during the 1930s, Franklin Delano Roosevelt was elected President of the United States. President Roosevelt also suffered from Polio. Suddenly the disease was nothing to be hidden, but one to be fought with all of the assets at the disposal of the government. So it was that in the autumn of 1937, the doors opened on New Mexico's new children's hospital. This new facility was named after Carrie Tingley, wife of then Governor Clyde Tingley, who felt a hospital was needed for the children of the state who were suffering from polio.

Again following the example of President Roosevelt, the Tingleys chose the site of Hot Springs, later named Truth or Consequences, located in southern New Mexico. It was known for its healing mineral waters, and it resembled the site in Warm Springs, Georgia, where their friend President Franklin Roosevelt was treated for polio.

As polio became less widespread due to new vaccines, the hospital direction began to focus on other orthopedic conditions such as scoliosis, clubfoot, cerebral palsy and spina bifida.

In 1981, the hospital moved to Albuquerque to align itself closer with medical services and consultants here. In 1987 the University of New Mexico (UNM) Board of Regents was appointed as the Carrie Tingley Hospital (CTH) Board of Directors. Subsequent legislative action merged Carrie Tingley Hospital with the UNM Medical Center.

Carrie Tingley Hospital is now a component of the University of New Mexico Health Sciences Center. CTH houses a 24-bed inpatient unit and conducts 21 specialized clinics for children from birth to 21 years of age. A community outreach program visits 16 communities throughout New Mexico, enabling rural patients to be seen by CTH doctors and staff.

Surgery is also performed at University Hospital. All children who are residents of New Mexico may receive services. Rehabilitation is in-house under the care of board-certified doctors and therapists. Carrie Tingley Hospital has a full service orthotics and prosthetics department to meet all the children's needs.

THE GHOSTS

Less well known are the stories of hauntings that have spread about the facility occupied by the hospital when it moved to Albuquerque. It is said that there are some unused portions in the hospital building that contain glowing rooms and strange figures.

Other former employees talk about invisible "force fields" that do not allow a person to pass into certain rooms. The force fields also make a static/hissing sound when encountered by an unsuspecting worker.

There have also been stories regarding voices being heard that cry out for help. At other times sounds similar to very loud heartbeats can be heard echoing through the silent halls. Several maintain that they have seen black robed figures walking about the hallways.

DESERT SANDS MOTEL
5000 Central Avenue, SE
Albuquerque, New Mexico

The Desert Sands Motel was built in 1957 and is comprised of 67 rooms on two floors. Once described as a first class facility in the 1960s, this motel has certainly seen better days. As has happened to many formerly top notch motels, it is now living out its days as a resting place for drifters and those with little disposable income. It also appears to be the resting place for many unseen residences.

The Desert Sands Motel is now ranked number 116 in a ranking of hotels/motels in Albuquerque. On the other hand it is a cheap and easy place to stay when you're headed west on Interstate 40.

THE HAUNTINGS

Several guests who stayed in the corner room on the first floor of the center building have reported that they had some very unusual things happen to them. Several said that almost as soon as they had entered their room and put their bags down on the bed, unusual things began to happen. There were cold spots in some parts of the room and unexplainable voices were heard coming from the bathroom.

In addition to the mysterious voices, the water in the bathroom ran by itself and the TV in the room kept turning on and off on its own. As if this was not bad enough, when it was not turning itself off, the television set was also changing channels by itself. The final straw for these guests was when the outside door kept unlocking of its own accord.

HAUNTED HILL
The end of Menaul
Albuquerque, New Mexico

The location called Haunted Hill is said to be located at the end of Menaul. This broad thoroughfare crosses the city of Albuquerque until it ends in the foothills.

Though who have ascended this haunted high ground report that they could hear the sounds of women screaming, footsteps crossing the hard packed earth and what sounded like bodies being drug through the dirt.

Others have reported seeing a lantern swinging in the darkness as if someone is walking down the trail and more than a few are adamant that they saw the apparition of an old man coming after them. According to the story, years ago, an old man lived in some of the many caves at the top of the hill. He hated prostitutes and would go out to some of the city's night spots after dark and kidnap women that he considered to be evil. He would then bring them back up to his home on the hill where he would torture and kill the scarlet women. It is said that after killing these unfortunate women, he would drag their bodies to graves that he had already prepared where he would then bury the evidence of his crimes.

ABANDONED INSANE ASYLUM
Corner of Edith and Osuna
Albuquerque, New Mexico

For whatever reason, it has long been felt that there was something healing about the air in the desert southwest. Perhaps this is the reason that there were so many hospitals and mental asylums built in Albuquerque. As might be suspected, many of these facilities have fallen into disuse.

There is an abandoned house located on the corner of Edith and Osuna that was once an insane asylum. The property is now owned by some of the neighbors who go to great lengths to keep trespassers from entering the property for a variety of reasons. As I made reference to earlier, this empty structure was formerly used as an Insane Asylum and there were several murders committed inside the building by some of the patients.

For those who have risked going into the empty building, it is said that they have sometimes seen a large black cloud hovering in one of the hallways. Interestingly enough, this unusual black cloud has appeared in several photographs taken by some of the more intrepid explorers.

It is also said that one of the patients confined in the building went so crazy that he went on a rampage and killed several patients and members of the staff. According to the story, after the murders, strange things began to happen in the asylum and many of the staff refused to work after dark. As a result, the management of the Asylum was forced to close it.

Currently, the neighbors of the deserted building that used to house the insane asylum are members of The Banditos Motorcycle gang. In typical biker fashion, they have made it clear that they would not hesitate to release their Rottweiler on anyone who enters their property.

THE KIMO THEATER
423 Central Avenue
Albuquerque, New Mexico

The KIMO Theatre, a Pueblo Deco picture palace, opened on September

Figure 3: The KIMO Theater.

19, 1927. Pueblo Deco was a flamboyant, short-lived architectural style that fused the spirit of the Native American cultures of the Southwest with the exuberance of Art Deco. Pueblo Deco appeared at a time when movie-mad communities were constructing film palaces based on exotic models such as Moorish mosques and Chinese pavilions. Native American motifs appeared in only a handful of theatres; of those few, the KIMO is the undisputed king.

The genius behind the KIMO was Oreste Bachechi, a motivated entrepreneur from humble origins. Oreste Bachechi came to the United States in 1885 and set up a business in a tent near the railroad tracks in Albuquerque. Bachechi's fortunes expanded with the city's growth; he became a liquor dealer and proprietor of a grocery store while his wife Maria ran a dry goods store in the Elms Hotel. By 1919, the Bachechi Amusement Association operated the Pastime Theatre with Joe Barnett. In 1925, Oreste Bachechi decided to achieve "an ambition, a dream that has been long in realization," by building his own theatre, one that would stand out among the Greek temples and Chinese pavilions of contemporary movie mania.

Bachechi envisioned a unique, Southwestern style theatre, and hired Carl Boller of the Boller Brothers to design it. The Bollers had designed a Wild West-Rococo-style theatre in San Antonio and a Spanish cathedral cum Greco-Babylonian interior in St. Joseph, Missouri.

Figure 4: The Balcony Stairs Where Bobby Darnall Is Said To Play.

Carl Boller traveled throughout New Mexico, visiting the pueblos of Acoma and Isleta, and the Navajo Nation. After months of research, Carl Boller submitted a watercolor rendering that pleased Oreste Bachechi.

The interior was to include plaster ceiling beams textured to look like logs and painted with dance and hunt scenes, air vents disguised as Navajo rugs, chandeliers shaped like war drums and Native American funeral canoes, wrought iron birds descending the stairs and rows of garlanded buffalo skulls with eerie, glowing amber eyes.

None of the designs were chosen at random. Each of the myriad images of rain clouds, birds and swastikas had historical significance. The swastika is an original Navajo symbol for life, freedom and happiness. Only later was the swastika copied by Hitler for use as a symbol in Nazi Germany. Like its abstract symbols, color, too, was part of the Indian vocabulary. Yellow represents the life-giving sun, white the approaching morning, red the setting sun of the West and black the darkening clouds from the North. The crowning touch was the seven murals painted in oil by Carl Von Hassler. Working from a platform hung from the ceiling, Von Hassler spent months on his creations.

The theatre, which cost $150,000, was completed in less than a year. The elaborate Wurlitzer organ that accompanied the silent films of the day was an extra $18,000. On opening night, an overflow crowd watched performances by representatives from nearby Indian pueblos and reservations. The performers, reported the New Mexico State Tribune in an advance story, included "numerous prominent tribesman of the Southwest who will perform for the audience mystic rites never before seen on the stage."

Isleta Pueblo Governor Pablo Abeita won a prize of $50, a magnificent sum for the time, for naming the new theatre. Reflecting the optimism of the time, "KIMO," is a combination of two words literally meaning "mountain lion" but more liberally interpreted as "king of its kind.

Vivian Vance, who gained fame as Lucille Ball's sidekick in the "I Love Lucy" series, performed at the KIMO. The theatre also hosted such stars as Sally Rand, Gloria Swanson, Tom Mix and Ginger Rogers. When the theatre was packed, the balcony—which spans the east to west walls without support and was designed to give and sway—would drop four to eight inches in the middle.

A year after the realization of his dream, Oreste Bachechi died, leaving the management of the KIMO to his sons, who combined vaudeville and out-of-town road shows with movies. Extra revenue came in from a luncheonette and curio shop on either side of the entrance. In later years, the Kiva-Hi, and second floor restaurant, and KGGM radio, housed on the second and third floors, were major tenants.

In 1951, the boiler in the basement exploded, demolishing a section of the lobby and killing a young boy. Ten years later, a fire destroyed part of the stage area. The movie house then closed in 1968, although the stage is still used by local performing arts groups.

The KIMO fell into disrepair following the exodus from downtown that so many American cities experienced. Slated for destruction, the KIMO was saved in 1977 when the citizens of Albuquerque voted to purchase this unrivaled palace to movies and one man's dream[10].

---

[10] http://www.cabq.gov/kimo/history.html

THE GHOSTS

There are actually several spirits that seem to haunt this historic old theater. According to those who have had a long association with the KIMO Theater, in 1951 a six year old boy named Bobby Darnall was killed when the boiler in the basement exploded, demolishing part of the original lobby. The boiler was located right beneath the concession stand in the lobby. Bobby, who had been sitting in the theatre balcony with some of his friends, suddenly was frightened by something he saw on the movie screen and ran down the staircase to the lobby. Just as he arrived, the boiler exploded killing little Bobby and completely destroying part of the lobby. It is the spirit of little Bobby who is said to continue to haunt the KIMO Theatre today.

There is also the spirit of an unknown woman, wearing a bonnet that has often been reported walking down the halls of the theatre appearing to be just going about her business. Nothing more is known of this ghostly presence, but seemingly she doesn't disturb anyone, she just likes strolling about the old theatre.

However, it is the spirit of little Bobby that is a much more prevalent force and has been known to play all kinds of impish tricks upon staff and guests of the old theatre. Often seen playing on the lobby staircase near the scene of his death, those who have seen the spirit of little Bobby report that he always wears a striped shirt and blue jeans.

According to the stories told about this old building, the impish spirit of Bobby Darnall causes the performers problems by tripping them and creating a ruckus during performances. To appease the spirit, the cast hangs doughnuts on the water pipe that runs along the back wall of the theatre behind the stage. Often, the treats are gone the next morning. Of those that are left, several people have said that bite marks made by a little mouth, can sometimes be seen.

One year, a crew preparing for a Christmas production took down the stale doughnuts. No sooner were the doughnuts removed, when the technical rehearsal started to become a disaster, with everything going wrong, from lighting, to sound problems, and more. When the treats were replaced, things began to run smoothly again. Staff no longer takes chances with rehearsals, as Bobby is well-behaved as long as he has his doughnuts. Now, they stay there. There are two other entities that seem to be much older than the young boy, seeming to date from the theater's opening night in the fall of 1927. These entities seem to be from that long forgotten era. Very little seems to be known about them.

JOB CORP BUILDING
Albuquerque, New Mexico

The Job Corps Program is a United States Department of Labor no-cost education and vocational training that helps young people ages 16 through 24 get a better job, make more money and take control of their lives.

At Job Corps, students enroll to learn a trade, earn a high school diploma or GED and get help finding a good job. When you join the program, you will be paid a monthly allowance; the longer you stay with the program, the more your allowance will be. Job Corps supports its students for up to 12 months after they graduate from the program.

To be eligible to enroll in Job Corps, students must meet the following requirements:

- Be 16 through 24;
- Be a U.S. citizen or legal resident;
- Meet income requirements;
- Be ready, willing and able to participate fully in an educational environment.

Funded by the United States Congress, Job Corps has been training young adults for meaningful careers since 1964. Job Corps is committed to offering all students a safe, drug-free environment where they can take advantage of the resources provided. Almost all major cities in the Untied States have a Job Corp presence.

The building that houses the Job Corp Offices in Albuquerque, New Mexico is a large warehouse that was once used by a major manufacturing concern in better times. Now it is home to a number of training programs designed to help young people find jobs.

As an additional assist to those preparing for these new jobs, if they have nowhere else to live, the Albuquerque Job Corp has a dormitory on the second floor of the building for student use.

THE GHOSTS

A number of those who have sought to utilize the services offered by the Albuquerque Job Corp have reported that by the lunch room in the building they have seen a nun that is sometimes said to be carrying a baby. It is also said that she can be seen when the lights on the light posts are turned on.

On the girls' side of the new dorms there have been reports of unseen people running up and down the hallway. Even if one of the girls looks out her door as soon as she hears the sounds of running, the hallway is always empty.

MARIA TERESA RESTAURANT & 1840 BAR
618 Rio Grande NW
Albuquerque, New Mexico

Figure 5: The Maria Teresa Restaurant.

The Old Savador Armijo House, which dates from 1840, is now the Maria Teresa Restaurant and 1840 Bar. The building has a long and varied history as it has been occupied continually since being constructed. A center piece in the Restaurant is the long bar which was originally removed from Fort Sumner, New Mexico and installed in this historic old building in 1970. This 1800s homestead is now the home of a romantic restaurant. The bar has the distinction of having quenched the thirst of, among others, the notorious outlaw Billy the Kid and members of his gang.

THE GHOSTS

This beautiful old hacienda, turned restaurant, is reputed to be one of the most haunted buildings in Albuquerque. According to a news article in the

Albuquerque Journal[11], customers often mention the strange energy of the historic building that houses this Old Town restaurant. Owner Rob Spaulding agrees.

"The first time I walked into the Armijo room, I was instantly covered in goose bumps," he says.

Creepy already, the Armijo room is made creepier still by a portrait of Dona Jesusita Salazar de Baca, whose eyes seem to follow you all over the room.

Spaulding says the restaurant is haunted by at least three ghosts — Maria de la Nieves Sarracino, the lady of the house; a youngish woman who wears a red flapper dress; and a mournful male presence, probably the ghost of a man who hanged himself there in the late 1800s. Spaulding says he had one bartender — an ardent nonbeliever — quit immediately after seeing the ghost in the red flapper dress.

The ghost of Maria is the most well known, according to Daniel Lamb, a 14-year employee of the restaurant and its resident historian. Lamb says Maria's family kept journals, which describe her apparition appearing not long after her death. Superstitious, they took down all photos of Maria in the building.

After Maria Teresa's was established, Lamb was invited to examine these family journals. He also got to see a lone photo of Maria — she was wearing a beaded white French dress and had her hair in a bun. Lamb says although there are no portraits of Maria in the building, customers repeatedly describe seeing a woman wearing a beaded white dress walking through the building.

One way Maria apparently amuses herself, Lamb says, is by taking dessert orders — she even brings her own dessert cart. This presents a bit of a problem when an actual member of the wait staff shows up a table and customers say the lady in the beaded gown already took their order.

"I have to explain that the woman was a ghost," Lamb says, "and that the restaurant doesn't own a dessert cart."

As with any house over a hundred years old, there have been a lot of emotions unleashed inside these four walls. These days the Zamora room seems to be the most active at the moment. Silverware placed on the tables in this room has been rearranged numerous times to form crosses. The glass shade to a light fixture shattered on its own, however the light bulb inside was not damaged.

In the Armijo Room a glass levitated off the table, flew across the room, hit the wall, bounced back and landed back upon the table. In this same room, another very unusual event was witnessed by the manager and five patrons who were enjoying the fine food served here. According to the reports, a waitress was carrying a tray of water glasses into the room when, one by one, they started exploding.

---

[11] Wheeler, Liza, N.M. Has Its Share of Haunts, Albuquerque Journal, Thursday, October 31, 2002.

A number of current and former employees of the Restaurant have reported hearing voices coming from empty rooms and hearing other odd noises as if invisible activity was going on around them. A number of the female employees have also reported experiencing the sensation of being touched by invisible hands.

Others have reported a piano that plays by itself, mirrors that show reflections of ghosts, silverware that moves on its own and many reports of apparitions.

RADISSON HOTEL
Albuquerque, New Mexico

As might be expected of a city with the age and history of Albuquerque, there are a large number of hotels and motels available to potential travelers. In addition to indoor plumbing, some of the rooms even come with live in spirits. One such hotel is the Radisson.

THE GHOSTS

There have been a large number of unusual happenings reported as taking place inside this hotel. Some have reported that while staying on the first floor of the hotel they have heard peculiar scratching noises and the loud slamming of doors from the floor above, even if there was no one renting the room above them.

Others have talked of stories that they have heard about loud yelling and screaming coming from rooms that are vacant and sometimes women who stay in some of these rooms report being shaken from a deep sleep by what seems to feel like children's hands.

All of the floors have been remodeled except the third floor. In fact, guests are not normally permitted on the third floor. A few hardy souls who have been able to gain access to this floor report that as soon as the elevator doors opened they were hit with a gust of hot air. As they walked further along the hallway on this floor there is an area that was originally outfitted as a bar. The top of the bar itself is in perfect condition but the rest of it is completely destroyed. Several individual who have had the opportunity to get into this area report that in the corner of the bar was what appears to be newly broken glass. No one had an explanation for the broken glass as the staff rarely goes into the area and none of the windows were broken.

RAMADA HOTEL
Albuquerque, New Mexico

The Ramada Hotel in Albuquerque is another hotel with a somewhat unusual past and some permanent guests who are not registered at the front desk.

THE GHOSTS

According to some of the hotel staff, one of the spirits resides on the first floor of this large hotel. She said to be a very pretty young broken hearted lady, who was murdered in one of the first floor corner rooms by her lover who wanted her out of his life. She is said to only be on the bottom floor of the hotel, dividing her time between the hotel lobby and the corner room where she was killed.

More than one chamber maid has reported the when housekeeping goes to clean the corner room where the young was murdered that invariably find it in disarray. Among the things reported to have been found in this room are the bed sheets torn off of the bed and thrown onto the floor, the television set knocked onto the floor and the curtains torn from the curtain rods.

This type of activity went on so long in this particular room that finally, the hotel management just closed off the room and do not even make it available for guests. However, out of curiosity, periodically, the staff still visits the room. They always find it is a shambles.

SAN PEDRO PUBLIC LIBRARY
5600 Trumbull Avenue, SW
Albuquerque, New Mexico

It has been my experience that many librarians are completely and totally dedicated to their jobs. They love the books and the building in which they are housed. It is also said that many of the librarians centered their lives around the books over which they had charge. So is it any wonder that some of them might return to haunt the library in which they spent most of their lives?

THE GHOSTS

I have had a number of people tell me that late at night, around closing, they have heard strange noises inside the San Pedro Public Library. Some have even said that they hear footsteps among the shelves and if they forget where they are at and talk to someone near them too loud, they hear a faint shushing as if someone wanted them to lower their voices.

Others have reported hearing the voice of one of the deceased librarians softly asking them to check out a book just as she was wont to do at closing time during her life. I also have in my files reports of several instances where the sounds of giggling were heard in this library as if children are playing among the many shelves of books.

There are also reports of the lights turning off by themselves.

XILNIX, INC.
7801 Jefferson Street, NE
Albuquerque, New Mexico

Like many firms are doing these days, the Xilnix Company moved into an older building and renovated it to suit their needs. In this particular instance, the old building selected by this computer firm started its life as a mental heath hospital. Of course, when this high tech firm purchased this building I am sure they had no intention on also purchasing a ghost.

THE GHOSTS

Former employees and others who have had cause to visit this historic building have reported that on several occasions banging noises have been heard. These sounds seem to echo throughout the building, but they seem to originate in the bathroom. Of course whenever anyone tries to track down the source of the sounds, nothing is ever found.

Others have reported seeing shadowy figures moving up and down the hallways, appearing to duck into rooms whenever someone tries to pursue them. Of course when the would-be ghost chaser dashes into the room the mysterious figures just entered, no one is ever found.

There is an outdoor courtyard from which groaning noises have been heard periodically. Others have heard low pitched voices coming form the back office area. Of course in both cases, investigators never find any sign that anyone caused the groans or the voices. Finally, there have been several instances when objects began to move all by themselves.

LAS MANANITAS
1800 Rio Grande Boulevard, NW
Albuquerque, New Mexico

There is no written record of when the adobe structure standing on the northwest corner of present day Indian School and Rio Grande, Albuquerque, New Mexico was built. Legend and word of mouth has it that some parts of the building are over 300 years old.

The current owners, Paul and Linda, took over Las Mananitas in 1991. Before Paul and Linda, it was a restaurant operated from 1985 to 1990 by a previous Albuquerque Mayor.

Before becoming a restaurant the property was owned and used as a residence by Sheila Garcia, The Kinney's, The Harrison's and the Gilstrap's. There are stories of huge social parties held by previous owners. Before its use as a residence, verbal history has it remembered as a brothel, saloon and billiards hall. Reportedly the structure was originally built as a stagecoach stop along the historic El Camino Real.

Neighbors and previous owners have told Paul and Linda some of the events and history of the building. At one time there was a farm and a blacksmith located on the property as well. Neighbors would hear the bang and clang of the blacksmith at work.

Original wooden ceiling beams and kiva fireplaces still exist. When the building was renovated in 1991 over five tons of dirt was removed from the original sod roof. There are light fixtures in many rooms and medicine cabinets in both bathrooms that were saved from the famous Albuquerque Hotel Alvarado. (The Alvarado Hotel was a fixture in Albuquerque from 1896 until 1945, when it was torn down.)

THE GHOSTS

Paul and Linda were told when they took over the restaurant in 1991 that it was haunted.

In their fourteen years at Las Mañanitas, Paul and Linda have witnessed and been told first hand of several occurrences. There does not seem to be any pattern. The building will be quiet for months at a time then there will be a flurry of unexplained activity for several days in a row.

Reportedly, one previous owner, Mrs. Kinney was plagued by what she thought were 'evil spirits'. She stated that plates flew out of the oven at her and that the doors inside the building would slam shut after she walked through them. The slamming doors unnerved Mrs. Kinney so badly that she had all of the interior doors removed and to this day they remain stacked in the garage.

Supposedly Mrs. Kinney brought in members of the church to perform an exorcism to no avail.

The wait staff employed when Paul and Linda took over the restaurant told them to be sure that they "left toys out for the kids". They were told that the ghost's of a boy and a girl were often seen playing out on the patio or heard playing in the house. Linda leaves toys in hidden areas of the building and then returns to find that they have been somehow broken.

One evening after closing, Paul entered the dining room to find the metal chandelier swinging wildly back and forth. All of the windows and doors were closed in the building, the heat and air conditioning were turned off, and there was no breeze or air flowing in the room. Paul called for Linda to come look. When Linda entered the room she too saw the chandelier swinging from side to side and asked Paul, "What are you doing?!" Paul stated, "I did not do a thing! It was moving when I walked in!" They could not explain the chandelier's movement.

Guests seated in the main dining room have witnessed "something flying in and out of the fireplace". Witnesses state that a "cloud" or "ball of smoke" shot out of the fireplace then moved extremely fast into the center of the room where it dissipated in front of everyone's eyes. One of the guests asked afterwards if they could perform a séance in the room but their request was denied.

Paul and Linda's cat often runs throughout the building as if it is playing with someone. It looks like it is chasing someone or being chased.

Several times Paul and Linda heard what sounded like a squeaky rocking chair rocking bath and forth, in what is now their office, when no one was in the room. A few months later a psychic visited Las Mañanitas. She asked if she could look around as she felt the presence of "spirits". She walked into what is now their office and told Paul and Linda that she saw a "sewing room with a rocking chair".

The psychic also stated that she felt that a man was hanged in one of the back, older rooms of the building. This is the only mention Paul and Linda have ever heard of a murder or death in the building. The hanging can not be proved but Paul and Linda state, "given the building's sordid past, it would not surprise us if it were true!"

The lights go on and off at random. One instance in particular, Paul noticed that the lights in the main dining room were turned off. Paul went and checked the light switch, which is a round dimmer type of switch, and found the switch still turned on. Paul turned the switch off, leaving the lights off, and left the room. A few moments later Paul looked at the dining room and noticed that the lights were now on! He checked the dimmer switch only to find it still in the "off" position. He left the lights on and left the building.

The building is made of adobe and retains heat extremely well. In fact, on hot a summer's day the temperature inside can be quite unpleasant. But at times, the staff will walk through what they describe as unexplainable "really cold spots".

One winter's morning Paul and another employee arrived at work, driving across the virgin snow, almost four inches high, in the parking lot. They were the first to arrive that day. The ground was beautiful with the untouched coating of fresh snow. As they entered the gate to the courtyard they noticed very large footprints in the snow in front of them, walking in a sort of oval route towards the house. However - the tracks seemed to just start and stop with no visible trail leading to or away from them. Paul says the footprints were "Huge - at least a size 14." And that it was "almost as if the person had been placed then lifted off of the ground and disappeared."

One busy afternoon Paul and an employee were frantically cooking in the kitchen. One of the waiters reported to them that they were out of clean coffee cups. The sounds of the dishwasher running and the rattling of dishes could be heard coming from the sink area of the kitchen. Paul assumed that Linda was in back washing dishes and he was a bit upset that she was not out waiting on customers. Just then, Linda walked into the kitchen from the dining room. Paul and the employee both asked, "Well then who is back there doing the dishes?" All three of them heard the noise and rattling coming from the back. They went to look but no one was there. However, they found that all of the coffee cups had mysteriously washed themselves and were drying in the rack.

Customers often ask, out of the blue, if the building is haunted. They state that they 'feel' a presence and that they 'know' it is haunted. Once, a male customer sat out in his car for over an hour and would not join his wife inside for dinner because he felt so uncomfortable.

A professional photographer, Allencort, once visited Las Mañanitas. She took a few pictures around the property. A copy of one of these photos now hangs in the hallway. The copy was sent to Paul and Linda from a Wisconsin Art Gallery where the original photo is on display. Many people report seeing the faint, hidden image of a Grandmother and a Cat in the photo. Allencort returned to Las Mañanitas several times attempting to take more pictures. However, every single photo she shot on subsequent visits never turned out; these photos were completely black.

Paul and Linda believe that there are two main ghosts who haunt Las Mañanitas. The first is a woman they call 'Priscilla'. Paul and Linda both state that they can "feel her presence". "You know when she is here", they say, "because you can smell her perfume throughout the entire restaurant." The building will be closed with only them in it and the over powering, strong, perfume will fill the air. At other times, customers have even complained about the strong smell.

A Mariachi who often played in the restaurant stated that once he entered the back dining room and saw a woman in a big, fancy, white dress. He looked away for a moment, and when he looked back, she had vanished.

A busboy once saw a blonde haired girl wearing a plaid colored sweater enter the men's bathroom. The bus boy waited and waited for her to exit the bathroom. He knocked on the door and got no answer. He tried the doorknob but it was locked. He waited outside the door for almost an hour then knocked and tried the door again. Now the door was unlocked and when he entered he found the room empty.

The second ghost is that of a large young man. "He is very, very big," states Linda, "But you can tell he isn't that old; he's a young man." He is often seen out of the corner of her eye and Linda often mistakes the shadow for one of the waiters. She will see someone walk by and will call out to who she thinks it is, then she realizes that no one is really there.

Often Linda and other female employees will feel a light breeze blow by them then they feel the touch of fingers on their hips, a friendly and flirty sort of gesture. They will turn around to see who is behind them and no one will be there. Linda even tells the new female wait staff in advance "not to freak out" if this happens to them. One time, a customer felt a hand on her shoulder. When she turned around, no one was there.

The young niece of a frequent customer said that she often talks to 'someone' while in the bathroom of Las Mañanitas. The girl states, that a boy is in there under the bathroom floor. He talks to me."

When asked how she talked to this boy under the floor she just said, "I don't know - but we communicate." The girl had never heard any of the stories about the shadow of a young man seen in the building.

One afternoon the young girl ran out of the bathroom squealing in excitement, "He told me his name! He told me his name! His name is Joaquin!"

It is believed by many that Priscilla, the woman seen in the fancy white dress, once worked in the brothel that is now Las Mañanitas. Priscilla became pregnant and had her child on the premises. Sadly, Priscilla died while giving birth to her son, Joaquin. To this day, Priscilla wanders the halls looking, in vain, for her son just as Joaquin still searches for his Mother.

PRIVATE RESIDENCE
Four Hills Area
Albuquerque, New Mexico

The residence is located in the Four Hills area of Albuquerque and is a two story single family dwelling with attached garage. The reporting party asks that we use only her first name in any web posts and do not specifically state her address.

Ashley has lived in the house for 2 1/2 years and states that there have been noises from upstairs since the beginning of occupancy. Since one year ago there has been an increase in activity. The house is 33 years old and has had three owners. Very little is known about the history of the house, except that a "mostly cosmetic" (floors, ceilings, paint) remodel was done about three years ago. The remodel did include some electrical work in the form of ceiling fan installations.

At the time of this writing, the house is for sale and has been on the market for about a month. No electricians or plumbers have been called to determine possible causes of the reported phenomena.

- General noises in upstairs section of house, mostly resembling footsteps or running children. The most common noise is the sound of running towards the master bedroom followed by rattling of the master bedroom doorknob.

- Locked doors will unlock and open themselves.

- Faucets will turn on by themselves.

- The bed in the master bedroom will shake, often enough to wake the occupant. This happens usually at night.

- Lights will turn themselves on.

- DVD player cords will unplug themselves.

- Orbs appear in pictures taken inside the house.

- A bizarre phone message was once left on the resident's voice mail. The speaker's voice was unintelligible, but seemed to transition from a little girl's voice to an angry man's voice. A tape of the message is not available, but was heard by a number of witnesses.

- Reported phenomena are "worse" when a group is in the house, and generally take place in the upstairs section of the house. Other witnesses have observed most forms of the reported phenomena.

Two psychic "cleansings" of this property were said to have been performed on April 4 and November 8 of 2003 by P. Burns, apparently a local person representing herself as a psychic or spiritual healer. Ms. Burns charged a substantial sum of money for each "cleansing" but the reported phenomena continued.

Heather, a friend of the resident, once burned sage and asked the "spirits" to leave. This reportedly made things worse. A Ouija board was also used to attempt contact with those responsible for the phenomena. No messages were received, but one person interviewed stated the board made a partial message along the lines of "you're not welcome."

LUNA-OTERO MANSION
The restaurant is twenty miles south of Albuquerque off I-25 in Las Lunas.
Las Lunas, New Mexico

Figure 6: The Luna-Otero Mansion.

Even though this historic structure is not inside the city limits of Albuquerque, it is close enough to that city and so involved in the history of the area that the distinction of being located in Las Lunas is really not important.

In 1692 Domingo de Luna came to New Mexico on a land grant from the King of Spain. A few years later, Don Pedro Otero came to Valencia County under similar circumstances. These two families grew, acquired fortunes in land and livestock, and became extremely powerful in politics and prominent in territorial society. The family heads became friends and business associates. The marriages of Solomon Luna to Adelaida Otero, and Manuel A. Otero to Eloisa Luna in the late 1800's united these two families into what became known as the Luna-Otero Dynasty.

In 1880 the Santa Fe Railroad wanted right-of-way through the Luna property. In return for this favor, and because the proposed railroad tracks went squarely through the existing Luna hacienda, the railroad agreed to build a new home to the specifications of Don Antonio Jose and his family. Legend has it that numerous trips through the South by the Luna family inspired the architectural design of the mansion. Whether or not this is true, the building is unique in that, while it is southern colonial in style, its basic construction material is adobe.

Because Don Antonio Jose died in 1881, the first family to occupy the mansion was his oldest son, Tranquilino. After Don Tranquilino's death in Washington while serving in the legislature, younger brother Solomon took the reins of the family. Although Solomon was probably the most famous of the Lunas, he was not very prolific. With no children in his family, control passed to his nephew, Eduardo Otero, in the early 1900's. It was during this time, specifically in the 1920's that the mansion truly became the outstanding building that now exists. During this period the solarium was constructed, the front portico was added, and the ironwork, which once surrounded about five times as much property as it now does, was erected. Responsible for these and other improvements was a talented and creative woman, Josefita Manderfield Otero, wife of Don Eduardo. Josefita, or Pepe as she is affectionately remembered, was a daughter of William R. Manderfield, founder of the Santa Fe New Mexican.

This fine lady ruled the mansion with a gentle and loving hand and spent her days caring for her magnificent gardens and applying paint to canvas. There are those in this area who still remember and speak highly of her.

The words "Los Lunas" in Spanish means, where the Lunas live. Before the arrival of the Santa Fe Railroad, Los Lunas identified a geographic location of the family's ranch headquarters and home. Growth as a town, and bustling bedroom community to Albuquerque that it is today, began after the railroad arrived.

THE GHOSTS

I can find no record of hauntings in this historic old home until the 1970's when the grand old mansion was remodeled into a restaurant. It was then that the ghost of one of the original family members, Josefita "Pepe" Otero, began to appear. Several employees have seen her ghost and describe her as very real looking, dressed in 1920's clothing. She haunts two former bedrooms on the second floor an attic storeroom and the top of the stairs which leads to the second floor bar.

One of the stories of the hauntings in this old home concerns the old rocking chair, which sits at the top of the stairs. Several employees have reported seeing the spectral figure of a woman seated in this chair, rocking slowly, as if she was taking a leisurely break. She looked so real that one evening one employee approached the figure as she sat peacefully rocking. Seeing the young man approaching, the woman stood up, then slowly vanished. This particular spirit has been seen many places in the restaurant, and many believe that it is Josefita, who still visits her old home.

It was also reported to me that one of the waitresses in the upstairs serving area had some encounters. According to the young woman in question, one evening she saw a man sitting quietly on one of the sofas, as if he was waiting to be served. She said that the man was dressed oddly. His clothing was more in keeping with what was worn many years ago. She also thought it somewhat unusual that he was not complaining about the fact that the staff seemed to be ignoring him. The waitress asked one of the other staff members why the man hadn't been served, and the other person said, "What man?" When the waitress looked over to the couch, the man just faded away.

The stairway that leads from the front door up to the second floor is a favorite place for Josefita. She walks up and down the stairs, and has been seen by employees and patrons alike. It was reported that one evening, the spirit of this indomitable old lady walked across the main downstairs dining room as if she owned the place. Of course, if it is the spirit of Josefita, she once did own the place. Why should death change that?

THE WOOL WAREHOUSE THEATER RESTAURANT
502 1st Street, NW
Albuquerque, New Mexico

The building in question began its life as a wool warehouse. Like most buildings in older areas of America's larger cities that are being considered for renovation and preservation of the historic buildings, this old building is now being used for something totally different than the purpose for which it was built.

In 1984, this abandoned old warehouse was purchased and converted into a dinner theater. Now the floors that used to groan under the weight of heavy bales of cotton resound to the sounds of the footsteps of the many customers that enjoy coming to this eatery and the wait staff that hurry from table to table. The stage area also now is a busy place as the actors and stage hands work to produce entertaining plays.

THE GHOSTS

In this particular instance, no one seems to know the identity of the spirit that haunts this historic building. However, no one seems to doubt his existence as he has been seen many times.

The unidentified ghost that seems fascinated by the plays that are part of the dinner theater entertainment is that of a man wearing a double breasted, cream colored suit. He has been observed by both customers as well as the actors standing near the stage during performances. Cold spots have also been reported in this same area, as well as the feeling of an unseen presence in the area around the stage.

CHURCH STREET CAFÉ
2111 Church Street
Albuquerque, New Mexico

Another haunted location in Albuquerque is the Church Street Café, built in 1709 as the home of the Ruiz family. This renovated 18 room hacienda is nestled in the shadows of the San Felipe de Neri Catholic Church and is the site of continuing unexplained activities.

There are those who say that Sara Ruiz is the cause of the hauntings in this historic old building. Sara was said to be a healer, well versed in the use of the many herbs that she collected. The locals could probably have tolerated this activity, as many placed more faith in homespun medicine than they did the early doctors of the area.

However, it was Sara's views on the conventions of the day that seems to have caused much of the gossip about her. She was definitely an unconventional woman. In a day and age when a proper woman married before having children, Sara never did marry, though she seems to have produced a large brood of children. In fact one of her children was the last of the Ruiz family to live in this beautiful old home. After the death of Rafinia Ruiz, the home was sold by the Ruiz family to Marie Coleman, the curent owner of the Church Street Café.

Of course, what no one thought to tell Marie was that Sara Ruiz had never left her former dwelling. A number of vents that have occurred convinced Marie that Sara Ruiz never got around to leaving the house she grew up in — despite being dead for more than a century.

It was during the renovation that Marie had her first brush with Sara. Since the old house required a great deal of renovation before it could be opened at the Church Street Café, Marie interviewed a number of contractors. TO her surprise, while she was taking one through the house, she could hear a woman's angry voice shouting at her to get that man out of the house at once.

Marie said later that she could feel the anger all around her as they moved from room to room and she rushed the contractor through the house barely giving him a chance to look at the work that needed to be done. Once outside the house, everything became calm. Marie had no idea who had been shouting at her, but she knew this man could not work on the house. She later learned that the prospective contractor was the grandson of a man Sara had been involved with long ago.

Marie finally convinced a friend to handle the work for her. She never mentioned the woman's voice she'd heard until the new contractor finally told her she'd have to do something about "that woman." "Tell her to stop kicking the buckets around," he told her. "Make her stop." Marie couldn't believe it, but Charlie was well aware of Sara. She asked just how she was supposed to stop her. He replied, "Talk to her."

Marie took his advice, and the spirit stopped kicking the buckets. That was the beginning of their relationship. Marie believes the spirit is Sara Ruiz and

Marie gives her the room and respect the former mistress of the house deserves. She greets her every morning and bids her good bye every night. Now and then, when Sara wants her attention, she tosses small pebbles at Marie. A waiter told Marie he saw the spirit of Sara in a long black dress, and customers have said they've felt a presence.

When Marie's brother Jim came in to help her, he would have none of this ghost nonsense. On the first night he locked up alone, he couldn't find his keys. The door was already locked, but he needed the keys to get out. He knew where he'd put them, but they weren't there. As he began an all out search, he heard a voice laughing. "All right, Sara," he said. "Leave me alone." He found the keys in his pocket. When he got to the door, it was unlocked. He quickly became a believer.

A number of people have said that they have seen Sara Ruiz performing daily chores — like feeding ghost chickens out back — and, at closing time, she is fond of engaging the owner in a battle of light switches: Marie Coleman turns them off, and Ruiz turns them on, ad nauseum.

There is a locked glass case in the lobby that contains figurines and pottery. There is one figurine from a nativity scene that Sara Ruiz apparently hates. Most mornings, when Marie Coleman arrives at work, that figurine is in a different position from where it was the night before. Sometimes, Coleman says, the figurine has been moved to the very edge of the glass shelf, so she has to maneuver carefully to keep it from falling when she opens the door. The employees all swear that they have not moved the figurines.

HIGH NOON RESTAURANT AND SALOON
425 San Felipe MW
Albuquerque, New Mexico

Another haunted building in Albuquerque's Old Town is a building that was originally built in 1785. During its long life, this historic old building has served as both a casino as well as a very successful brothel.

There are those who believe that this popular restaurant/saloon is haunted by the spirit of a trapper, who may responsible for customers and employees feeling a tap on the shoulder by an unseen presence or smelling the fireplace burning when it's not.

The ghost is often absent for long stretches, but when he is in residence, the spirit makes himself known by rattling dishes and, disconcertingly, calling out the wait staff's names.

The building in which the foyer and Santo room of the High Noon Saloon are located is one of the original structures in historic Old Town Albuquerque.

The date of August 20, 1850, is listed in the building's original territorial deed as the date of the first recorded sale of the building, when Quereva Griego De Chavez purchased it from Jose Delores Chavez. It changed owners four additional times between 1884 and 1965 when the present owner, George Sandoval, purchased the building from Carlos Vigil. Leonardo Huning, whose family built the famous Huning Castle which stood nearby on Central Avenue for many years, owned the structure from 1887 to 1894.

LA PINATA
2 Patio Market Street NW
Albuquerque, New Mexico

According to what I can find out, the building that houses the La Pinata once housed a school. The primary ghost that haunts this location is believed to be the spirit of a very hungry little boy who once attended this school. There were apparently a number of spirits who once visited this location, but after one spirit became especially violent, a psychic cleansing ceremony was held at the request of the owner in order to eject the spirits. Apparent his uninvited guests were making his life hell and hurting business. The psychic cleansing was only partially successful. All of the spirits except one were banished. Now only the little boy seems to be in residence.

There seem to be several areas of disturbance within the structure. In the bathroom there have been a number of electrical problems. This might be expected in an old building, but it seems to be very intermittent. In a back storeroom, an unseen presence knocked the owner off of a ladder. This event might mean that the violent spirit has not left, but is now much weaker in ability.

I am also told that the owner left a bowl of candy on the counter one evening as an offering to the little boy. When the owner left, the bowl was full of candy. The next morning, the owner, who was the first on to arrive, noticed that the bowl was half empty. Apparently the little boy enjoyed the candy.

LA PLACITA RESTAURANT
208 San Felipe Street NW
Albuquerque, New Mexico

The building that houses the La Placita Restaurant was supposedly built

Figure 7: La Placita.

around 1706 by Don Juan Armijo y Maestas and then later sold to Ambrosio Armijo. The building was constructed as what is called the classic placita (little plaza) style, developed for defense against raiding by Indian War Parties as well as various military units that fought across the desert southwest over its turbulent history.

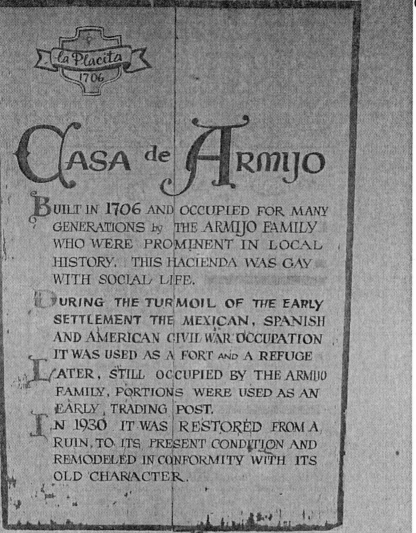

Figure 8: The History of La Placita.

According to the many stories about this historic old building, it is believed that the Casa Armijo is haunted by at least four different spirits, according to those who have worked at the restaurant. All would agree that the vast majority of reported phenomena seem to occur in the women's restroom and the upstairs area.

Almost everyone who would talk about their adventures at the former Casa de Armijo agree that it is was almost routine that they would hear their names called by someone who sounded as if they stood very close to them. When they would turn around the answer the call, there would be no one there.

A number of female employees would see the apparition of a young girl reflected in the mirrors of the women's restroom. When they would turn around to see who the young girl was, there would be no one in the restroom but themselves. Several who had experienced then reported that what is now the women's restroom was once a part of the bedroom of one of the young Armijo girls who is said to have died in the room of an unknown disease in the early 1900's.

Several people reported that they experienced cold spots can be felt at certain times throughout various locations in the building. Glowing lights have been seen floating in the hallways on the second floor near the manager's office.

BOTTGER KOCH MANSION
110 San Felipe Street NW
Albuquerque, New Mexico

The Bottger Mansion has a storied history, involving famous entertainers (Elvis, Sinatra), one known mobster (Machine Gun Kelly), and three ghosts who still visit frequently. The Mansion has won numerous awards and has been featured on PBS and QVC television programs. This year, an award-winning gladiator with a beautiful mind has spent time at the Mansion.

Construction was started in 1905 and completed within two years. Charles Bottger was a wool exporter originally from Germany who made his fortune after migrating to New Jersey. He moved to New Mexico – close to the Native American sheep ranchers– and built the Bottger Mansion in Old Town. There were four original mansions in Old Town, and only the Bottger remains, intact, virtually as it was when built.

Charles Bottger owned a saloon west of the Mansion (now the parking lot) and a toll bridge over the Rio Grande River. His saloon advertised "Fine Whiskeys, Fine Cigars, Fine Women and Billiards."

The Mansion was used as living quarters by three generations of Bottgers, then sold several times.

During the forties it was used as a home for a small colony of Buddhists. Later it was used as a restaurant downstairs, a boarding house and beauty salon upstairs. In 1955, a young Elvis Presley (along with Bill Black and Scotty Moore) performed two shows in Albuquerque and stayed at the Bottger, leaving the next day for a show in Amarillo.

In the late 50's, a prominent Italian family rented the Bottger for a large wedding. Frank Sinatra was a guest, who performed in the courtyard after the wedding dinner was served.

In the 40's, the FBI's Most Wanted criminal, Machine Gun Kelly, was being hunted by lawmen everywhere. Kelly, his girlfriend and his gang were headed back to Memphis from California and checked into the Bottger under assumed names. They had dyed their hair and purchased new clothes to help conceal their identities. After several days, the owners became suspicious when they noticed that the group always sent a neighborhood boy out to purchase the meals and bring them back to the Bottger for consumption in the rooms. They decided to notify the police, but were overheard by one of the gang members. They quickly left just ahead of the law. However, they were captured shortly thereafter and imprisoned.

The Garcia family purchased the Bottger and converted it to a B&B in the 80's. They did a great business for many years, before selling it to the Koch family in 1997. The Koch's changed the name to the Bottger-Koch Mansion during their ownership. The previous owners, Gary and Carole Millhollon purchased it from the Koch's in 2003, and reverted to the original, historic name. Steve and Kathy Hiatt purchased the Mansion in 2004.

THE GHOSTS

Depending on which past owner (or Old Town resident) you speak to, there are at least three ghosts (and some say six) living in the Bottger.

All are harmless, but do play pranks. "The Old Man" (whom many assume is Charles himself) is a regular. He will occasionally pace in the parlor or stairway, usually late at night.

The "Grandmother" ghost just sighs. She is most often heard in the Linda Lee and the Carole Rose suites. No one has ever reported seeing her, but many, many guests report hearing her sigh from time to time. Some believe that she is Charles' granddaughter who died as a very old lady and lamented the fact that her children intended to sell the property after her death (which they did).

One story has it that they locked her out of the house one night after her bath; she caught pneumonia, and died, thus assuring their inheritance.

The "Lover Ghost" is often featured in the Old Town Ghost Tour. He reportedly joins young, pretty women in the bedrooms at night. Since we've been owners, no guests have reported his presence, but stories are legend about his past visits in which he just wants to lie down next to the young ladies. When they turn on the light to see who has joined them, no one is there.

The famous Ghost Detectives of Los Angeles rented the Bottger for a week and explored the many ghosts in Old Town including the ones here in the Mansion. Their visit, complete with strange electrical devices, recorders of all types, and special photographic equipment can be reviewed over the internet. According to them, there are "at least 4, and perhaps more, ghosts living in the Bottger Mansion.

This bed and breakfast has it all: flying objects, strange sounds, cold spots, mysterious smells (like men's cologne or rose toilet water) and apparitions.

Owner Yvonne Koch says one morning a guest came down with pieces of a soap dish in her hands. The rattled guest swore that she didn't break it — she saw it go flying across the bathroom and crash into the wall.

Koch confesses she feels the ghosts more often than seeing them. She says there are six spirits at the mansion, including a native woman who fell down the stairs to her death; Charles and Miquela Bottger; and their daughter Dorothy Bottger, who died from pneumonia after being locked out of the house.

There have also been a number of other manifestations that have been reported. Such as:

- A dessert plate on a top shelf levitated up and fell to the floor
- Cold spots have been felt while sitting in the chair in the lobby.
- The toilet lid in the downstairs bathroom moves and objects on top of it fly off and across the room.

- One guest reported a "white fog" that came under the door to her room and tried to enter her mouth.
- Guests have reported the feeling of an unseen person breathing on their arms.
- The apparition of a woman has been seen on the first floor.

BERNALILLO COUNTY COURTHOUSE
Albuquerque, New Mexico

Bernalillo County was established 8 January 1852. It was one of the seven Partidos, established during Mexican rule. It may have been named for the Gonzales-Bernal family that lived in the area before 1692. The county seat is Albuquerque.

The first courthouse in Albuquerque was built in 1886 at a cost of $62, 053.81 and was constructed of gray stone with a peaked shingled roof exterior tower reaching three stories high. The courthouse stood at the current San Felipe Elementary School site in Old Town. Once the demand for another school surfaced, the courthouse was relocated to New Town (present day downtown area).

This "new" courthouse was built in 1926 with bricks imported from Colorado. Built in the center of its own park, the symmetrical design gave the building a Grecian, temple of justice effect. In 1964, the historic courthouse was remodeled and expanded. Its outer surface was also refinished with sheets of marble (Photo at left). A more modern courthouse was built and completed in 2001, leaving the older building empty.

THE GHOSTS

In 2003 the Community Service group has been cleaning out the old courthouse downtown. In the basement rooms they've been collectively witnessing strange things. A worker reported seeing a little girl standing in one of the dark halls; she was a blonde with braids, wearing a school uniform. When the witness smiled at the little girl, she vanished.

A cold spot in another hall was experienced by the lead-man himself. He was unable to find a vent or source to explain it. All of the JDC "clients" that were doing the CS work were taking a break in one of the rooms, and an old law book circa 1920's went skittering down the hall. It came to a stop in the cold zone. Nobody's been willing to touch it.

Two people reportedly died in the building - both of heart attacks. One was the Sheriff who suffered his heart attack while sitting at his desk in the basement and the other person to suffer the same fate was another man on an upper floor. Reportedly employees have tried doing little 'tests' - placing objects in certain places and placing a dry eraser on a door knob, etc and then returning to find these objects moved.

Other things that have been expedited are cold spots, hot spots, lights being turned off, doors being closed and locked when a key is required and boxes that were taped closed being opened and contents strewn about.

QUARAI MISSION
The ruins of Quarai are southeast of Albuquerque in the Manzanos Mountains at Punta de Agua.
Mountainair, New Mexico

As with the Luna-Otero Mansion, the ruins of the Quarai Mission are very close to the city of Albuquerque. For this reason, I am including them in the Albuquerque section of this book.

Quarai was a thriving pueblo when Don Juan Oñate first approached it in 1598 to "accept" its oath of allegiance to Spain. Since Onate was on a journey of exploration and treasure hunting, giving its "oath" to the King of Spain would probably have made little difference to the inhabitants of this area except along with Onate came the dreaded Inquisition. Unfortunately for the natives, the Spanish decided that Quarai was a good spot for a Mission.

Three of the Spanish priests assigned to the Quarai Mission were head of the New Mexico Inquisition during the 1600s, including Fray Estevan de Perea, Custodian of the Franciscan order in the Salinas Jurisdiction and called by one historian the "Father of the New Mexican Church." Despite the horrors associated with the word "Inquisition," records from the hearings show that the early inquisitors, in New Mexico at least, were compassionate men capable of separating gossip from what the church regarded as serious transgressions.

In one case, tensions between church and state reached a peak when

Figure 9: Quarai Mission

Perea charged the alcalde mayor of Salinas with encouraging the native Kachina dances. That case was dropped, but the alcalde's continued disruption at the mission prompted the Inquisition to banish him. Quarai was the base of operations for the Inquisition here in New Mexico.

What appear to be low hills around the ruins are actually the remains of a large masonry Indian village or pueblo. The few scattered walls above ground are the results of limited excavations in the 1950s. There has been little archeological research in the pueblo, so we only the barest outline of Quarai's prehistory is currently known. From ground surveys of the area, and occasional mention in Spanish records, it would appear that the population of Quarai in the 1600s was around four hundred to six hundred people. Not all of the house blocks were occupied at the same time; some were abandoned while others were thriving.

Quarai was on the southeastern fringe of the pueblo world. Tiwa-speaking Indians migrated through mountain canyons from the area around present-day Albuquerque before A.D. 1300. They established settlements along the eastern slope of the Manzanos Mountains at Chillily, Cacique, and here at Quarai.

The inhabitants of this area farmed, hunted, and gathered salt from saline lakes in the valley beyond. They also took advantage of their location between Rio Grande pueblos and the Plains Indians to become traders.

Also called the church of Nuestra Senora de La Purisima Concepcion de

Figure 10: Inside the Mission.

Cuarac, enduring symbol of the early Spanish presence in this valley. Quarai is probably a later phonetic spelling of Cuarac. The red sandstone walls, once protected by adobe plaster, are forty feet high on foundations seven feet deep and six feet wide. The interior length of the church is one hundred feet. The nave is twenty-seven feet wide, and the transept fifty feet.

Since we have no plans or drawings of these early Franciscan missions, we must envision how they looked by studying the physical clues which remain. The square holes above the entry are sockets for beams. They hint that a porch extended across the front of the church, although no traces of it remain. The splayed entrance held wide doors which swung inward on iron pivot hinges providing light and easy access.

It is believed that Fray Juan Gutierrez de la Chica, a priest assigned her in 1628 probably started construction of the church. Although Quarai was on a frontier, remote from the hearth of the Spanish Empire and the Catholic Church, every detail of the church's conception and construction reveal careful planning and attention.

These massive stone walls enclosed a vast space which contrasted sharply with the modest rooms familiar to the Indians. The kiva located nearby is a ceremonial chamber of the pueblo religion. This kiva is a shape more familiar than the square kiva in the patio of the convento. However, in Tiwa pueblos both square and round kivas are common. The flat roof of a kiva was supported by posts. On the floor was a fire pit, and the hatchway above served as both an entrance and an opening for smoke to escape. As warm air and smoke rose out the hatchway, cool air descended through a ventilator shaft on the east side. Thus fresh air circulated through the kiva making it a reasonably comfortable place for the various activities carried out below.

This kiva was here before the church and convento were built. It was buried by mission construction, implying that the Spanish structures were built on a mound of pueblo ruins similar to those you see along the trail today. It was never in use during the mission period.

The architectural contrast between these Tiwa and Spanish structures is clear; and it suggests an even greater gulf between the social and spiritual worlds of the cultures which created them. Oddly enough, this is where we obtained the majority of our unusual readings. By the 1670s, the people of Quarai were suffering all the problems of drought, disease, famine, and hostile tribes that plagued the Salinas Jurisdiction as a whole.

As a result of the drought and the illness, coupled with the inability of the Procurator General to send sufficient supplies, in 1677 Fray Parraga made the decision to abandon the mission and move his charges to another area.

Today these ruins yield clues to the relationships between Spaniards and the Salinas pueblos. What affect the Spanish had upon pueblo life is also hinted at by the archeological information unlocked here at Quarai. Many remnants of life in that time still survive as part of the cultural tradition that is New Mexico today.

THE GHOSTS

Along with a vast feeling of age, it is said that this seventeenth century mission is haunted by the ghost of a conquistador that still guards the ruins. There are many who claim to at least known someone that has seen this relic of a bygone age. It is said that he enters through one of the gaps in the adobe walls and is surrounded by a blue white light. He wears a tabard bearing the symbol of the Calatrava, a Spanish military religious group.

This ghost of the conquistador was first reported in 1913. The first to see him was startled when the man from the past pointed his finger at a startled tourist and said (in Spanish): "Frequent this place, traveler on a mystic journey."

Since that time, not only the conquistador but several dark clothed monks have been seen moving about the ruins.

CHAPTER SIX

ANTHONY, NEW MEXICO

Anthony, New Mexico is a small town with a very big history. Railroad promoter and diplomat James Gadsden negotiated the purchase from Mexico of 77,000 square miles for ten million dollars. In 1854, the U. S. Senate ratified the deal by a narrow margin. This odd-shaped strip of land now forms extreme Southern New Mexico and Arizona south of Gila. The eastern most portion of the Gadsden Purchase includes the Mesilla Valley that lies on either side of the Rio Grande River, where the villages in this story are located.

Residents had been given the choice, following the Hidalgo Treaty, of living in Mexico or the U.S. However, these events in history took that choice out of their hands, and the Gadsden Purchase set new international boundaries. Thus, those in these villages who had lived in Mexico, although they had not moved, suddenly lived in the United States of America, in what is now New Mexico. The Spanish language is heard there more often than English, and some do not speak English at all.

On the eastern end of the Gadsden Purchase, the town of Anthony, that is divided by an invisible state line, has become known by locals as the "best little town in two states." The early center of commerce developed around a flour mill located about 1/2 mile north of the state line and slightly east of where the railroad now runs. Farmers would visit and conduct business when they brought grain to the mill to be ground. The first post office was established in New Mexico in 1884, and still, in 1999, both sides of town are served by one post office in New Mexico. The post office, as well as other state and county offices, form the service center for small towns between Sunland Park and Mesilla.

Anthony, New Mexico was at one time called Halfway House because it is located half-way between Las Cruces, New Mexico and El Paso, Texas. Two stories of how the post office in 1884 became Anthony exist. One says a local lady built a chapel in her home and dedicated it to her patron saint, San Antonio. When a post office was requested under that name, another city in New Mexico had already claimed it, so the English form, Anthony, was chosen. The other story is that it was named by a Catholic priest who had established a church there. At one time it was a stop on the Butterfield Stage route.

When the Santa Fe Railroad was built in 1881, they located the train depot on the Texas side of the state line and called it La Tuna. It is said that name was chosen due to the large number of prickly pear cactus that grew in the area. The Spanish name for prickly pear is La Tuna. The name was also given to the Federal Prison built at Anthony in the early nineteen thirties.

The area between Las Cruces and Anthony contains some of the richest farm land in New Mexico. Early crops of cotton, alfalfa and grape vineyards have been joined by large pecan orchards and onion, lettuce, and chile fields. The many dairies make insulage, alfalfa, and grain crops popular. Population estimates of this area are about 15,000 people living in the little hamlets and the wide open spaces, and encroaching seriously on the farm land in the Mesilla Valley.

On the New Mexico side, the Gadsden Independent School District is reported to have more bus miles than any other school district in the United States. The district extends from Sunland Park on the southern end to San Miguel and Mesquite on the north and across the mountain to Chaparral on the east. In contrast, the Texas side of Anthony makes up the Anthony Independent School District, one of the smallest school districts in the state. Anthony, New Mexico is not incorporated and is governed by Doña Ana County. The Texas side of town was incorporated under the name of Anthony, Texas in 1953, and is somewhat of a bedroom community for El Paso.

In 1988, Mary Ann Brown, a member of the Anthony Chamber of Commerce and born on Leap Year, founded the Worldwide Leap Year Birthday Club. The Chamber voted to proclaim the New Mexico/Texas town "Leap Year Capital of the World" and to sponsor the one and only World-Wide Leap Year Birthday Club and celebration. Then New Mexico Governor Gary Carruthers and Texas Governor William B. Clements joined in the special proclamation. Senator Pete Domenici read it into the Congressional Record Vol. 134, No. 146, Friday, October 14, 1988, of the 100th Congress. Quadrennial celebrations were held in 1992 and 1996. The Leap Year 2000 celebration is planned to be the biggest one yet. The dates set for it are February 26-29, 2000.

GADSDEN HIGH SCHOOL
6301 Highway 28
Anthony, NM 88021

The Gadsden Independent School District may be known as having more bus miles than any other school district in the country, but one of its schools, Gadsden High School is also known for serving as home to a number of ghosts. This school is located at a crossroads of Highway 28, out in the country. The setting could not be better for a haunting.

The campus of Gadsden High School is fairly large, all of which is enclosed by a large chain link fence. The school campus is actually composed of a number of buildings that are connected by walkways. The older structure, which is named Old English was the original high school and is the building that is said to be haunted as you shall read.

Figure 11: The Old English Building at Gadsden High School.

According to those who gave me the information on this haunted location, in the Old English Building, located in the front of the campus near the end of Washington Street, is the spirit of a very pretty girl who was lured into a deserted part of the rambling old building by two male students during a school dance. Once they had her alone, the two drug her to the basement where she was stripped, raped and murdered.

Those who have seen the unfortunate young woman report that she still wears her white prom dress just as she did the night of her murder. Staff, janitors and students have reported seeing and hearing her in the building. It is said that she can also sometimes be seen from the street as she walks from one end of the building to the other just as if she was passing through the solid walls.

CHAPTER SEVEN

ALCALDE, NEW MEXICO

The town of Alcalde, New Mexico is actually a very small village in northern New Mexico. Alcalde may actually the oldest viticulture site in North America.

Don Juan de Onate brought settlers to the Los Luceros area in 1598, reportedly bringing grapevines with him. The grapevines were planted and watched over by the early settlers who planned to produce wine. The winemaking industry is wide spread in New Mexico and the quality of the wine rivals the best that California's wine country has to offer.

This area of New Mexico is best known for The Los Luceros Winery building appears to be a classic adobe structure, but is in fact the first stable winery in the southwest. There are those who say that this building is over four hundred years old. It is in this old historic building that shadows are seen to move and faint voices of the past are still heard. It would seem that the ghosts are very much at home with the "other" spirits.

THE OLD COURTHOUSE
Alcalde, New Mexico

According to the story, a lovely senorita from Spain was given in an arrange marriage to her new husband who happened to be of French descent. The lovely hacienda in which the couple lived was large and well appointed in befitting the wealth of the couple.

What no one knew was that the husband was a very jealous and abusive of his lovely young wife. During one argument, the husband became enraged and through his wife down the broad staircase. She broke her neck and died. Suddenly realizing what he had done and knowing that his father-in-law would be looking for revenge, the husband committed suicide. He was found lying beside the body of his dead wife.

Some years later, the town acquired the property and the large hacienda was converted into the first Courthouse. Those found guilty of hanging offenses would be hung from the limbs of a giant tree that grew near the building. Those who worked in the courthouse claimed to see a woman dressed in colonial period costume walking around the second floor of the building. Others have seen a man pacing the floor in an angry manner on an office that was once a bedroom. Other witnesses have since bodies hanging from the tree in front of the property where the guilty once paid the ultimate price for their crimes. There are also those that claim that they have seen lights burning in the old house even though there is no electricity running to the old building.

CHAPTER EIGHT

ARTESIA, NEW MEXICO

Like the American Frontier, Artesia's history is rich in discovery: the fertile Pecos Valley, the artesian waters and its oil and gas fields.

The first settler, Union soldier John Truitt, homesteaded along the famous Chisum Trail, at Chisum Springs Camp which is now just three blocks from the heart of Artesia's main business district.

With the completion of the Pecos Valley Railroad in 1894, Artesia's first given name was Miller's Siding. The community had yet another name change when promoter Baldwin Stegman settled in Miller's Siding and married the famous cattleman John Chisum's niece, Sallie Roberts. Together they established a post office, naming the town Stegman.

In 1903, the town adopted a new name, Artesia, for its Artesian wells and the township laid out. That same year the Artesia Town site Company joined with the Artesia Improvement Company to drill the first Artesian well in the community. By November, a well 830 feet deep with a six inch casing was completed three miles outside of town making it the world's largest Artesian well at that time. The age of the big water well had come and each weak saw a new well surpassing the last. From 1905 to 1907, the ample water for irrigation brought over 1,200 people to area farms.

1923 - a record year for Artesia when two men from Robinson, Illinois hearing of the oil traces in the Artesian wells, brought a steam powered cable tool rig to drill for oil. After several dry holes, Van Welch and Tom Flynn were ready to pack up their drilling rig when Martin Yates II acquired state leases east of the Pecos River. Yates talked the two into drilling one more well which was more promising. The next well was gas, while not marketable then, supplied energy for equipment on future wells. By April of 1924, the company brought in well Illinois No. 3 which was the first producing well in New Mexico and the third in the oil-rich Permian Basin.

The next four decades were a period of steady growth for Artesia. Its agricultural production flourished with the ample water supply and great soil conditions. Oil and gas production and processing helped to meet the needs of an energy-hungry world.

The first Urban Renewal project in New Mexico, the ever flooding Eagle Draw was turned into a 35 acre city park which catches excess water in times of heavy downpours and offers a complete recreational facility.

But, Artesia is rich in more than natural resources . . . for it's the people which make a community. Artesia treasures the solid American traditions of family and country, and people move to Artesia confident that it's a good place to live and raise their families.

ATOKA SCHOOL
Artesia, New Mexico

In Artesia there stands an old deserted building that once housed a school. No one knows for sure what happened to cause the school to close, but it happened very quickly. Other businesses that have tried to use the old building quickly move to other quarters and refuse to discuss the reasons for the move. The old building has been sitting empty for a long time. As with every old empty building, there are young people who find ways to enter the old building looking for adventure. Many of them have claimed to have heard strange noises to include the sounds of footsteps in the empty hallways as well as voices that seem to be coming from a great distance.

CHAPTER NINE

AZTEC, NEW MEXICO

On the west bank of the Rio de Las Animas Perdidas stands the Aztec Ruins National Monument, the remains of a great prehistoric town built in the 12th century. The creators of the Ruins used materials of stone and mortar to create massive masonry and huge apartment houses. The main ruin at the monument covers two acres, stands three stories high and contained 500 rooms averaging 10 by 12 feet.

This terraced pueblo is seven rooms wide at the base and four and five rooms wide across the wings. An enclosed plaza is dominated by the Great Kiva. Tree ring dating provides evidence indicating that most of the pueblo was built between AD 111 and 1115. Cultural and Architectural evidence indicates that the builders who abandoned the site by the middle of the 1110's were related to the people of the Chaco Culture located at Chaco Canyon to the south. By AD 1125, people reoccupied Aztec Ruins whose culture resembled that of the people of Mesa Verde, Colorado. These people remodeled and enlarge the ruins and occupied the area until they too abandoned the ruins in the late 13th century.

The Animas River, which flows through Aztec, is derived from the Spanish name, Rios de Los Animas Perditas that means "River of Lost Souls." Two tales arise from why the river was named such. One being that the Spanish fought a number of Indians in a battle and tossed their bodies into the river, the second story suggests that it was named such because of the number of Indians and early explorers who lost their lives while trying to cross the river. Regardless of how the river got its name, it has continually provided the valley with the sustenance so needed in a semi-desert environment, water.

The name of Aztec can also be attributed to the misguided notion of Escalante's visit to the San Juan Basin and finding large ruins, now known as Aztec National Monument, that were thought to have been built by the Aztec Indians. However, we know today that the Anasazi were responsible for the construction of the ruins. Yet with an early Mexican population settlement, the name remained with the city.

The recorded history of Aztec does not start until the summer of 1776. The arrival of Father Francisco Atanosio Dominquez and Father Francisco Velaz de Escalante, two friars who were seeking a shorter trail route from Santa Fe to the missions in California. On route to find a suitable trail, the two friars and several explorers passed through the San Juan Basin. Don Bernardo de Miera y Pacheco, a mapmaker and surveyor, was a member of the exploring party. It is from his maps that many of the names of the rivers and the valleys were documented and are still in use today. Such names as Rio Florida (River of Flowers), Rio de Las Piedras (River of the Stones), Rio de Los Pinos (River of the Pines), and Rio de San Juan (River of St. John) are taken directly from the original maps. Despite their efforts, Father Dominquez and Father Escalante never did find a suitable trail to the missions of California. However, their efforts did provide a route for all other explorers and early settlers into the San Juan Basin region.

Aztec was established in the late 1800's. In its infancy, it was only a trading post in Taos County in the 1880's. It was not until 1887 that Aztec became an established community. San Juan County was formed by cutting the west portion of Rio Arriba off. By 1890, the Aztec Town Company was formed and was in need to divide 40 acres of land for laying out a town. Aztec was born. Unlike the rest of the Wild West, the earlier Anglo-settlers of Aztec were of agriculture and horticultural backgrounds.

Though cattle raising and herding became prevalent later in the area, the farming of the valley took root sooner and hence allowed Aztec to develop a character quite different from the rest of the Southwest. For the most part, the citizens of Aztec were law abiding and quite proud of their peaceful community.

The citizens of Aztec were struggling to produce income to help boost the economy of their newly found town. In 1894, the Territorial Legislation financed a program called the "Experimental Farm". This "experimental farm" was set up to teach local farmers the best crops that will grow in this area. The program was a great success for the Town of Aztec. However, the program ended in 1901 due to the lack of appropriations by State Legislation.

In 1895, Main Street was created with incoming businesses such as a blacksmith, a drugstore, barber shop, livery barn, a flour mill operated by water power, two lawyers, a doctor and a dentist, all of which were located on the East Side of Main. A meat market and a saloon with a mercantile store were located on the central block of Main Street.

The economy of Aztec was sustained by activities of new people coming in to build homes and farms. The older citizens were on pensions from the Civil War and consequently their income added to the economy.

By 1900, the City of Aztec was a beautiful town of homes with picket fences, flower and vegetable gardens. Aztec quickly became a well-established town, growing with sufficient businesses to supply the needs of the people.

The agricultural forum was sound and sufficiently maintained the economy of the town. The future of Aztec was bright and full of optimism. In 1900, daily delivery to the post office was a standard. By 1903, telephone exchange service began and by 1905, the Denver & Rio Grande Railroad had a standard rail constructed between Durango and Aztec. Aztec became the shipping point for hundreds of head of sheep and cattle. In 1908 electricity found its way to Aztec, but since it was DC current, it was limited to sundown until midnight. It was not until the 1920s when the outfit was purchased by a Chicago company and converted over to AC current that electricity was available 24 hours a day. That same time in 1908, the Alturian Club was formed by several women of the community who donated time in the refinement of their community. They were the founders of the present city library.

Though Aztec for the most part was a peaceful town, it would occasionally have its debacle with a rowdy kid on occasion. As such, Aztec built a one-room jailhouse in 1910 for delinquent kids so as not to house them with "adult" lawbreakers. The jailhouse is currently on display at Pioneer Park.

By the end of the 1910s, Aztec had approximately 30 businesses, including general merchandise, grocery, meat market, two newspapers, a bank, two lawyers, a bake shop, three doctors, two dentists, several carpenters and painters. Aztec was well on its way to becoming a busy town with well-stocked stores and many services such as jewelry and clock repairs.

In 1910 the population for Aztec was a steady 700 people and supported another 300 people living in the surrounding farming communities in Blanco, Bloomfield and La Plata. Aztec was the most convenient place to shop.

During the depression, Aztec did not feel the ill effects as much as the rest of the nation. The bank did not close and citizens were able to sustain the daily lives by working the land for food and supplies. Aztec was stagnant during the 1930's and the 1940's.

MISS GAIL'S INN
300 South Main Street
Aztec, NM 87410

Built in 1907 by George Stone, this building housed the first hotel in

Figure 12: Miss Gail's Inn.

Aztec. Upon entering Miss Gail's Inn, you enter a time long forgotten of country charm and creatively decorated theme rooms. Located downstairs in this two-story hotel are Rooms 1 through 4, the main foyer, and Giovanni's Restaurant where one can have an exceptional home-made lunch from 11am to 2pm, or Italian Specialty Dinner from 6pm to 9pm by reservation only on Friday and Saturday evenings only.

THE GHOSTS

There are several ghosts that are said to occupy Miss Gail's Inn. One spirit is that of a lady who is seen to float down the stairs. Room number seven, located on the second floor of this historic old hotel is occupied on a sort of permanent basis by a very cantankerous old man.

There is a tree growing in front of the hotel that was used as a hanging tree in the early days. It is said that from time to time, bodies can still be seen swinging in the wind from the limbs of this old tree.

CHAPTER TEN

BAYARD, NEW MEXICO

Two miles east of Santa Clara, Bayard, now the center of the Mining District, began its history as a railroad station serving as a supply terminal for Fort Bayard. Bayard gained prominence when the company town of Santa Rita was literally consumed by the expansion of the open pit mine. Bayard's status was again enhanced when the Cobre Consolidated School District was formed and the administrative offices, the district high school, a middle- school, and an elementary school were located in Bayard.

CHINO MINES CREEK
Bayard, New Mexico

There are those who hold that there is an old lady seen in the creek crying and yelling for her child. A flood had supposedly gone through this woman's home and washed her son away. Though she is long dead, there are many who maintain that she is still heard and seen in the area calling for her son.

Another story related that she was a beautiful Hispanic woman, but she was very poor. One day she was in the village and met a handsome man. They started dating and ended up getting married. Then one day she noticed that he had changed. Instead of spending time with her, he was always finding excuses to leave town, leaving her alone to tend to her children. She noticed that he would leave town more and more. Finally, she caught him cheating on her with another woman. Instead of getting even, she that she would get back at him by not letting him see the children. So she drowned them in the local creek.

When doing this she realized what she was doing, she tried to stop her children from drowning, but she lost control and let the kids go. They started to float down the creek, she tried to run after them and save them but it was no use. They had drowned and she had lost them forever. However, while running after them, she tripped over a root in the ground and hit her head on a rock. She died instantly.

According to the locals, she tries to save her children each night and you can hear her crying and yelling for her children. This is the one that they call the "Llorna" which means crying lady. Since that had happened it is said that you can hear her crying all over searching the riverbeds for her children.

CHAPTER ELEVEN

DEMING, NEW MEXICO

The town of Deming is located in the Southwestern part of New Mexico, 33 miles north of the Mexico border, a land of an ever present sun and flowing desert rocks and cacti. Deming has been named a "Rock-Hunters Paradise."

The history of the area dates back nearly 1,000 years ago, when the Mimbres Indians, the first people known to inhabit the area, lived in villages along the Mimbres River and farmed the area. Primitive though they were in other respects, the pictures of daily life they painted inside their pottery reflect their gifted creativity and unsurpassed skill in reproducing likeness of animals and birds. Known throughout the world, some beautiful samples of the magnificent Mimbres Pottery are on display in the Deming Luna Mimbres Museum.

It was about 1800 that the Americans entered Southwest New Mexico. Deming's first years were hard ones, with the usual problems of a small Western town. It had such a bad reputation that some outlaws rounded up in Arizona were given one way tickets to Deming. Back in 1850 it was a Butterfield Stage Trail stop.

Deming is the county seat of Luna County and was founded in November, 1881. Named for Mary Deming Crocker, wife of a railroad magnate of the Southern Pacific Railway system the town was the result of railroad expansion to the West. The Southern Pacific, building toward the Pacific coast, reached this point in late 1881, and made preparations for the construction of a round house and repair shops. This activity furnished the incentive for the erection of a city of tents and shanties. Six months later, the Atchison, Topeka and Santa Fe completed its junction with the Southern Pacific at Deming, thus assuring Deming a prominence in the Southern part of New Mexico.

During the year of 1882, settlers flocked in, and substantial buildings were erected. E. Germain and Company opened the first store in Deming, using old boxcars for storerooms. Pictures of Deming's growing up years can be found on the picture page.

The business district of Deming is located on what was a Wayndotte Script Location. As the result of treaties with the Wayndotte Indians on March 17, 1842 and January 31, 1855, the U.S. government issued land warrents, later termed "Wayndotte Script." which were good for land in the public domain.

With a population of 1600 persons in 1887, Deming had two schools, one private and one public, a Methodist and a Congregational Church and four hotels. By 1891, there were in addition to the other churches an Episcopal and a Catholic church which was under construction. There were two newspapers, the Headlight (which is still in existence) and the Advance. This same year a "City Club" was organized, composed of the citizens of Deming, and having for its object the establishment of a library and the promotion of social, commercial and scientific development for the community.

In 1923 and 1924, a serious economic decline hit the Deming area. Deming's two banks, The Bank of Deming and the First National Bank were forced to close their doors. Recovery was slow. Like many other towns, Deming had its problems during the depression. The coming of World War II stimulated growth in the community. As a part of the war effort, the Deming National Guard was called into federal service and was sent to the Philippines. This unit was the 200 Coast Artillery commanded by C.G. Sage, the publisher of the local paper. Altogether, there were about 246 men from Luna County in the regiment. In the Philippines, most of these men participated in the infamous Bataan Death March where several Deming soldiers lost their lives. Most of them remained prisoners of war until 1945.

During the first World War, the War Department established Camp Cody near Deming, as a training encampment that covered over 2000 acres. At the termination of the war, Camp Cody was used for a tuberculosis sanitarium for ex-soldiers. It was operated by the Catholic Sisters of the Holy Cross. In 1939 Camp Cody was completely destroyed by fire and the sanitarium closed at the same time. During World War II, an Army Air Force Base was installed in Deming, located at what is now the "Municipal Deming Airport and Industrial Park." This base trained bombardiers and there were over 5000 men stationed at this base.

There was not a serious decline in Deming's economy following World War II as there had been after WW I. Deming's industry and farming grew and its population increased to its present day size of 14,116 (Census Bureau 2000)and Luna County is 25,016 people of mixed nationalities. Deming has grown 20% and Luna County has grown 38% since the 1990 Census. Today Deming is a full service community with low cost of living, affordable taxes, taxi service, municipal airport, hospital/ambulance service, nursing home, senior citizens center, library, over 40 churches, over 80 listed organizations, 18 hole golf course, civic center, public auditorium, schools and a community college.

Many thanks to the Deming Chamber of Commerce and The Luna County Historical Society for directing me to the website.

GREENSANDS FACTORY
Deming, New Mexico

There was once a factory called Greensands in operation outside of Deming. During one of the economic downturns, the factory was closed, though the empty shell of the once thriving business was left for the desert creatures and the elements. On the site of the old Greensands Factory witnesses have reported seeing shadowy figures moving in and around the old factory.

Nearby there is the remains of an old abandoned house. Those who are bold enough to explore Greensands late at night have reported hearing screams coming from the abandoned old house. However, if someone investigates, there is nothing found but an old deteriorating house. Outside the old house, people have reported seeing a young girl holding a doll. She stands near the rear door as if waiting for someone to come home. Someone who never comes.

DEMING MIDDLE SCHOOL
500 West Ash
Deming, New Mexico

Figure 13: Middle School

Deming is a small town in southwestern New Mexico better known for its historical sights than for its violence. However, the following story will show that we are not really safe no matter where we live. The Deming Middle School, which contains grades 6 & 7, has always been known as a quiet school where students could just be kids. However, that is now changing.

DEMING, N.M. (AP) - Holding hands and praying, about 150 students and adults formed a human chain halfway around Deming Middle School Monday to remember a 13-year-old girl gunned down on campus last week. Candles, red roses and half-dozen teddy bears adorned the school grounds for the vigil in memory of Araceli Tena, who died of a bullet wound to the back of her head.

A fellow student, Victor Cordova Jr. of Palomas, Mexico, is charged with the Friday shooting. Erica Orozco, 11, a seventh-grader whose locker was next to Araceli's, said she wanted to return Monday "to see how all my other friends are, to get used to coming back." She did not witness the shooting, but said, "I feel like it's going to happen again. I feel very scared." "You don't know how to cope with something like this here," said Mary Alvarado, 35, whose 11-

year-old daughter, Amanda, attends the school. "Eventually, we'll get over it, but this is way overwhelming for everybody."

Superintendent Carlos Viramontes said 40 to 50 counselors were available on campus Monday when classes resumed. It wasn't immediately known how many of the schools' 750 students were in attendance. Some parents wanted Deming to remain closed until after the Thanksgiving holiday. One of the students' classmates said in Sunday's Albuquerque Journal that Cordova had boasted the day before the shooting that he would open fire on his school. Richard Ramirez said Cordova brought .22-caliber bullets to Deming Middle School to show them off Thursday, the day before police say he shot Tena. "He (Cordova) told us, 'Watch, I'm going to make history blasting this school,'" the 13-year-old told the newspaper. Ramirez said he did not report the incident to school authorities because he feared Cordova would seek revenge. "I was scared," he said.

Victor Cordova Sr. said his son told him during a visit at the Luna County Juvenile Detention Center in Deming that he had planned to kill himself, but his arm was bumped and the loaded .22 caliber Colt revolver he held discharged. Police said they had no information that would corroborate that version of events. The boy's family said he has experienced several difficult years dealing with depression, a violent temper and the loss of his 31-year-old mother, Emma Armendaris, who died of cancer in February. Police declined to comment on Ramirez's statement and would not discuss where the younger Cordova obtained the gun.

The boy - police said he is 13, but family members say he is 12 - has been charged with attempted murder, and various assault counts. Police said the charges would likely be amended because of the girl's death. Under state law, children under 14 years old cannot be charged as adults. The boy lives in Palomas and commutes to school 33 miles away in Deming. He has dual citizenship because he was born in Deming, and he is one of many children living in Palomas who are allowed to cross the border each day to attend classes in Luna County. Tena was the oldest of three children, her uncle Beto Tena said. "She was a very good girl," he said in Spanish. "She was the best girl she could be. Her brother and sister are very sad. They don't even want to eat

THE GHOSTS

Even before the senseless death mention above, there have been strange happenings within the walls of this school. Students and staff alike have reported unexplained loud sounds coming from the basement of the old building while some of the computers in the office and class rooms turn themselves on and off with no one near them.

HOLY CROSS SANATORIUM
Deming, New Mexico

The Holy Cross Sanatorium was located on part of what had been known as Camp Cody. The U.S. War Department in 1917 established a 2000-acre training camp near the town of Deming, New Mexico during World War One. The garrison of soldiers assigned to this base, called Camp Cody, was made up of National Guardsmen from Nebraska, Iowa, Minnesota and the Dakotas.

Official opening of Camp Deming was on December 29, 1916. The day was marked with a flag raising ceremony. The camp was renamed in honor of William "Buffalo Bill" Cody on July 20, 1917. William Cody was born February 26, 1846 and died on January 10, 1917.

The 34th Infantry Division was called the "Sunshine" Division at first, but this was in conflict with the 40th Division formed at Camp Kearney, California at the same time. So Camp Cody's 34th became known as the "Sandstorm" Division. Base quarters were built for 36,000 soldiers and the hospital had 800 beds. Camp Cody closed on June 20, 1919.

When World War One ended, the facilities at Camp Cody were converted for use as a tuberculosis sanitarium for ex-soldiers. Later the buildings on Camp Cody were turned over to the Catholic Sisters of the Holy Cross who continued to operate the Sanatorium. In 1939 most of the other buildings on Camp Cody were destroyed by fire. It was also about this same time that the Sisters decided to close the Sanitarium.

In the mid 70's there was a devil-worshiping cult that used the abandoned Sanitarium as the site for their rituals and the sacrifice of animals. There is currently only one building still remaining on the site, the others having either burned in 1939 or been torn down due to deterioration.

THE GHOSTS

There are many who maintain that the one remaining building is definitely haunted. Many intrepid individuals who have explored this old building have heard noises from the upper floor and seen lights near the fountain at night.

There are stories that tunnels run from this building in the northwestern part of town to the southeastern side of town. It is claimed that the tunnels come out at the airport. As is usually the case, these tunnels were discovered by the local teens and used as a party place. As a result, most of them have been caved in to keep trespassers out.

A number of people have claimed to have experienced something in the part of the old building referred to as the "Altar Room". Several people have said that they have seen a shadowy figure lurking just inside the doorway. The sound of footsteps also echoes through the empty hallways.

There is also a cemetery just to the north of the building. Some of the old graves have been disturbed and a large cross has been cut down. There is an urban legend in Deming that holds that all of the teenagers involved in cutting down the cross in the 70's all died that same year.

The hauntings are also said to not be contained within the walls of the old Sanitarium, but to also extend to some of the newer houses that have been built around the area. Shadowy figures are seen moving through the homes and residents have heard voices coming from empty rooms.

The Holy Cross is said to have become a very dangerous place, with a string of deaths having occurred there. It is reported that a gang with satanic beliefs actually sacrificed one of their own members in an attempt to call upon Satan to grant their wishes. Others say that a couple sought privacy within its walls and as a result of a quarrel, the man was killed, his body stuffed into a drain pipe.

Sheriffs patrol it often now and run people off who are in there and occasionally arrest them for trespassing.

MEMORIAL ELEMENTARY SCHOOL
1000 South Tenth
Deming, New Mexico

Memorial Elementary School contains grades Kindergarten through the fifth grade. By all reports the school is well run and the students are happy – but, there are those who say that there are spirits that walk the halls of this relatively modern school.

I am told that two students reported find a large knife lying in the gym. One moment it was there and the next moment it was gone. There have also been reports of shadowy figures being seen moving about the hallways and strange noises coming from parts of the building that are supposed to be empty after the students go home for the day. Sometimes, it is said, flickering lights can be seen inside the building after the doors are locked for the night.

A former employee has said that a number of people have reported hearing a piano playing in the third grade hallway when no one was there. More than one student has reported catching sight of what appears to be two young girls looking in the windows of the school. However, whenever someone tries to see who the girls might be, there is no one there.

CHAPTER TWELVE

SANTA FE, NEW MEXICO

The City of Santa Fe was originally occupied by a number of Pueblo Indian villages with founding dates between the years 1050 to 1150. The "Kingdom of New Mexico" was first claimed for the Spanish Crown by the conquistador Don Francisco Vasques de Coronado in 1540, 70 years before the founding of Santa Fe. Coronado and his men also traveled to the Grand Canyon and through the Great Plains on their New Mexico expedition.

Spanish colonists first settled in northern New Mexico in 1598. Don Juan de Oñate became the first Governor and Captain-General of New Mexico and established his capital in 1598 at San Juan Pueblo, 25 miles north of Santa Fe. When Oñate retired, Don Pedro de Peralta was appointed Governor and Captain-General in 1609. One year later, he moved the capital to present-day Santa Fe. New Mexico was part of the empire of New Spain and Santa Fe was the commercial hub at the end of the long road which linked Mexico City with its northern province.

During the next 70 years, Spanish soldiers and officials, as well as Franciscan missionaries, sought to subjugate and convert the Pueblo Indians of the region. The indigenous population at the time was close to 100,000 people, who spoke nine languages and lived in an estimated 70 pueblos, many of which exist today.

In 1680, Pueblo Indians revolted against some 2,500 Spanish colonists, killing 400 of them and driving the rest back into Mexico. The conquering Pueblos sacked Santa Fe and burned most of the buildings, except the Palace of the Governors. Pueblo Indians occupied Santa Fe until 1692-93, when Don Diego de Vargas reestablished Spanish control.

When Mexico gained its independence from Spain, Santa Fe became the capital of the province of New Mexico. Trade was no longer restricted as it was under Spanish rule and trappers and traders moved into the region. In 1821 William Becknell opened the 1,000 mile-long Santa Fe Trail.

On August 18, 1846, in the early period of the Mexican American War, an American army general, Stephen Watts Kearny, took Santa Fe and raised the American flag over the Plaza. Two years later, 1848, Mexico signed the Treaty of Guadalupe Hidalgo ceding New Mexico and California to the United States.

In 1851, Vicar Apostolic, and later Archbishop of Santa Fe, Jean B. Lamy, arrived in Santa Fe. Eighteen years later, he began construction on the Saint Francis Cathedral, one of 45 churches he built in New Mexico. Built in the French Romanesque style, the building is alien to the Spanish heritage of Santa Fe, but is still one of its greatest landmarks. Constructed on the site of an adobe church destroyed in the Pueblo Revolt, the Cathedral was built of locally quarried stone. Portions of the old adobe parish church (La Parroquia), remain in the form of the Chapel of Our Lady of the Rosary, which houses a wooden stature of the Virgin know as La Conquistadora, Our Lady of the Conquest. La Conquistadora was first brought to Santa Fe in 1625 and was returned to the city by the armies of Don Diego de Vargas during the reconquest of 1692-93.

For 27 days in March and April of 1862, the Confederate flag of Brigadier General Henry H. Sibley flew over Santa Fe until he was defeated by Union troops. With the arrival of the telegraph in 1868 and the coming of the Atchison, Topeka and the Santa Fe Railroad in 1880, Santa Fe and New Mexico underwent an economic revolution. Corruption in government, however, accompanied the growth, and President Rutherford B. Hayes appointed Lew Wallace as a territorial governor to "clean up New Mexico." Wallace did such a good job that Billy the Kid threatened to come up to Santa Fe and kill him.

New Mexico gained statehood in 1912 and Santa Fe has been the capital city since statehood.

Ten years before Plymouth Colony was founded by the Mayflower Pilgrims, Santa Fe, New Mexico was established as the seat of power of the Spanish Empire north of the Rio Grande. Santa Fe is the oldest capital city in the United States and the oldest European community in the U.S. west of the Mississippi. The Palace of the Governors, on the north side of the Plaza, is the oldest public building in the United States. Santa Fe has been a seat of government under the flags of Spain, Mexico, the Confederacy, and the United States of America.

Courtesy of City of Santa Fe

THE GLOW HOUSE
Santa Fe, New Mexico

I was given this story by a friend who swore that it was true. According to his information, there is an abandoned church that the locals call "The Glow House." This church was once headed by a priest who began to lose is mind as the number of his parishioners began to shrink. The neighborhood was one a downward slide and the local kids were causing a great deal of mischief which was chasing away those that he looked on as his "flock". Blaming the local kids for his problems, the priest was especially annoyed by those children who continually disturbed the solitude of the church with the noise fro the playground nearby.

One afternoon, the priest snapped and went on a killing rampage. He killed the children at the playground and hid their bodies in the basement of the old church. Regaining his reason, the priest was so horrified by what he had done that he took his own life in atonement. Investigators late found the priest's body lying among the dead children.

It is said that there is a light that burns inside the church than does not go out. Strange sounds are heard from the old building and if someone tries to enter, a shadowy figure will chase them out and slam the door behind them.

THE COLLEGE OF SANTA FE
1600 St. Michael's Drive
Santa Fe, New Mexico

The history of The College of Santa Fe dates to the days of the Old West. It was in 1859 that four Christian Brothers left France for Santa Fe at the request of Reverend J.B. Lamy, first bishop of New Mexico. They traveled for two months by boat, train, horseback and wagon train along the Santa FeTrail to open a school for boys in Santa Fe.

St. Michael's College opened in impoverished conditions on Dec. 15, 1859. The Brothers taught in an adobe hut near the

Figure 14: Library Building

"oldest church" on the Pecos Trail (later College Street and today Old

Santa Fe Trail). For a long time it was the sole source of education for boys in the Territory of New Mexico.

When the territory granted a charter to the "College of the Christian Brothers of New Mexico" in 1874, St. Michael's had expanded to include a program of higher education. At New Mexico's constitutional convention in 1910, 22 of the delegates (more than 20 percent of the convention) boasted St. Michael's as their alma mater. After World War I, however, the college program was dropped.

While St. Michael's continued to flourish as a preparatory school, the Christian Brothers dreamed of reinstating the collegiate program, bringing the option of independent higher education back to New Mexico. Through the efforts of Brother Benildus of Mary, their dreams came true in 1947 with the acquisition of the World War II Bruns Army Hospital on the edge of town. On Sept. 15, 1947, St. Michael's College (today's College of Santa Fe) opened with 51 converted barrack buildings, 15 Christian Brothers faculty members and 148 students.

In 1950 the College graduated its first class of 23. Upon the untimely death of Brother Benildus in 1957, Brother Raymond Ogden became acting president for one year. In 1958, Brother Cyprian Luke was appointed the College's third president. He led the institution as builder president. He led the institution as builder and innovative problem solver for 24 years until his retirement in June, 1982. There were many improvements during this growth period. After the achievement of accreditation in 1965, the student population, number of faculty and educational offerings increased rapidly.

In 1966 the name of the school was changed from St. Michael's College to The College of Santa Fe to show the close rapport between the school and the city it serves. The College began enrolling women that year.

The College continued to evolve under the direction of Brother Donald Mouton, who was appointed by the Board of Trustees in 1982 as fourth president of the College. To meet the needs of local working adults, the Graduate and External Programs (GEP) division opened in 1980.

In 1985, the College's first graduate program, the Master of Business Administration, received accreditation from the North Central Association of Colleges and Schools.

One of the most significant changes was the College's expansion into Albuquerque following the closing of the University of Albuquerque in 1986. In a cooperative effort, the College agreed to assume the responsibility for programs of the University of Albuquerque to assure that students could complete their degrees. Today, the College of Santa Fe at Albuquerque continues to serve the community through two campus sites.

When Brother Donald Mouton resigned from the presidency to return to teaching in December 1986, Dr. James Fries was selected as interim president. On June 5, 1987, the Board of Trustees appointed Dr. Fries president.

During President Fries' tenure, CSF has grown both academically and physically. A master's program in education was implemented, a new major in environmental science was started, and an exchange program with Universidad de La Salle in Mexico City was initiated.

Improvements at CSF continue to reflect social and student developments. The Lasallian philosophy of a caring, personalized education and a strong liberal arts curriculum remains unchanged.

THE GHOSTS

There are those who claim that there are a number of ghosts that haunt this campus. There is one ghost in particular who seems to be the best known. This figure is seen continually walking in the shadows late at night.

Another well known ghost is that of a decapitated nurse that many students claim to have seen late at night. According to the story, during World War II, an insane asylum was located in Bruns Army Hospital, the building that became the College of Santa Fe. During the time it was an Insane Asylum, a patient suddenly went berserk and went on a killing rampage. Before he could be restrained, the patient had cornered a nurse, cutting off her head. Now this decapitated nurse is sometimes seen walking in the hallways that lead to the cafeteria.

GRANT CORNER INN
122 Grant Avenue
Santa Fe, New Mexico

The Grant Corner Inn is located in a very elegant three story colonial style home built in 1905 for Judge Arthur Robinson and his wife for many, many years. It was then used as an office building in the 1950s and became an inn in 1982. It is located in the heart of downtown Santa Fe. The Inn proper contains nine rooms that are furnished with antiques. According to the literature on this charming little hotel, it prides itself on its friendly, warm atmosphere. What is seldom mentioned is that in addition to the charm and antique furnishings, is that this old home also comes with a few spirits.

THE GHOSTS

Custodians, guests, and visitors have reported a number of ghostly encounters over the years. Unexplainable sounds of heavy objects falling to the floor, doors banging shut, and loud footsteps are heard throughout the building. Police have been called on several occasions.

According to all reports, rooms 4 and 8 and the hallway on the second floor are the primary haunting sites. There have been incidents of the sounds of heavy objects falling on the floor, footsteps, and slamming doors. Later investigations reveal nothing has fallen and no explanation for the footsteps or slamming doors. Some witnesses have claimed to have seen a grayish figure in the hallways that always seems to vanish right before their eyes.

In "Adobe Angels: Ghosts of Santa Fe and Taos," Antonio Garcez interviewed Art Garcia, former caretaker of this B&B. Garcia's account was terrifying — he endured deafening noises, a blast of freezing air that killed his house plants, the stench of rotting meat. He tried to convince friends to stay with him, only to have them leave hurriedly, frightened for their lives.

According to owner Louise Stewart, the spirit that haunted her house so violently has since quieted down. Extensive remodeling has been done since Stewart bought the building ("We gutted it," she says), and she thinks the unhappy spirit may have left.

Then again, maybe it's just waiting for the right guest to torment[12].

LA FONDA HOTEL
100 East San Francisco Street
Santa Fe, New Mexico

When Santa Fe was founded in 1607, official records show an inn or Fonda was among the first businesses established. More than two hundred years later, in 1821, when Captain William Becknell completed the first successful trading expedition from Missouri to Santa Fe - a route that came to be known as the Santa Fe Trail - he enjoyed the hospitality at the inn (la fonda), where the Santa Fe Trail terminated at the town's central Plaza.

The current La Fonda was built in 1922 on the site of the previous inns. In 1925 it was acquired by the Atchison, Topeka Santa Fe Railroad which leased it to Fred Harvey who operated it as one of his famous Harvey Houses. For more than 40 years, from 1926 to 1968, La Fonda was one of the more successful Harvey Houses, a renowned chain of fine hotels.

Since 1968, La Fonda has been locally owned and operated and has continued the same tradition of providing warm hospitality, excellent service and modern amenities while maintaining historic integrity and architectural authenticity.

Throughout its long history, La Fonda has changed and evolved many times, but it continues to be the true heart of Santa Fe for visitors and locals alike.

---

[12] Wheeler, Liza, N.M. Has Its Share of Haunts, Albuquerque Journal, Thursday, October 31, 2002.

THE GHOSTS

The present La Plazuela Dining Room in this lovely old hotel was originally an enclosed courtyard that was situated around an old well. Over 100 years ago, during the period of time in which a casino operated in this historic old building, a salesman who had a streak of bad luck and lost all of his company's money left the gambling tables and leapt to his death into the old well. From time to time, guests in the dining room sometimes report seeing a man walk to the center of the room and then jump as if into an invisible hole and simply disappear.

This building is old — it was already built when the city of Santa Fe was founded in the early 1600s. Alan Jordan, president of About Walks and Tours in Santa Fe, says that at one point, court was held in the building, and the public hangings of those found guilty took place in the lobby.

Besides the hangings (as if they weren't enough), there were plenty of other documented deaths in the La Fonda. In 1867, when La Fonda was known as the "Exchange Hotel," building records show Judge John P. Slough was killed in the lobby by Captain Rynerson, a member of the Territorial Legislature representing Dona Ana County. Rynerson shot him in the stomach after Slough called him a liar and a thief. He was later acquitted. Many people believe the judge still haunts the building today.

The hotel archives also document the hanging death of some poor soul by a lynch mob in the hotel's back yard.[13]

LA RESIDENCIA
820 Paseo De Peralta
Santa Fe, New Mexico

La Residencia, located at the corner of Palace Avenue and Paseo de Peralta is a long term nursing facility that has been operated by Presbyterian Medical Services since late in 1983. On October 14, 2003, the facility closed its doors for the final time. The move meant the 101 residents had to find new quarters within a short period of time and the 106 employees either had to look for new jobs or move into new quarters.

The facility that housed this nursing home was originally the site of the original St. Vincent Hospital, the Santa Fe community hospital.

---

[13] Ibid.

THE GHOSTS

There are a number of former staff and, not a few residents, who talk of strange sounds coming from empty rooms as well as ghostly dark clad figures being glimpsed in the hallways at night. Others whisper of malevolent inhuman figures sticking their heads into rooms to glare at the terrified residents.

The muffled crying of a little boy who died in Room 311 when this as still the community hospital is still heard by nurses. The child and his father both died of injuries suffered in an automobile accident on Interstate 25. The eerie sounds from Room 311 are so frequent that the nursing home administrators try to keep the room unoccupied.

The hauntings of the upper floors seemed to be taken in stride by the nursing staff. However, almost all of them wanted nothing to do with the basement of the building. The staff was almost unanimous in their belief that something evil lurked in the darkened corridors of the bottom floor.

When the State Museum, which is located in the building next door, began storing Indian artifacts in part of the huge basement, some nurses absolutely refused to enter the area. Those that would speak of their experiences claimed that they saw shadowy figures moving about the hallways and heard strange sounds such as banging and voices talking rapidly emanate from the basement rooms.

As usually happens in every organization the old timers thought it was fun to require the newcomers to the staff to go through a "rite of passage" that required them to spend some time in the basement. One of the staff members would take the new employee to the basement on the elevator and then required the rookie to cross the darkened basement to the stairway and then ascend to the third floor.

However one evening, a new staff member, a very young, inexperienced, nurse's aide, was taken to the basement and given her assignment. The one that had taken her to the basement then returned to the third floor to await the rookie's arrival. Traditionally, the newcomer always arrived shortly with some truly bizarre stories of thinks in the dark. This time, the new staff member did not arrive via the stairs; in fact, she did not arrive at all.

Concerned that something had happened to the young girl, two nurses went to the dark basement to look for the nurse's aide. They searched the main part of the basement, but found no sign of the aide. Finally, in desperation, they begin to call her name. Finally, she answered, her voice faint and far away. With the aid of a flashlight, the two nurses finally located the newcomer, in a small dark room, far down one of the hallways, crouched in the corner.

The very scared young lady confessed that she had become disoriented in the dark and lost her way. When she heard something moving in the darkness, she had run until she found the small room in which she was hiding. The older nurse calmed the young aide and the two started for the door. Then they both froze – oozing down the wall beside the doorway of the small room was fresh blood. The nurse later said that it covered most of the wall and seemed to actually be coming from then wall. Not waiting to see anything else, the two ran for the elevator where the other nurse was holding the car.

Later, the nurses discovered that St. Vincent's had once had a small incinerator in that same room where hospital maintenance personnel had cremated amputated limbs.

LA POSADA DE SANTA FE
330 East Palace Avenue
Santa Fe, New Mexico

Located on land originally owned by one of Santa Fe's first families, the establishment now called the La Posada de Santa Fe Resort & Spa was long known as The Staab House, named after an early Santa Fe settler, Abraham Staab, who built the original mansion for his wife Julia. The original part of the hotel was originally the Staabs' Victorian mansion built in 1882.

Later the elegant structure was adobeized, in other words, an adobe structure was literally built around the original structure. Now the original Victorian presence is found only within the charming bar, the original staircase and four rooms upstairs, which still maintain the original brick and high ceilings.

It is said that Julia Staab, who died in 1896, continues to haunt the place. Mischievous but good-natured, Julia is said to be Santa Fe's best-known and most frequently witnessed ghost, normally seen on the second floor of the hotel in Room 256.

According to the hotel's archives, the house was built for her shortly after the Civil War by her husband, Abraham, who had amassed a fortune as a major supply contractor for the U.S. Army. Room 256 was originally Julia's bedroom in life and reflects much of its original charm. It is a large room, comprised of over 600 square feet and in keeping with the history of the room it is furnished with king sized brass bed, antique furniture and beautiful area rugs.

After the latest renovation of her former bedroom in the 1980s, Julia now seems to prefer the dining room on the second floor[14]. Staff members have reported that a strong gust of wind will blow through the room as they set the room up for parties. If there are candles burning on the table after the guests depart, somehow they are all extinguished. It would seem that even in death Julia Staab is a good and careful hostess.

---

[14] Norman, Michael and Beth Scott, Haunted Heritage, TOR, New York. 2002.

One staff member was cleaning the floor in the dining room when he looked up to find Mrs. Staab standing nearby watching him work. He said that she had the most intense eyes he had ever seen.

In an unidentified magazine clipping titled "The Ghost" that La Posada keeps in its archives, Mary Lee White writes that Julia Staab entertained endlessly and "was such a socialite that few recognized her dedication to her family." But after her infant son died of an illness, Julia's hair turned prematurely white. "People then realized," White writes, "that she was a sensitive and conscientious mother as well as a prominent wife, hostess and socialite."

White goes on to explain that many more unsuccessful pregnancies probably contributed to her early demise at age 52. The obituary that ran in The New Mexican gave scant details about the death.

"The official record contained nothing untoward about Mrs. Staab's demise," White writes. "But rumors afoot in Santa Fe had it that Julia had gone crazy and was kept in her room the last few years of her life."

Given the uncertainty surrounding Staab's death, it doesn't surprise some that her spirit seems to remain in her old house, interfering with La Posada's employees and guests.

Bartender Judy Vanderbeck says last Mother's Day, before a packed house, glasses flew off the shelf one by one, crashing to the floor; the fireplace kept turning on and off; and seasoned waitresses dropped trays as if someone pushed them up from underneath. Perhaps Julia Staab didn't go gently into her eternal sleep[15].

There may well be another ghost in residence at the La Posada De Santa Fe. One evening as a security guard was making his rounds, he heard the sound of a man's voice talking in the closed lounge area. He was unable to understand what was said, but there was no doubt that someone was talking. However, when he opened the dor for a quick peek inside, the lounge was empty.

There is also other evidence regarding a male ghost in the hotel A young hotel guest awoke one night to see a man wearing a waistcoat standing over her bed. When she asked who he was, the man vanished.

Finally, an employee working in the hotel's office, which is off of the main lobby glanced up from her work to see a man standing by the front entrance. She looked back down at what she was doing and then realized that there was not supposed to be anyone in the lobby so late at night. When she looked back up, the man was gone. A search did not reveal anyone roaming the hallways or outside the front doors.

Others have also heard pots and pans making noise in the empty kitchen as if someone was cooking. A heavy cut glass chandelier in one of the dining rooms will periodically begin to swing back and forth though no one or nothing is touching it. Then most unnerving of all, staff and guests alike have heard the

---

[15] Ibid.

sound of a woman sobbing that seems to come from everywhere in the old building.

SANTA FE INDIAN SCHOOL
1500 Cerrillos Road
Santa Fe, New Mexico

The federal government's treatment of the Native American tribes has been called nothing short of shameful. As if dealing with a defeated country, the United States government even went so far as to take the children of the Native Americans and send them to special schools designed to eradicate their native culture and replace it with the culture of main stream America. In many cases, Native American children were forcibly taken from their parents to be sent to these schools. Many of these unfortunate children died in these schools.

One such school was the Santa Fe Indian School which was founded in 1890 as a federal boarding school to culturally assimilate Indian children through education and isolation from their families. In 1962, the Santa Fe Indian School merged with the Albuquerque Indian School, and the Santa Fe site was taken over by the Institute of American Indian Arts. A series of events beginning in the mid-1970's led to the Albuquerque Indian School being transferred to the Santa Fe Indian School, and the Institute of American Indian Arts permanently relocating to a neighboring site in Santa Fe. As a result of the passage of the Indian Self Determination Act in 1975, administration of the school transferred from the U.S. Government to the American Indian Pueblo Council. The school has evolved into a community school with the missions of fostering traditional Indian culture, while teaching the skills necessary for students to thrive as individuals.

THE GHOSTS

There are those that believe that the Santa Fe Indian School is one of the most haunted places in New Mexico. The spirits that haunt this site are those of the young Native American children who were, sometimes, forcibly, taken from their homelands in the late 1800s to be taught in the Indian School system.

Over the many yeas that this school has been in existence, some of what are now dormitories were once hospitals where these Indian children were treated for illnesses, some buildings were churches where they were taught a new religion and sadly, some of these buildings were morgues where some children were taken who caught the dreaded small pox and died.

There are stories that the children who died of small pox were buried in one huge grave behind the track field and not sent home for fear that the rest of the tribes would be infected with this deadly disease. Many former students say that there are balls of light that can be seen jumping around behind the school. Others have been adamant that they have heard children's voices coming from the top floors of the dorms where no students are housed. Still others talk of things moving by themselves, radios changing, showers turning on, beds shaking and the unbelievably eerie feelings that they are not along when they have entered certain rooms.

Some also tell stories of seeing the shadows of being hanging from the ceiling as if they had been hung and the sounds of voices screaming as if in agony.

PENITENTIARY OF NEW MEXICO, STATE FE
P.O. Box 1059
Santa Fe, New Mexico

The Main Unit of the Penitentiary of New Mexico at Santa Fe was opened in 1956 to house long term offenders. In 1980, there was a major rebellion at the New Mexico State Penitentiary, though it was said to have been an inmate rebellion without a plan, without leadership and without goals. Once the uprising began, a sort of mob mentality seemed to overcome the rioting inmates. There were few heroes, plenty of villains and many victims.

When State Police marched into the Penitentiary of New Mexico on Feb. 3, 1980, they didn't retake the prison from rioting inmates so much as they occupied the charred shell after the riot had burned itself out.

Thirty-three inmates were found dead inside -- some of them horribly butchered by their fellow prisoners. The emergency room at St. Vincent Hospital in Santa Fe was overwhelmed with more than 100 inmates -- some beaten, others suffering from drug overdoses. Eight of the 12 guards who had been taken hostage were treated for injuries, though, amazingly, none of the guards had been killed. It was a black mark on New Mexico history as the nation was captivated by the horror stories that dribbled out of Santa Fe.

The riot began in the early morning hours of Saturday, Feb. 2, when guards entered dormitory E-2 on the south side of the prison.

For some unknown reason, the door to the dormitory wasn't locked, in violation of prison security procedures. Neither was a hallway gate that led to the prison control room. Four guards were taken hostage during the first few minutes of the riot. In all, there were 15 guards on duty inside the prison that night, supervising more than 1,100 inmates.

Inmates rushed down the main corridor and broke the shatterproof glass at the control center. The guard on duty fled, leaving behind keys that could open most of the prison gates and doors.

Once the inmates assumed control of the cellblocks, the inside of the prison became a nightmare of violence. One Associated Press reporter later described it in a story distributed worldwide as a "merry-go-round gone crazy." A large number of fires were set as other inmates ripped out plumbing fixtures, flooding parts of the prison. Other inmates got into the infirmary and began taking drugs while still others began hunting their enemies and found them.

Sometime around 8 a.m. that Saturday morning, inmates began using tools from the prison to gain access to cellblock 4, which housed the "snitches" and inmates in protective segregation. The "snitches" housed in that cellblock all met a horrible end. One was hung from the upper tier of the cellblock, another decapitated. Most of the 33 inmates killed were from the segregation unit.

Early Saturday morning, fitful negotiations began with some inmate leaders. Ambulances shuttled the dead and injured to St. Vincent Hospital in Santa Fe. Smoke continued to pour out of the prison gymnasium.

It became clear later that neither the inmates nor the state had a single spokesman during the negotiations. This resulted in a great deal of confusion in the attempted negotiations. Eventually, however, the prison inmates made 11 basic demands. Some concerned basic prison conditions like overcrowding, inmate discipline, educational services and improving food. They also wanted outside witnesses to the negotiations such as federal officials and the news media.

Guards who had been taken hostage when the riot started were finally released. Some of the guards had been protected by inmates; others were brutally beaten. "One was tied to a chair. Another lay naked on a stretcher, blood pouring from a head wound," a Journal reporter wrote. Negotiations broke off about 1 a.m. Sunday and state officials insisted no concessions had been made. But the riot, fueled by drugs and hate, was running out of gas.

Later Sunday morning, inmates began to trickle out of the prison, seeking refuge at the fence where National Guardsmen stood with their M-16s. Black inmates led the exodus from the smoldering cellblocks, staying in groups large enough to defend themselves from other inmates. The largest riot in New Mexico Prison History was over.

THE GHOSTS

Many have said that violent emotion can produce hauntings and this prison riot released emotions that had been suppressed for years. Inmates went on a killing spree unprecedented in New Mexico prison history.

The most active areas of the prison are Cell Blocks 3, 4, the Tool room and the laundry room. Cell Block 3 was the maximum security ward which also contained the Solitary confinement cell. Some of the ghostly activity reported here includes unexplainable noises, doors that open and close by themselves, and lights that turn on and off without any apparent cause.

Cell block 4 was the area where the "snitches" and other prisoners held in protective custody were contained. Upon entering the cell block, there are marks on the floor where rioters used power tools to decapitate the snitches and several other inmates. Also visible are the outlines of scorch marks where other inmates were burned to death with propane cutting torches. Another inmate was hung from the upper tier of the cell block with sheets that had been tied together. The activity reported here is similar to those reported in Cell Block 3. Twenty three of the inmates that were murdered during the riot were killed in Cell Block 4.

The laundry was the site of several murders, although they occurred long before the riot of 1980. It is located in a labyrinth of corridors that lie underneath the prison. These corridors also link to the gas chamber, many mechanical rooms and the tool room where the inmates stole the propane torches and other tools that were used during the riots. Uneasy feelings and whispers are often reported down there as well as unusual human shaped shadows.

THE OLDEST HOUSE
215 East De Vargas Street
Santa FE, New Mexico.

The house at this address is said to be the oldest house in Santa Fe. If true, this would probably make it one of the oldest houses in the United States as Santa Fe is next to the oldest European settlement in the country.

According to legend, at one time this house was inhabited by two women who were said to be "brujas" or witches. Whether either of these two women were actual card carrying witches is not important, but they had gained a reputation for making a love potion that was said to be very effective. Most of the young men of wealth came to this house to purchase what they believed was the key to true love.

One young man came to see the two witches and purchased the love potion that had become so famous for paving the way for wealthy marriages in Santa Fe. He paid the price demanded by the two witches and received the potion. He then went to see the young woman he desired for his own and arranged for her to drink the potion. To his shock, even after drinking the magic potion that had been so successful for so many other suitors, the young woman chose to marry another man. The young suitor felt that he had been cheated.

The disappointed young man returned to the house on De Varas Street and demanded his money back. Apparently this conversation became very heated because one of the two women grabbed a large butcher knife and with one swing, separated the spurned suitor's head from his body.

It was said that the witches dumped the body and the head in the nearby Santa Fe River. Some have said that the spurned lover searches for his head as he can never know peace in death until his body is whole again. Though the body was found, the head was never recovered.

One of the streets that runs toward the Santa Fe River is called Alto Street. Not too much is known about this street that runs down toward the river. It is said that this street is haunted by the headless caballero. This cursed young man is said to brandishes a sword over where his head should be as he rides his phantom horse down the road to the Santa Fe River.

CASA REAL HEALTH CARE CENTER
501 Galisteo Street
Santa Fe, New Mexico

The Casa Real Health Care Center is a senior health-care facility that was built in 1985. In spite of the relatively new age of this building, it seems to have become endowed with the violent history of the ground upon which it was, perhaps unwisely, built. Of all of the things that contractors take into consideration when constructing a new facility, what might have previously occupied the land is certainly not of prime importance. In this case, perhaps, it should have been given more attention.

This building, designed to be a shelter and a place of care for the aged and the infirm was built on top of an old penitentiary graveyard next to another haunted building. Later happenings made it clear that something had lingered in the cemetery that found an outlet for its rage and violent emotions in the newly built Healthcare Center.

Employees, patients, and visitors to the 112-bed convalescent center have complained of an oppressive, uncomfortable feeling that seems to emanate from the place. The moment a person steps through the front door, they are assaulted by what seems to be waves of emotions. Strange cold spots move through the rooms, and unexplained moaning sounds have been heard in the north and south wings.

THE SCHOOL OF AMERICAN RESEARCH
606 Garcia Street
Santa Fe, New Mexico

Figure 15: The Admin Building on the historic campus.

The historic campus of the School of American Research is located on Santa Fe's east side. Built by sisters Amelia Elizabeth White and Martha Root White in the 1920s, the estate became the home of SAR in 1973. Canyon Road, with its many galleries and shops is within walking distance and the Santa Fe Plaza, the heart of the city, is one mile away[16].

Martha Root White and Amelia Elizabeth White were the very wealthy spinster daughters of the well known New York publisher Horace B. White. They were also two women with a love for the southwest in general and Santa Fe in particular. During the 1920s the two women came to Santa Fe and built an estate that they called *El Dilirio*[17].

In keeping with the lifestyle that they had become accustomed to while living in New York as the only children of Horace White, the two women made it a point to cultivate those in the arts living in Santa Fe. As a result, El Delirio became known as a popular gathering place for Santa Fe writers and artists. The two sisters were very generous supporters of the arts and were also among those who loved the art of the southwest Native Americans. The White sisters were the ones to open a gallery in New York City dedicated solely to the art of the Native Americans of the Southwest.

---

[16] http://www.sarweb.org/home/directions/directions.htm.
[17] Norman, Michael and Beth Scott, <u>Haunted Heritage</u>, TOR, New York. 2002.

Martha White died in 1937, but Amelia Elizabeth White lived on at El Dilirio until her own death in 1972 at the age of 96. No one was surprised when her will was read. She had stipulated that her estate and all of her other properties in and around Santa Fe be donated to the School of American Research.

The School of American Research was established in Santa Fe, New Mexico in 1907 as a center for the study of the archaeology and ethnology of the American Southwest. In the early years of the twentieth century, archaeology was a young discipline with roots in the art historical studies of Old World antiquities. The unveiling of the treasures of Troy, Ephesus, and the Valley of the Kings held the world spellbound.

In 1906 Alice Cunningham Fletcher, a pioneering anthropologist and ethnographer of Plains Indian groups, was on the American Committee of the Archaeological Institute of America. The AIA, founded in Boston in 1879, had schools in Athens, Rome, and Palestine that sponsored research into the foundations of classical civilization and promoted professional standards in archaeological field work. Fletcher wanted to establish an "Americanist" center with three aims: to train students in the profession of archaeology, to engage in anthropological research on the American continent, and to preserve and study the unique cultural heritage of the Southwest. Her aims coincided with those of Edgar Lee Hewett, an innovative educator and passionate amateur archaeologist whom she met in 1906 in Mexico.

Hewett, nicknamed "El Toro," was a flamboyant and controversial figure. He served as president of New Mexico Normal School in Las Vegas (now New Mexico Highlands University) from 1898 to 1903, where he taught some of the first courses in anthropology to be offered at any U.S. college. Hewett transformed himself from an amateur to a professional archaeologist, undertaking a doctoral program at the University of Geneva in 1903 and writing his dissertation, "Les communautés anciennes dans le desert américain," on the distribution and social organization of archaeological peoples in the greater Southwest and northern Mexico. His work as a lobbyist for the protection of archaeological sites led to the creation of Mesa Verde National Park and the passage of the Preservation of American Antiquities Act of 1906.

In December of 1907 the American Committee of the AIA accepted Fletcher's plan to establish an American program and appointed Hewett the director of the new School of American Archaeology. Alice Fletcher was named the first chairperson of the School's managing committee. From this institutional base, Hewett became a key architect of the discipline of Southwestern archaeology over the next forty years.

THE GHOSTS

There are many stories both about the White sisters as well as the property upon which they built their famed estate. There are those who believe that El Dilirio was built upon the site of an ancient Indian Pueblo. It is said that a number of relics found on the property from this ancient site are inside the mansion.

Additionally, there is no question that the White sisters were somewhat eccentric. The bodies of these two wealthy women are buried under a gazebo on the property as well as the bodies of some twenty rare Afghan and Irish wolfhounds raised by the sisters.

Whatever many be the cause, there is also no question that spirits roam this palatial estate. Some of the staff swears that late in the evenings, they have heard the voices of women talking outside the building. However, when they try to find the source of the conversations, there is never anyone found. On another occasion, an employee working late heard the front doorbell ring. She then heard the front door open and footsteps come down the hallway to the very room in which she was working. She heard the footsteps enter the room and then retreat back toward the front door and then the door open and close. During this entire time, she saw no one through the steps came to within a few feet of where she sat.

More than one person who has spent time in or around the gazebo beneath which the White sisters rest for all eternity report having felt like they are being watched even though they can find no one about. Perhaps the White Sisters are curious about the new comers using their beloved estate.

Another individual, a professor always felt as if someone was following her around and then reading over her shoulder as she worked though she never saw any sign of anyone. She would usually find her office door open when she knew very well that she had closed it the night before. Her dog also reacted as if there was someone in the room that had become her office that she was not able to see. Many times she found items in her office rearranged and the furniture showed signs of being cleaned; through no one would admit to cleaning her office.

Someone staying in what had been Amelia White's bedroom left for several days on vacation. Though the door had been locked when the occupant left, upon her return, she found the door open and the room had the appearance that it had been cleaned in her absence.

Finally, there is an arroyo near the school that has the reputation of being haunted. Many times, people have heard the sounds of conversations and laughter coming from this area, but they never find anyone that could account for the sounds.

LEGAL TENDER SALOON
Just off of Paseo de Peralta
Santa Fe, New Mexico

This historic old building was built in 1881 and has been used for a number of purposes over the years. Of course, being located across the street from the train depot, it was a natural spot for a commercial establishment. The first of these ventures was first called the Pflueger General Merchandise Store and Annex Saloon. It is also known that after serving its time as a general retail establishment and a bar that it became a vaudeville house for a time.

Then in the 1950s, the building was home to the Pink Garter and then in 1969, it became known as the Legal Tender Saloon and Restaurant.

THE GHOSTS

This old saloon and vaudeville hall is haunted by several ghosts.

There is a lady dressed in an elegant white gown who is seen floating up the steps to the balcony in the Parlor Room. No one seems to know her identity. There is also a little girl ghost in a long dress that sits all alone on the stairs. She looks so lonely that a lot of kind hearted people who do not realize that she is a ghost try to comfort her, but if anyone approaches her, she fades slowly away.

There is also a man dressed all in black who had the misfortune to be killed by a stray bullet fired in the rowdy gambling hall. This gentleman has been seen helping himself to a drink at the bar. Once again, no one seems to know who this mysterious figure might be.

NIGHT SKY GALLERY
826 Canyon Road
Santa Fe, New Mexico

This one-story building is now the fashionable Night Sky Gallery catering to the artsy crowd in Santa Fe. It is also said that this building has long been haunted by strange voices and unexplainable sounds for many years. Gentle voices are heard during the winter months carrying on conversations though no one is seen. Many who have visited this building that have heard the voices say that they have experienced feelings of tremendous fear. According to director Kate Norton, there is an uneasy feeling about the place after hours, and employees refuse to spend the night in the building.

ST. VINCENT HOSPITAL
Santa Fe. New Mexico

St. Vincent Hospital, established in 1865, has been caring for the communities of Santa Fe and northern New Mexico for more than 130 years. Originally run by the Sisters of Charity, today's St. Vincent is a non-profit, non-affiliated hospital with a board of directors.

Many things have changed since the hospital opened its doors in 1865, but its mission remains the same, to care for all the people of Santa Fe, northern New Mexico, and southern Colorado regardless of their ability to pay.

THE GHOSTS

The ghost of a very short Hispanic man dressed in old fashioned clothing, appeared several times to a nurse on the top floor of this three-story modern hospital. The ghost of a woman wearing a black mantilla was observed with the man. The ghostly couple seemed confused and in need of some kind of help. The hospital was built in 1977 on top of an old penitentiary graveyard. A more recent hospital operated on this same tract of land also reported paranormal activity.

THREE SISTERS BOUTIQUE
211 Old Santa Fe Trail
Santa Fe. New Mexico

Years ago, the Sisters of Loretto operated a Catholic school in the area that is now occupied by the Inn of Loretto. Nearby there is a row of very elegant shops located in the 200 block of the old Santa Fe Trail. There is a great deal of evidence that the structure that houses these expensive shops was once used by the school as chicken coops.

In addition to the stories about the chickens that once occupied these quarters, it is also said that there are now said to be permanent residents who, from time to time, make themselves known to those among the living.

There is a printing shop occupying one of these historic buildings. Many nights, members of the staff who worked late heard the sound of women's laughter and the sound of someone walking when no one could be seen.

Topping this, however, are the antics that took place in the Three Sisters Boutique, a clothing store along this row of haunted buildings. Though these buildings many have once housed chickens, it was also once the Old Opportunity School Building. However, today, this particular section of this historic old structure now houses a modern Western-wear shop.

The Boutique is owned by two women who had high hopes for their business in the tourist mecca that is Santa Fe. The first night when they counted their receipts, they came out with ten dollars too much. No matter how hard they tried, they were unable to account for the extra ten dollars. However, to their amazement, for the week, each evening they found that there was ten dollars too much in the register. No explanation has ever been found.

THE GHOSTS

Those who had lived in the area said that Sister George, a member of the Sisters of Loretto Order, known for her unselfish assistance to those of need in the community was responsible for the extra money that appeared in the register each night. She was always helping out those in the community and she had spent many years teaching in the old building.

Many said that after she died in the early 1970's her spirit started manifesting in the old Opportunity School building, where she had spent many years. The old school was purchased by Best Western Corporation and turned into upscale shops. The company spared no expense to make the old building comfortable quarters for the shop owners.

However, several tenants complained of hearing footsteps when no one was around, and of noticing strange electrical problems such as lights going on and off for no reason. There are also some shop owners who have reported than an extra ten-dollar bill regularly appears in their cash registers. Today, most of the ghostly activity seems to be cantered around the Three Sisters Boutique. The clothing shop was named for Sister George and two other nuns who ran the original school.

CAMACHO HOUSE
507 Apodaca Hill Street
Santa Fe, New Mexico

The Camacho House is old, but no one is sure exactly how old it might be. Not a lot of detailed information is known of its history, except that during the 1920s it is known that this house was used as a brothel and a gambling hall.

The old house also has a reputation of being very haunted by a number of spirits. There have been stories of a mischievous presence that likes to grab ankles and trip people who walk through the house.

Patricia Camacho was one tenant in this house that reported that she has seen the impression of an invisible person in the comforter on her bed and has heard the voices of a group of people in conversation coming from the empty basement of the house. These unearthly voices have also been heard by visitors to the house.

CHURCH OF SAN MIGUEL POR BARRIO ANALCO
Old Santa Fe Trail
Santa Fe, New Mexico

The city of Santa Fe was founded in 1610, and El San Miguel (St. Michael's) Mission Church was built between 1610 and 1628. Foundations of the first church remain observable under the sanctuary of the present structure. Archaeological investigations beneath these foundations reveal evidence of Native American occupation of the site as early and 1300 A.D. In 1680, during the pueblo rebellion, the church vigas in the ceiling were burned, and in 1692 De Vargas ordered the church rebuilt. In 1710 the church was reconstructed and a sacristy was added to its south side in 1714. Repairs to the structure were made between 1798 and 1805 and again in 1830. In 1853 Archbishop Lamy installed the altar stone[18].

In 1859 the church served as the chapel for the newly arrived Christian Brothers who took over control of St. Michael's School. In 1881 the Christian Brothers purchased the church, a recently completed school building, an adobe building and the land upon which they were situated from the Archdiocese of Santa Fe. Over the years repairs were affected to the roof, walls and floor. In 1955 archaeological investigations were made, the altar reredos and artwork were restored.

Since its creation, San Miguel has been used as a chapel and shrine to St. Michael, a military chapel, an oratory for the Christian Brothers, a school chapel and a barrio church. Today, in addition to being an historical treasure, cultural heritage and tourist attraction, it still serves as a shrine to St. Michael and a chapel where Mass is celebrated weekly.

This particular story concerns not a ghost, per se, but rather the story of a miracle that has defied explanation to this day. It was actually the old bell at this church was the source of a miracle that took place in the mid-1800's.

According to local legend, a blind man attended the church at noontime every day. His fervent prayers for the return of his sight are said to have caused the bell to ring with no one pulling the rope. To the shock of not only the man but also the rest of the parish, it was said that during the time that the bell was

---

[18] http://www.cbnosf.org/Old%20Church.htm

ringing loudly, the man regained his sight. He was later able to accurately describe statues and icons inside the church that he had never seen, but to his sorrow, he became blind again as soon as the ringing of the bell stopped.

Catholic Church officials were initially puzzled, but finally described the miracle as a visitation of the Holy Ghost. The bell that caused the miracle was cast in Spain in 1356 and placed within this church. In 1872, the bell of the miracle fell from the old spire. It was left where it landed and is currently on display on the church grounds.

THE DEVIL HOUSE
934 Lopez Street
Santa Fe, New Mexico

A young man who engaged in devil worship in this house got more than he was bargaining for; Michael joined a gang of Satanist from Cerrillos and was soon overcome by evil. He performed rituals in his bedroom and once sacrificed a dog there. Then one evening, two figures, like "huge, winged birds or bats" appeared in his room and beat him unconscious. When he was released from the hospital, Michael tried to quit the group, but never succeeded. In September 1988, the twenty-three-year-old committed suicide by slitting his throat. Prospective tenants inspecting the house reported feeling uneasy there, and a few felt they were being slapped by an invisible hand. A priest blessed the house, and current residents have reported no problems.

LUGUNA PUEBLO MISSION
Santa Fe. New Mexico

The coffin of the murdered priest keeps popping up through the church floor here. Father Juan Padilla was murdered by Indians in 1733 and was buried beneath the floor at the Isleta Pueblo Church. Before long, his coffin, hollowed out of a cottonwood tree, rose out of the earth in front of the altar. It rose again twenty years later, and again in 1889. Then, on Christmas Even 1914, it poked through the floor again. Two investigations were conducted by the Bishop o Santa Fe, but no conclusion was reached as to the nature of the phenomenon.

PERA BUILDING
1120 Paseo de Peralta
Santa Fe, New Mexico

In April of 2001, New Mexico's Governor, Gary Johnson authorized the General Services Department to purchase the Public Employees Retirement Association (PERA) Building as part of a new office building in the West Capitol Complex[19]. Many locals consider the Public Employees Retirement Association (PERA) building to be haunted.

Some will not go near it because both the building and the parking lot were built on the site of an old Spanish-Indian graveyard. In fact, two levels of the five floor building were constructed below ground in the middle of the graveyard. Unseen hands are said to reach out and trip people on stairs, and unexplained cries and moans echo through the halls. Once the ghost of a tall, thin, woman appeared in a third floor corridor. At least one janitor quit because of the ghostly activity.

Another ghost has been seen by a number of people in the parking lot adjoining the building. According to all reports, the spirit of a small lady in a black dress with a mantilla pulled tightly about her head had been seen moving quickly across the parking lot. She looks so real that a number of people who have met her speak to her, though she never acknowledges the friendly greetings.

It seems that the lady's son was a student at the old St. Michael's College in Santa Fe. St. Michael's was a boarding school with students from many distant and isolated New Mexican towns.

While at the school, the lady's son contracted the dreaded smallpox and died. Not wanting to alarm the citizens of Santa Fe with the thought of a possible smallpox epidemic, City authorities buried the young boy very quickly and in an unmarked grave in the cemetery upon which the PERA Building is now located.

The boy's mother was long in learning of his death due to the isolated location of her village. She came to Santa Fe as soon as she could, but the boy's body had long been buried and City authorities refused to tell her the location of his grave. She was heart broken at the death of her only child and refused to return to her home without his remains. She eventually died of a broken heart, but even today, she still searches for the remains of her son.

---

[19] Norman, Michael and Beth Scott, <u>Haunted Heritage</u>, TOR, New York. 2002.

VILLAGRA BUILDING
408 Galisteo Street
Santa Fe, New Mexico

There is another building in the Capitol Complex that is reputed to be haunted. As the first building constructed with New Deal money in New Mexico in 1934 this building was designated as the Public Welfare Building. For many years it played an important role as the headquarters for state and federal relief programs during the New Deal.

Architecturally, the Villagra Building represents the maturation of John Gaw Meem's Territorial Revival work, the signature style of Santa Fe's state government buildings. The original 1934 section, along with an addition that was added in 1953 was built of poured concrete frame finished with cream-colored stucco walls, brick coping, pedimented window and door surrounds and classically inspired columns across the front entry.

In September 2001, the Historic Preservation Division (HPD) learned that Property Control Division (PCD) was planning to demolish the historic Villagra Building on Galisteo Street, as part of their Capitol Complex Master plan, and build in its place a brand-new facility to house government offices. Their reason for the demolition was their belief that the building was no longer suitable for re-occupancy without substantial work, after its tenant of 30 years, the state Game and Fish Department decided to vacate the building in early 2001. HPD staff quickly acted to facilitate an Emergency State Register Listing for the structure, to temporarily protect it from its demise, while trying to negotiate possible alternatives with PCD and its architectural consultants for the project. As a result of the listing on October 5, 2001, PCD and HPD entered into an agreement to save the majority of the original 1934 Public Welfare Building, while permitting the demolition of the entire 1953 addition and a portion of the northwest wing of the original structure.

THE GHOSTS

What was not widely known and was certainly not mentioned nor considered in any of the high level negotiations over the fate of this historic old building was that it is haunted.

The employees of the Department of Game and Fish, the primary tenant in this old building for many years, reported that they had often seen an old woman wearing a gown from the late 1700s era walking down the hallway. Even more unusual, witnesses said that the old woman always had a small dog perched on her shoulder.

It was also reported that whenever someone met her, the old woman would beckon them to follow her. But as soon as she invited someone to follow her, it is said, the old woman, and her dog, would vanish.

Inquiries about this story will result in some saying that the old woman whose spirit is seen in the building was a witch who was hung in the 1700s. The place where she was hung was located where the Villagra Building now stands. Of course, others swear that there was an early cemetery located where the building now sits and the old woman was one of those buried in the cemetery. These people say that the building of the structure disturbed the old woman's rest and now she comes back to try and chase away those who disturbed her.

CHAPTER THIRTEEN

LAS CRUCES, NEW MEXICO

It was an Apache ambush on settlers that gave Las Cruces its name. When travelers from Taos were killed along the El Camino Real in 1830, the grieving survivors marked the graves with crosses. Thus, La Placita de Las Cruces, or the Place of the Crosses, became the frontier settlement of Las Cruces in 1849, when the first streets were marked with rawhide rope.

However, during the two centuries preceding the 1850s, the Rio Grande Valley changed hands several times. Resisting the termination of their tribal customs, the Pueblos overthrew their Spanish oppressors in 1680, and maintained their autonomy until defeated in 1692.

More than 100 years later, Mexican revolutionaries overthrew the Spanish rulers and established the Republic of Mexico in 1821. Within 25 years, America's resolute westward expansion prompted a war against Mexico. The 1848 Treaty of Guadalupe Hidalgo and the Gadsden Purchase of 1854 claimed much of Mexico's northern land as U.S. domain.

The area became Confederate soil briefly in 1862, when 3,000 Texas troops marched into the Mesilla Valley en route to Santa Fe. Union soldiers later defeated the Confederates north of Santa Fe.

After the Civil War ended in 1865, the U.S. Army built Fort Selden to guard against the Apache. The Buffalo Soldiers of the 125th (African-American) Infantry were among the first troops to defend the fort. Later, a young captain named MacArthur commanded the post, while his son Douglas, played among the adobe, flat-roofed buildings. The expanding railroad and the increasing influx of new immigrants abated the Apache threat, and the fort was officially abandoned in 1891.

In 1973, Fort Selden became a state monument, and it is now the summertime site of weekend portrayals of the life of a frontier soldier. An interpretive trail also winds through the historical ruins, which are located about 15 miles north of Las Cruces.

During the late 1800s, Las Cruces began supplying goods to adventurous miners who came into the mountains seeking wealth. Fort Selden soldiers also came into town for supplies. Mesilla had become a major stop along the

Butterfield Overland Stage route, which carried passengers through much of the western U.S. Also, innovative irrigation techniques spurred agricultural growth along the Rio Grande.

A colorful local character of this Wild West timeframe was Henry McCarty, a.k.a. William Bonney, a.k.a. Billy the Kid. During the Lincoln County cattle range wars in 1878, Billy the Kid killed a county sheriff, for which he was captured and sentenced to hang. Remarkably, he escaped from the Mesilla courthouse. Within a couple of years, however, he was tracked and killed by the Dona Ana County Sheriff, Pat Garrett. Ironically, the well-known sheriff was later shot outside Las Cruces by an unknown gunslinger; Garrett's body was buried in the local cemetery.

Today, Las Cruces proudly displays the national historic districts of the Alameda Depot and Mesquite Street, which marks the town's original 1849 settlement. Significant buildings include the former Amador Hotel, built in 1853, now a county office, and the Armijo House, built in 1877, most recently a law office. Both the charming adobe buildings of the frontier settlers and the elegant mansions of the railroad tycoons reflect two distinct, local lifestyles of the latter 19th century. On January 6, 1912, New Mexico became the nation's 47th state. The area grew quietly and inconspicuously until July 16, 1945, when scientists involved in the war effort exploded the first atomic bomb north of Las Cruces near Alamogordo. The earth shattering, life-changing explosion occurred on Jornada Del Muerto, long ago marked as a valley of death.

Following World War II in 1946, Las Cruces was incorporated as a city. Since then, it has grown to be New Mexico's second largest city and the Dona Ana county seat. Its current population of 78,000 has increased fivefold since 1950. The U.S. Census Bureau ranks Las Cruces among America's fastest growing urban areas. It has also been selected by Money Magazine as the 10th best small city in the West.

In addition, Las Cruces and its unusual environs continue to be popular for shooting a variety of movies. One of the earliest films ever made near Las Cruces was the 1911 feature "The Dude." During the 1990s, "Mad Love," "Homage" and "Lolita" were filmed in and around Las Cruces. The music videos of Toby Keith, John Michael Montgomery and Boys II Men have also been produced in the area. Most recently scenes from the Michael Douglas movie "Traffic" were filmed in Las Cruces.

In 1998, Las Cruces celebrated its 150th birthday with a gala of events that extended into the year 2000. This festive community spirit as well as the city's sunny climate, spectacular views and tricultural heritage make Las Cruces an amiable and enviable place to live.

HAUNTED AIRPLANE HANGER
Hangerlake Road
Las Cruces, New Mexico

There have been a large number of stories making the rounds about this old hanger. It is now said to be off-limits and guarded almost all of the time. No one seems to know for sure what it is used for at this time.

Witnesses have said that they have seen what appear to be bodies hanging from the rafters of the old hanger. Others talk of secret gatherings and what sounds like chanting issuing from this old building. Still others have spoken of strange sounds and banging noises being heard t odd times of the day.

More than one person has mentioned voices coming from outside the hanger when there has been no one around to account for the sounds. Some residents of the area have also had odd happenings inside their homes; to include hauntings and what has been described as demonic activity, which they believe are as a result of whatever is going on inside that hanger.

BANKS OF THE RIO GRANDE
Las Cruces, New Mexico

Las Cruces has its own variation of the La Llorona spirit. According to the local story, in the days when the Rio Grande ran a mile wide and was deep and fast flowing, a woman became sic and tired of her kids and drowned them. Legend says that at her death she was sentenced to search for her lost children until judgment day.

Witnesses say that when she is near, a faint greenish glow can be seen along the river bank and her pitched screaming for her children is heard.

THE T.R.H. SMITH MANSION
909 North Alameda Boulevard
Las Cruces, New Mexico

There seems to be something about buildings in El Paso, Texas designed by Henry C. Trost that attracts mysterious happenings. So too does it seem to be the case in Las Cruces. Las Cruces was clearly a town with a future and as the town prospered, its more affluent residents built homes in the up-scale Alameda Depot District.

One of those who built homes here was First State Bank of Las Cruces president T.R.H. Smith. Banker Smith built his dream home there just two years after New Mexico entered the Union in 1912 as our 47th state. He retained well-known Southwestern architect Henry C. Trost, a Frank Lloyd Wright contemporary, to design it in prairie style.

Figure 16: The T.R.H. Smith Mansion.

However, almost as soon as the magnificent home was completed in December 1914, Smith and his bank declared bankruptcy. The resulting investigation and commotion involved the city, the county, the state including the governor, as well as banks in surrounding states that played a major role in the conspiracy.

Even the New Mexico College of Agriculture and Mechanic Arts, now New Mexico State University, was affected. The College had maintained a $73,000 deposit in Smith's bank, perhaps $1,168,000 in today's money, which was frozen. Another local bank quickly loaned them enough until the state could send a replacement amount.

After all of the risks he took to build the house, Smith apparently never got to live here. His fate is still being researched. It took three years of litigation before the receiver was able to transfer ownership to William W. Cox, well-known local rancher, county treasurer and also a bank president. It was this Cox who, at one time, controlled 150,000 acres of ranch land, now part of the White Sands Missile Range.

He also was the Cox who owned the mortgage on famed sheriff Pat Garrett's neighboring ranch in the Organ Mountains at the time Garrett was ambushed. Garrett's fame, of course, was gained because it was he who killed William Bonney, "Billie the Kid," in the 1880's following the Lincoln County War.

Cox's employee, Wayne Brazel was acquitted of Garrett's murder in 1908 with help from famous lawyer Albert Fall. Fall was New Mexico's first senator appointed by the state legislature in 1912, and was U.S. Secretary of the Interior who was blamed for the Teapot Dome naval oil reserves scandal which erupted in the 1920's.

Soon after it was completed and for many years, stories spread of buried treasure somewhere in the house, also of its being used as a high-class brothel! The home cost $15,000 to build in 1914. Cox owned it until 1922, when he sold it to his wife Margaret for $10,600. She then sold it to Edward and Elizabeth Snow for only $7,000 in 1929.

In 1954, Mrs. Snow sold it to the Browns, who maintained it until 1986 and did considerable retrofitting. A physician family and a college professor owned it for 5-year periods until 1995. The current owners are 7th in this group of prominent owners.

Stories of buried or embezzled treasure hidden in or around the house as well as stories of ghosts that haunt this 5,700 square feet home have long been the fare of the curious in the city. There are a large number of stories that maintain that there is a tunnel running from the basement of the house to one of the houses across the street. According to the various stories, this hidden tunnel was used both in smuggling and to allow visits to the brothel by those who had rather not be seen entering and leaving the house.

.There is no question that the mansion is a beautiful building. It boasts lovely spacious gardens and lawns, a sun porch and deck - while the oversized honeymoon suite features a king bed, fireplace, loveseat and mountain views.

THE GHOSTS

I have been told of footsteps being heard in the night as well as the sounds of doors slamming in parts of the house that were empty. Others talk of soft voices that call out their names in an urgent tone. However, those so summoned never find anyone that could have been the cause of the voice.

Then there are those stories of the hidden treasure. Did Banker Smith actually spend all of the money he embezzled on the house? Or is some of it still hidden in the secret tunnel?

TOYS R' US
2532 E. Lohman
Las Cruces, New Mexico

Can a chain of stores be haunted? There seem to be a large of the toy stores in the well known chain that have permanent residents. In the store located in Las Cruces, New Mexico Las Cruses many former employees report that there is the spirit of a little boy about five or six years old that haunts the store in the night. Those who work late restocking the shelves or cleaning have reported that they have heard his laughs and heard the sounds of his running footsteps as he races up one aisle and down another.

Though the floors are clean and everything is neatly organized when the last staff member leaves for the night, early arriving employees are always finding toys strewn about floor as if someone has been playing with them during the night.

During the day employees have no doubt that this mischievous youngster has been playing with the toys as employees have a hard time keeping the toys off the floor. In one case, an employee replaced a toy on the shelf that had been found on the floor and even though no one was seen to go into that particular aisle, a few minutes later, the same toy was found back on the floor.

DRIPPING SPRINGS
Las Cruces, New Mexico

Dripping Springs has long been an area enveloped in mystery. Col. Eugene Van Patten originally built the Dripping Springs Resort in the 1870's. A native of New York State, Van Patten came to Mesilla at the invitation of his uncle, John Butterfield, who operated the Butterfield Stage Line. Van Patten worked at the Picacho Stage Station and probably elsewhere after the stage line ceased operations in the Las Cruces area in 1861. During the Civil War he joined the Confederacy and saw action in the Battle of Glorietta Pass near Santa Fe.

Dripping Springs Resort was originally called "Van Patten's Mountain Camp." It had approximately 16 rooms, a large dining room and a concert hall. It was very popular around the turn of the century and many famous people, including Pat Garret and Pancho Villa, have stayed there. Van Patten was married to a local Piro Indian woman and a number of Indians lived and worked at the resort. The Indians hand-carried water from the spring to the rooms in "ollas" attached to long wooden poles and, from time to time, held dances for the amusement of the guests.

In the late 1800's a stage line brought guests to the hotel from Las Cruces, 17 miles away. The stage would deliver the guests to the front of the hotel and then return to the livery. The wagons and horses for the stage line, as well as the personal livestock of the guests were kept in this area. In the 1900's guests began to arrive by automobile as well as by horse and wagon.

The resort had its share of exciting times. When Albert J. Fountain, a prominent figure in the Lincoln County War, was murdered on the East Side of the Organ Mountains in 1896, his daughter was notified of the murder at the resort. Van Patten led a large posse to investigate but Fountain's body, and that of his 12-year-old son Henry, were never found.

In 1917 Van Patten went bankrupt and Dripping Springs was sold to Dr. Nathan Boyd who homesteaded on a parcel of land adjacent to the resort. Boyd was a physician in San Francisco who later married the daughter of a wealthy Australian engineer. Boyd joined his in-laws' business and became involved in large engineering projects all over the world. He and his wife came to Las Cruces to promote, design and build a dam on the Rio Grande whose floods often devastated the countryside. Local farmers whose lands would have been inundated by the lake behind the dam stopped the dam. Ironically, the U.S. Bureau of Reclamation, creating the state's largest man-made lake, Elephant Butte Reservoir, eventually built a dam farther north. By the time Boyd had acquired Van Patten's resort, his wife had contracted tuberculosis. Deciding to remain in Las Cruces, Boyd converted Dripping Springs into a sanitarium. New structures were built in different parts of the canyon to provide housing and care for the patients.

The Boyd family eventually sold the property to another physician, a Dr. Sexton of Las Cruces, who continued to operate it as a sanatorium. As late as 1946 the resort was still in relatively good shape and a group of local citizens attempted to raise $4,000 to purchase it for historic preservation. Unfortunately, their effort failed and unknown persons scavenged the resort for building materials.

Today, the ruins of Dripping Springs Resort lie scattered along the canyon, preserving the memory of Col. Van Patten, the doctors Boyd and Sexton, and the many famous and not so famous who visited there.

THE GHOSTS

The complex that was once known as Boyd's Sanatorium sits silently, brooding over the deserted canyons, still mostly hidden from view behind clusters of rocky outcroppings and pockets of thick, thorny desert fauna. These buildings, which were once all part of a tuberculosis sanatorium, were constructed around 1910 by Dr. Nathan Boyd, medical doctor and international businessman. Legend says that Dr. Boyd had a beloved wife who was suffering from the terrible disease, and that he built the place, up in the rugged yet beautiful mountains, for her.

There are other, darker, rumors about Boyd's Sanatorium, as well. Rumors of a more... unknown element. Some say that this canyon is filled with restless spirits, and that some of them happen to be the spirits of the patients who passed away up at the mountainside sanatorium.

The deserted building known as the Caretaker's house had a wooden porch with a breath-taking view of the valley below. It is not hard to imagine that there might be spirits here. The trail leading up to this place is officially closed every day well before dark, earlier in fact than all of the other trails in the area. And, there have been reports of campers in the nearby canyon campgrounds being terrified by strange visions and horrific nightmares featuring torturous treatments undergone by gaunt and ghostly "patients," even though some of the campers are said to have no prior knowledge of the nearby sanatorium's presence.

There have been various paranormal investigations at this location; one group even claims to have gotten photos of "shadowy figures" in the ruins. In fact, it was here at Boyd's Sanatorium where a number of new cameras failed to work. In each case, the camera had worked fine at the Van Patten ruins, and it began to work once again as soon as the would be photographer went a little ways down the trail away from the sanatorium... it just would not function while in the vicinity of the sanatorium.

A hand-hewn stone stairway heads up the mountainside to where the patients housing used to stand. All that remains of these buildings now are the foundations and low stone walls that outline the shapes of where they once existed. On this pathway can be found the remains of an old drinking fountain designed to aid those who took this way up the canyon. Water was piped in from the springs nearby to a holding tank above the terraces where the patient's housing stood; piping carried the water down to the residences and the drinking fountain below. The kitchen and dining hall was located in a separate structure, perched high atop stilt-like beams along the mountainside.

In the early 1900's, Dr. Boyd was involved in a court case that would eventually deplete his funds; the sanatorium was sold to a Dr. T.C. Sexton from Las Cruces in the 1920's. It was intermittently run as a sanatorium and resort for several more years. Nathan Boyd's son, Earl, bought the place back in the early 1930's and moved onto the land, living in the Caretaker's house. In 1940, while Earl Boyd was away serving in the military, the remote structures were subjected to heavily damaging vandalism and looting by unknown parties. The place has been vacant ever since, despite changing hands one more time before being acquired by the Bureau of Land Management in 1988.

In spite of Federal government ownership, there are still figures that are seen moving about in the shadows as evening falls. Locals still say do not be caught around the Sanitarium after dark.

LA CUEVA
Organ Mountains
Las Cruces, New Mexico

The man they called "El Ermitano" ("The Hermit") - whose real name was Agostini-Justiniani- was born of noble Italian parents around 1800. He may have spent years studying for the priesthood, but when the time came for him to become a full-fledged priest, he refused his vows and instead spent many years wandering thousands of miles on foot across South America, Europe, Cuba, and Mexico. He accumulated a great amount of knowledge about botany and the healing powers of flora and fauna, and became a very skilled healer.

At age 62 he found himself near Las Vegas after walking many miles with a wagon train; he made his way to a hill to the northwest called Cerro Tecolote, where he lived in solitude for awhile. To this day, that hill is still known as "Hermit's Peak." In 1867, he moved again, traveling on foot with another wagon train which led him to San Antonio Texas, Juarez Mexico, and eventually, New Mexico. He made friends with a family by the name of Barela who lived in Mesilla; he would visit them often, and his miraculous healing powers became known far and wide. One day, he announced his plans to trek across the desert to the remote cave in the Organ Mountains now known as La Cueva ("The Cave"), with the intention of making it his home.

Despite his friend's misgivings, the old man followed through with his plan, and this cave became home to the mysterious hermit for the last few years of his life. Believers would make the trip to his cave to be healed from various ailments; he would often gather herbs and flowers from the lush desert landscape right outside his haven for the potions he concocted for his cures. He seemed quite content in the isolated home he shared with the cacti and the lizards... however; he did issue this strange warning to his friends in Mesilla, "I shall make a fire in front of my cave every Friday evening while I shall be alive. If the fire fails to appear, it will be because I have been killed." Unfortunately, he never mentioned who he thought might kill him.

One Friday night in the spring of 1869, the light of the fire failed to appear at the mouth of the cave as it usually did. A posse went up the mountain to check on El Ermitano; they were shocked to discover him dead on the floor of La Cueva. His body was facedown on a large crucifix and he was wearing a penitential "girdle of spikes"; a gleaming knife protruded from his back. Nobody ever figured out who killed the mysterious old hermit, or even why anyone would want him dead. His murder remains one of New Mexico's most infamous unsolved mysteries to this very day.

Since the unsolved murder of the old hermit, there have been a number of local ghost stories that claimed there is still phantom firelight spotted out in front of La Cueva on the occasional moonless night. Those who have explored the cave where the old man lived his last years all have reported a feeling of being watched.

CHAPTER FOURTEEN

TAOS, NEW MEXICO

The area around what is now known as Taos is a mysterious land of towering mountains and broad mesas. It is thought to have been continuously inhabited for approximately 6,000 years. During prehistoric times, nomadic hunter-gatherers roamed the valley. The ancestors of present-day Pueblo Indians, the nomads, eventually adopted a sedentary lifestyle, becoming the first farmers of the region.

Taos Pueblo, thought to be the oldest continuously inhabited structure--- from 800-1,000 years--- evolved into a trading center by the 13th century. The "trade fairs" of that time drew members of the Apache, Navajo, Kiowa and Comanche tribes, and caravans from Chihuahua, Mexico.

Taos Valley changed dramatically with the arrival of the Spanish in the 16th century. When their search for gold yielded only the glint of straw in adobe structures, the New World conquerors began to colonize the valley. Attempts to dominate the Indians and convert them to Christianity, and the inevitable intermarriage, resulted in rebellion. In the Revolt of 1680, Pueblo Indians rose against their Spanish masters and drove them out of the Rio Grande Valley. The Spanish would not reconquer the region for 12 years. Despite the hostility between Spanish and Indian, they had to join forces against marauding tribes from the north and west in an uneasy interdependence.

Yet another newcomer emerged in the 18th century with the arrival of French and American traders. Taos, no more than a tiny mountain village, was transformed into a bustling trade center as wagon trains, frontier scouts and Mountain Men gathered.

Rapid-fire change continued. Following New Mexico's entry into the United States as an official territory in 1847 came another Indian revolt.

Territorial Governor Charles Bent and 20 others were killed in a bloody massacre.

The once geographically-isolated village became more accessible when the Atcheson, Topeka and the Santa Fe Railroad reached Santa Fe. The era of American's love affair with the West had begun. As tales of the region's beauty spread, tourists, writers and artists from the east discovered Northern New Mexico's uniqueness. Some settled permanently.

In 1898, two artists with a broken wagon wheel ushered in the period that would lead to Taos' reputation as a world-famous art colony. That tradition continues, as does the legacy of the primary three cultures of Taos: the Indian, the Spanish and the Anglo.

GOVERNOR BENT HOUSE & MUSEUM
117 Bent Street
Taos, New Mexico

Charles Bent was a highly respected, much loved figure of the Old West. He was a trader and owner of a number of wagon trains on the Santa Fe Trail. He owned trading posts in Santa Fe and Taos and had many dealings with early mountain men. He provided them with supplies and bought their furs and buffalo hides. He, his brother William, and Ceran St. Vrain built Bent's Fort in Colorado, famous throughout the West as a trading center for the Indians and early mountain men[20].

According to the writings of his daughter, Governor Bent was killed In January 19, 1847 about six in the morning. The family was in bed when the Mexicans and Indians came to the house breaking the doors and windows while some of them scaled the walls of the house to begin tearing off the roof. With little choice in the matter, the family got out of bed and Governor Bent decided to speak to them.

His wife was afraid for his life and urged him to jump on one of those horses that he had in the corral and go somewhere until the danger was over. Governor Bent replied that it would not do for a Governor to run away and leave his family in danger, if they wanted to kill him, they could kill him here with my family. Without another word, he stepped out onto the porch to ask the mob what they wanted.

The ringleader of the mod responded that they had come for his head as they did not want any gringos to be in charge over them. Governor Bent asked

---

[20] http://www.laplaza.org/art/museums_bent.php3

what he had done to wrong them as he had worked hard to help the people of Taos and the surrounding area. The ringleader replied that he had done nothing to hurt them, but that he had to die so that no gringos would be placed over them.

Before Governor Bent could say anything else, some members of the mob fired arrows and fired guns at the Governor standing on his own porch. Though he was wounded, Governor Bent managed to get back inside his home and lock the door.

Mrs. Carson and Mrs. Boggs, and a female Indian slave had dug a hole through the adobe wall to the next house; so between the four women they helped the wounded man get to where they had dig out the wall.

Though he was seriously wounded, the Governor insisted that his children go through the gaping hole in the wall first, then Mrs. Carson and then Mrs. Boggs. He wanted his wife to go next, but she told him, you go first, as she did not think they wanted to kill her but rather him.

He finally gave in and went first, but when he was going through the narrow hole, the arrows in his head scraped against the wall and hurt him terribly. In frustration, he pulled the arrow out and threw them on the floor. As his wife was going through, an Indian burst into the room and forced his way through the hole. The Indian came through almost at the same time as Mrs. Brent and was going to shot her, but the Indian Slave girl interfered, jumping in front of the Governor's wife. She was killed instead. Enraged at accidentally killing the Indian girl, their attacker then struck Mrs. Brent on the back with the butt of his gun.

The Governor and his family moved into a little room, where he sat and began to write. Suddenly the mob burst into the room here they commenced to attack the governor once again. This time, they killed and then stripped him of his clothing. When the Governor was dead, the mob wanted to kill the family, but cooler heads prevailed and the rest of the family was spared.

The American response was somewhat slow in coming to Taos as there had been violence in many places in New Mexico. American forces arrived in Taos on February 3, 1847 which was about fifteen days after Governor Bent was murdered. On February 4, 1847, they began a roundup of the mob and fighting broke out. According to records, soldiers killed about 250 there In the Pueblo, and hung 6 Mexicans in the middle of the Plaza that were said to be the ringleaders of the Governor's murder. There were an additional sixteen Indians hung elsewhere in town.

At the same time that the Governor was murdered, rioters also killed they killed Sheriff Luis Estaven Lee, Cornelio Vigil, Mrs. Brent's Uncle, Provost Judge Lawyer Lea, Pablo Jaramillo, Mrs. Brent's brother and Narcizo Beaublen. In Arroyo Hondo they killed Turley the owner of the Distillery and seven men more that were working there.

THE GHOSTS

It was violent emotions that led to the uprising that resulted in the murder of Governor Brent and it is said that violent emotions can lead to hauntings. So it should not be a surprise that among the spirits that are said to haunt the Brent House are those of the men who killed the Governor They were caught and hung not too far from the scene of their crime and as a result, their ghosts still haunt his house. Their dim outlines and angry voices have been reported late at night by staff members.

KIT CARSON HOUSE MUSEUM
113 Kit Carson Road
Taos, New Mexico

The Kit Carson Home and Museum is a complex of buildings which includes a portion of the original four room home of Kit Carson and his wife Josefa, an 1855, three-room structure known as the Romero House, and two, 1952 structures that house the museum's retail shop and additional exhibition space. Carson arrived in Taos in 1826, at the age of fifteen; Taos was to be his base of operation and home until just before he died in 1868. Carson became a trapper and mountain man and traveled extensively through out the West.

Built in 1825 with 30-inch adobe walls and traditional territorial architecture, the home's 12 rooms are today furnished as they may have been during Carson's days. The Kit Carson Home and Museum was originally opened to the public in 1952. Since that time nearly a million people have been through the Museum this has taken a toll on structures that were never intended to be more than single family homes!

Kit Carson came to Taos in 1825. He died in this house in 1868 at the age of fifty nine.

THE GHOSTS

A number of museum employees and patrons have detected the ghost of Kit Carson in his former home. The friendly ghost of Kit Carson has been detected in the part of the museum that was his former home. The original three room house in which Carson lived was eventually expanded to accommodate his children. Though a rough and tumble frontiersman, those staff and visitors who have seen Carson's ghost say that Carson's spirit is a very domesticated ghost and is very kind to women and children.

LAS PALOMAS DE TAOS ADOBE
240 Morado Lane
Taos, New Mexico

This historic adobe house located in the northern part of Taos was the private residence of New York socialite and heiress Mabel Dodge and her husband Tony Luhan. Mabel Dodge came to the Hispanic, Pueblo and artist community of Taos in 1916. She came to the Southwest seeking "change". Here she met the man she was married to for over 40 years, Tony Luhan, a full blooded Taos Pueblo Indian.

Mabel was "the most common denominator that society, literature, art and radical revolutionaries ever found in New York and Europe." This claim was made by a Chicago newspaper reporter in the 1920's of Mabel Dodge Luhan, a woman who attracted leading intellectual and literary figures to her circle for over four decades. Mabel was mistress of a grand salon, an American Madame de Stael. She was also a leading symbol of the New Woman, self determined and in control of her destiny. Luhan found her final and best-loved home in Taos. Here she married a Taos Pueblo man, Tony Luhan, and set out to establish Taos as the birthplace of a newfound Eden. She brought writers like D.H. Lawrence and Willa Cather, painters like Georgia O'Keeffe and John Marin, and activists like John Collier to help her celebrate and preserve it[21].

Mabel and her husband, Tony started construction of the "Big House" in the 1920's, enlarging the original 160 year-old home to its present size. The 22-room house is sequestered behind an adobe wall whose gates are ancient altar pieces. Huge cottonwood, beech and elm trees shade the residence and the flagstone placita. In traditional Spanish Colonial style, a long portal crosses the house, opening to the living room, bedrooms and the log cabin studio. All main rooms have ceilings of viga and lattias construction, arched Pueblo-styled doorways, hand-carved doors, Pueblo fireplaces and dark hardwood floors. Credit for gathering many of the era's creative luminaries in Taos goes, however, to Mabel Dodge Luhan, a New York heiress, socialite, and counterculture activist. Tony Luhan, her fourth husband - to whom she remained married for more than 40 years - was an illiterate, full-blooded Taos Pueblo Indian.

Celebrated artists, writers, and thinkers of the day flocked to Mabel and Tony Luhan's home, and some of them later made their own homes in northern New Mexico, including D.H. Lawrence, Andrew Dasburg, Georgia O'Keeffe, and Leon Gaspard. Ansel Adams, Mary Austin, Robinson Jeffers, Laura Gilpin, Jean Toomer and many others were housed, fed, and nurtured in the Luhans' "Big House."

After the death of the Luhans, there have been a number of subsequent owners, which include Dennis Hopper (Easy Rider, Blue Velvet) and Las

---

[21] http://www.mabeldodgeluhan.com/history.html

Palomas (a center for global studies which occupied the home until August of 1996). It is now the Mabel Dodge Luhan Lodging and Conference Center.

THE GHOSTS

Though Mabel was a world traveler and extremely well read and Tony Luhan was said to be illiterate, the two had a marriage in which both were apparently extremely happy. They also loved their home since both are known to haunt it.

The ghosts of Mabel Dodge Luhan and her husband Tony have been seen moving through a wall in the hall outside the bathroom and their laughing apparitions have also been observed floating in another room.

Former residents have blamed Mabel's presence for moving statues and furniture in the house. The privileged matriarch lived in the house for forty-four years, until her death in 1963.

The Rainbow Room in the old adobe home was used by Indians for various rituals, and the ghost of an Indian girl has been seen there. She is said to have died of natural causes in this very room many years ago.

THE GARDEN RESTAURANT & BAKERY
127 Historic Taos Plaza
Taos, New Mexico

The very popular Garden Restaurant and Bakery began in the historic Taos building at 127 Historic Taos Plaza around 1987. Prior to becoming a fashionable restaurant and bakery, this old building had been occupied by an indoor flea market and even earlier it had been a large grocery store.

It was shortly after the purchase of the building and prior to the opening of the restaurant that the owner discovered an ancient Native American skeleton hidden away in a dark corner of the basement. A few years after this gruesome discovery, the restaurant changed hands and the new owners had a priest come bless the bones. An archeologist also examined them, finding that the bones were those of a Native American female. When notified of this fact about the bones, the owners decided to give the skeleton the name of Snowflake. They also had the bones buried properly. After the burial, most people put the skeleton out of their mind and got down to the serious matter of running the business. However, the spirit of the skeleton had not forgotten them.

THE GHOSTS

The management of the restaurant has heard various stories of strange noises and other unusual events happening to the staff, however, the bakers who spend most of their time in the basement where the skeleton was found have experienced these events on a first hand basis.

There is a story that one of the bakers would always make Snowflake, as the ghost is called, her own loaf of bread and hide it on a high shelf so that no one would take it. After a day or so, when the baker would check, the loaf would always be gone. There has never been any doubt in the baker's mind that the ghost takes the offered loaf of bread.

The bakers always come to work in the very early hours of the morning so that the baked goods are ready for the business day. As they work, many times they will hear footsteps in the restaurant above them. However, when they check, the building is always found to be empty.

Due to the heat given of by the large ovens, the temperature in the basement is always very hot. However, sometimes, the bakers will feel as if someone else is there with them and blasts of cold air will fill the basement, cooling them down. They have also found that if they speak of the ghost or call her name, they will be immediately hit with a blast of bone chilling cold air.

One morning, the bakers were working hard when they suddenly heard footsteps above them in the restaurant and the sound of something loud and metal falling on the floor. Then they heard something being drug across the restaurant floor. Thinking that a burglar had broken into the business, the bakers came up the stairs and searched the building. They found no one, nor did they find anything that had fallen or that was out of place.

Others have talked of pots and pans being thrown across the room or sliding across the floor. Perhaps Snowflake just wants some company and feels that she had to get everyone's attention. After all, she spent a long time in the dark corner of that basement and no one paid her any attention at all.

CHAPTER FIFTEEN

MONTEZUMA, NEW MEXICO

Montezuma, New Mexico is basically a ghost town. The primary inhabitants are those that attend the Montezuma Seminary. The Seminary is now the Armand Hammers United World College of the Southwest which occupies the old Montezuma Hotel Site. The town is basically a farming community on NM 65, 6 mi NW of Las Vegas. This is the site of Montezuma Seminary, which occupies the building formerly known as the Montezuma Hotel.

The name Montezuma was given to the community by employees of the Atchison, Topeka & Santa Fe Railroad. The community was named for Montezuma's castle which in turn was named for Montezuma (Moctezuma) the pre-Spanish Aztec ruler of Mexico, who was conquered by Cortez.

MONTEZUMA'S CASTLE
Montezuma, New Mexico.

Montezuma's Castle, originally known as the Montezuma Hotel, was designed by noted Chicago architects John Root and Daniel Burnham for the Atchison, Topeka & Santa Fe Railroad, which had built a spur from nearby Las Vegas, NM to Montezuma in 1882. For a decade, the resort was a major attraction and visitors included Rutherford B. Hayes, Ulysses S. Grant, William Tecumseh Sherman and Theodore Roosevelt before the Montezuma closed as a hotel in 1903.

The Castle was later owned by the Baptist Church and served as the site of its Montezuma College and then by the Catholic Church which ran a seminary for Mexican priests from 1937-1972. Once the Catholic Church closed the seminary, the Castle was left empty and became easy prey for a decade of vandalism. In 1981, the Armand Hammer Foundation bought the property in order to found the United States campus of the United World Colleges.

The Castle remained an empty but picturesque backdrop to the UWC-USA campus until 1997 when it garnered national attention. First, the National Trust for Historic Preservation recognized the building as one of America's most endangered historic places. In 1998, the White House Millennium Council named it one of "America's Treasures", the first property west of the Mississippi to receive that honor.

In 1998, the UWC-USA launched its first capital campaign, Save the Castle-Serve the World, raising funds for scholarship endowments, program development, campus improvements and the restoration of the Montezuma Castle.

In 2000-2001, the building underwent a $10.5 million renovation, transforming it into an international center with student and faculty housing, dining facilities, offices, a campus store and student social center. The Castle also holds the Bartos Institute for the Constructive Engagement of Conflict.

While many of the building's magnificent interior and exterior details were restored, modern treasures were added, including two eight-foot glass sculptures designed specifically for the Castle's enormous dining room by artist Dale Chihuly.

THE GHOSTS

A large number of people have reported seeing the figure of a woman in one of the towers at night. She seems to be watching for something or someone. Others have reported hearing strange sounds coming from some of the empty rooms of this massive structure. There have also been voices heard when there was no one around the account for them.

CHAPTER SIXTEEN

CARLSBAD, NEW MEXICO

In 1884, Charles B. and John Eddy formed a livestock company with Amos Bissell to operate in southeastern New Mexico. One of their first ventures was the Halagueno Ranch, which covered the area from Seven Rivers to La Huerta, NM.

In 1887, Charles B. Eddy built the Halagueno diversion ditch on the Pecos River 3 miles above the later site of Avalon Dam and incorporated the venture as the Pecos Valley Land and Ditch Company. He was seeking funds from a Swiss bank to attract European settlers to the clean air and sunny climate.

In 1888, former sheriff Pat Garrett (who gunned down Billy the Kid) and promoter Charles Greene joined with Eddy to create a system of canals and flumes for diversion of water to their properties. Greene secured potential investors from the east including Robert W. Tansill, manufacturer of the Punch five cent cigar. Eddy and his partners laid out plans for a new town on the south bank of the Pecos River, which was incorporated as the town of Eddy on September 15, 1888.

In 1889, the first school in Eddy opened on South Main with 35 pupils. In 1890, the Witt brothers completed construction of a wooden flume near Eddy for irrigation, and the county seat moved from Seven Rivers to Eddy. In 1890, the bridge over the Pecos River at Greene Street was completed, and Avalon Dam with its many canals was completed. On January 10, 1891, the first railroad train arrived in Eddy on the newly completed line from Pecos, Texas.

In 1899, by a vote of 83-43, the city residents voted to rename their community Carlsbad, after the famous European health resort, Karlsbad, Bohemia (now the Czech Republic). The mineral content and related healing properties of the water in the two cities, continents apart, was virtually identical.

Carlsbad Spring still flows today in the northern corner of the city, near the Pecos Flume, one of the most impressive structures in Carlsbad. The concrete aqueduct is Carlsbad's own "Believe It Or Not" entry -- the river that crosses itself. Originally built of wood, the flume was rebuilt with concrete following the 1902 flood, and at the time of construction, was the largest concrete structure in the world. It is still in use, carrying Pecos River water from Lake Avalon across the river.

GERMAN TOWN
Carlsbad, New Mexico

Carlsbad is located on the Pecos River and much of the life of this community depends upon the water from this river. 1890, the bridge over the Pecos River at Greene Street was completed, and the Avalon Dam with its many canals were completed.

There is an old Dam Works still in existence that is complete with an overseer's house and a garage and storage building. There are many stories told about people hearing very strange noises and seeing lights coming from these old buildings late at night. Some very strange photos have been taken of this complex.

CHAPTER SEVENTEEN

BLOOMFIELD, NEW MEXICO

CHACO CANYON NATIONAL HISTORIC PARK
State Route 4
Box 6500
Bloomfield, New Mexico

A thousand years ago the valley that contains the Chaco Canyon ruins was the political and economic center of the Anasazi, a people's whose legacy is forever shrouded in mystery by their disappearance some 700 years ago. Much of what is known about the Anasazi has been learned from the approximately 1,200 ruins found in the park. The complex system of homes and roads, abundance of turquoise jewelry, and cryptic petrogplyphs reveal precious few secrets of this puzzling culture.

Exactly 1,000 years ago Chaco Canyon flourished under the able hands of Anasazi artisans, builders, and farmers. Though the high desert environment of Chaco seems an improbable place for any culture to take root, the Anasazis seemed able to adapt to the elements. It is estimated that as many as 5,000 people lived in Chaco Canyon at one point. The people farmed the lowlands, built multistory stone and mud buildings, and traded as far south as Mexico.

The ruins are an inextricable part of this beautiful landscape. The mind's eye fills in holes and rebuilds the fallen walls of the pre-Columbian structures. Take the time to see them and respect them as the historical and environmental treasures they are.

THE GHOSTS

There are many who like to hike the many trails that run through the canyon. The ruin closest to the visitor center is Una Vida, which can be reached by trail from the parking lot. Only partially excavated, it looks much as it did when Lt. James H. Simpson of the U.S. Army described it in 1849. Construction was underway by AD 930 and continued until late in the next century. There are 5 kivas and about 150 rooms in the structure.

The core of this Anasazi complex lies farther down the canyon. The largest and best known of the great houses is Pueblo Bonito, which was occupied from the early 900s to about 1200. Built in stages, this pueblo in its final form contained some 600 rooms and 40 kivas and rose four stories high. The pueblo was first excavated at the turn of the century and again intensively in the 1920s. It is considered the "type" site for the Classic Bonito Phase (AD 1020 to 1120) of Chacoan culture.

Chetro Ketl was begun about 1020. Completed in most respects by 1054, it was remodeled and enlarged in the early 1100s. It holds an estimated 500 rooms and 16 kivas. The enclosed plaza is a typical feature of great houses from this period.

Pueblo del Arroyo was built in stages over a relatively short time. The central part was started about 1075; north and south wings were added between 1095 and 1105; the plaza and the tri-welled structure were constructed about 1110. The building had about 280 rooms and more than 20 kivas.

Kin Kletso seems to have been built in two stages. The first one dates from about 1125, the second from 1130 or later. This pueblo had about 100 rooms and 5 enclosed kivas and may have risen three stories on the north side.

Casa Rinconada on the south side of the canyon is the largest "great kiva" in the park. The trail leading to this ruin passes by several villages contemporary with it and continues up the mesa to the great house Tsin Kietsin, with its panoramic view.

The hiking trails also lead to a number of other ruins. Pueblo Alto, on top of the mesa, is important as the junction of several prehistoric roads. Casa Chiquita and Penasco Blanco can be reached by hiking from the central canyon. Wijiji, built in a single stage in the early 1100s, is notable for its symmetrical layout and rooms of uniform size.

There are many visitors who have hikes these trail who feel eyes watching them form the ruins the entire time they are in the canyon. Others talk of seeing the fleeting shape of figures that disappear whenever the hiker tries to get a better look at them. While still others have felt that someone was walking beside them as they toured the many ruins scattered throughout the area.

Finally, there have been a number of reports of a strange naked ghost haunting this national park. Visitors and employees have seen the apparition of a very tall naked man emerging from the Sipapu, sacred holes in the ground inside ceremonial kivas. The holes are said to be connecting points to the other side.

At other times, the phantom is seen to be bathed in blue light and dripping with moisture. Once, a park ranger tried to arrest the naked man, only to see him disappear into thin air.

Hopi Indians believe the naked ghost is a genius loci; a spirit of place that feeds off the energies of Mother Earth. Other Spirits are sensed here also (the ancestors of the Anasazi people?). Psychics consider Chaco Canyon to be one of the centers of Harmonic Convergence on the earth

CHAPTER EIGHTEEN

CLOVIS, NEW MEXICO

The known history of the area now known as Clovis begins approximately 12,000 years ago with the Llano culture of the Paleo-Indians who hunted the huge mammoth and other animals. Archeological findings in the Blackwater Draw near the Curry-Roosevelt county line have traced man from the Llano culture (more commonly called "Clovis Man") through the Archaic group of the period 2500 to 500 B.C. From here, there is a gap until about 1200 A.D. when an early Pueblo group appeared. From the 1200's through the advent of white men, Plains Indians and buffalo roamed over what is now known as Curry County.

The cowmen were the first permanent white settlers in the area. They chose the semi-shallow draws which were watered by a few springs to dig dug-outs, later erecting rock homes and barns, letting their longhorn cattle drift over the open range.

In 1906, the Santa Fe Railroad chose this area to locate their "Eastern terminal" of the Belen cutoff. The site was surveyed, and the new town was quickly established. The naming of the town was no small task. Although many felt it should have a Spanish name, there was no Spanish background to the area. The story goes that a railroad official's daughter, who had been studying French history, suggested the town be named after an ancient Christian King of the Frankish Empire. Finally, the Santa Fe Railway designated the name "Clovis" after this ancient King (Clovis I), who founded the empire, and was King of the Salian Frankish Empire, from 461 to 511 A.D.

In 1929 an airfield was developed west of Clovis for T.A.T. train-plane travel across the United States. The airfield became Clovis Army Air Field in 1942, where B-17, B-14 and B-29 bomber crews trained. The field was deactivated after World War II, but reactivated in 1951, and in 1957, was renamed Cannon Air Force Base, which has since become one of the major jet fighter training sites for U.S. Air Force. With the establishment of Cannon Air Force Base, Clovis stepped into a diversified economy that spurred growth of our modern colleges, healthcare facilities, and businesses.

Deep well irrigation beginning in the early 1950's turned the southeast third of the county into one of the most productive areas in New Mexico. Curry County grows more wheat and sorghum than any other county in the state. Land use of the other two-thirds of the county can roughly be equally divided between dry- land farming and grassland. The grassland and wheat pasturing supports the oldest industry in the county, that of raising livestock. Recently large Holstein dairies have come into the agricultural scene, and what is being billed as the largest cheese plant in the country is currently under construction.

Culture may not be the first thing that comes to mind when talking about Clovis, but we do have our share. "Clovis Music," with its small, world-famous recording studio, made history in 1957 when Norman Petty recorded and made the first hits for Buddy Holly, Roy Orbison, Waylon Jennings and the Fireballs. Today, music history continues to be made by stars such as LeAnn Rimes.

Clovis is situated at 4,260 ft. altitude and has a mild climate and low humidity that makes for year-round comfort. We average 335 days of sunshine and 18 inches of rainfall annually, making our climate hard to beat with no floods, no forest fires, no landslides, no quakes, no smog, and no hurricanes or volcanoes.

NORMAN PETTY RECORDING STUDIOS
1313 West 7th Street
Clovis, New Mexico

Of course, everyone has heard that New Mexico is the place where the

Figure 17: Sign for the Norman Petty Recording Studios.

UFOs came to visit in 1947. But strange happenings have ranged well beyond Roswell, New Mexico.

Ten years later, in 1957, Buddy Holly recorded his hit song, Peggy Sue, at the Norman Petty Studios in Clovis, New Mexico, first located in an abandoned Texaco station on 7th Street and later re-situated in the old Mesa Theater.

A musician who made sounds recordings there has reported that on several occasions tapes would come up blank after a recording session, there would be absolutely nothing on them. The musicians would have to re-record the whole sequence.

Billy Stull, who became the owner after Norman Petty had passed away, swore "that Norm's spirit watches over the studio, and helps out on occasion." In other words, the ghost of Petty hangs around to make sure the musicians get it right, erasing bad tracks. There have been a number of unusual stories to come out of this well known studio.

This first story came from an internet site that is dedicated to ghosts. It is called the Ghost of the 7th Street Studio. I don't even know the name of the author, but I called some people in Clovis who assured me that the story was true.

The Ghost of the 7th Street Studio[22]

It's been almost ten years since I last set foot in Norman Petty Studios. It's been almost nine since I last performed for money. Well, unless you count the donkey show, then it's ... er ... was that out loud?

What I'm trying to say is, it's been a long time. I think I remember the history of Norman Petty's original 7th Street Studio, but memory may falter. Sue me.

The studio itself was originally a gas station. A Texaco, I think. The gas station moved to a busier street and the property came up for sale. Norman bought it and proceeded to turn it into a studio. The front of the building became the studio proper: What used to be the sales area was converted into the foyer and the engineering booth, and what had once been part of the garage and the office was opened up and became the performance area. Unlike the Mesa Theater studio where we recorded -- with the separate booths for each instrument as well as a vocal booth -- the 7th Street Studio was wide open. Everyone played together.

On occasion, Norman actually had to move the Crickets' drummer out into the foyer. Apparently, he was so skin-happy that his drumming was bleeding onto all the other tracks. He was, therefore, excommunicated.

One of the major renovations Norman did to the studio, however, and what seemed to make recording there a most pleasurable experience, was the addition of a kitchen and sleeping quarters off the back of the studio. To get there, you had to squeeze through a long narrow hallway. (I am skinny and my shoulders only had a few inches breathing room when I walked through.) The hallway spilled out into the kitchen, which in turn led to the beds. (When I went on the tour, they still had the original two sets of trundle beds: Just enough space for the four musicians.)

Well, time went on. The world lost Buddy in February 1959 to a famous plane crash. Norman went on to do work with The Fireballs. He bought the old Mesa Theater in Clovis and turned it into his dream studio. The old 7th Street Studio became a museum.

Shortly following Norman's death in 1984, a journalist from England called Billy Stull (our producer and then head of the studio). Apparently, Buddy

---

[22] http://www.globalprovince.com/letters/10-6-04.htm

Holly was experiencing a huge rebirth in England. Would it, then, be possible to come take a tour of the old studio for an article?

Billy didn't see why not. When the journalist arrived in Clovis, Billy greeted him and proceeded to give him a VIP tour of the old studio. Afterwards, the journalist asked if it would be okay to sleep there that night.

Billy was concerned about this. He'd never been asked to grant such privilege before. After discussing it with Vi Petty, Norman's widow, it was decided that he could stay, but that Billy would have to lock him in the building -- you know, security. The journalist was very pleased.

The next morning, Billy headed straight for the old studio. He made a point to inspect everything on his way through the studio back to the bedroom, where the journalist was surely still sleeping. Nothing seemed out of place and no equipment appeared to be missing.

He squeezed through the narrow hallway and into the kitchen. The kitchen light was still on and as he moved closer to the bedroom he noticed that the lights were still on back there, too. When he stepped into the room, he found the journalist sitting up in one of the beds, back firmly against the wall, eyes wide open, skin white as a sheet, forehead dripping sweat.

Initially, Billy feared the man was having some sort of seizure. He rushed quickly to his side and took his face in his hands. "Are you okay??"

The journalist grabbed tightly onto Billy. "Just let me outta here!" he demanded.

Billy quickly led him out to the parking lot. After a chance to calm down, the journalist explained:

"About half an hour after you left, I heard the front door of the studio open and close. I was working on the outline for this article there on the bed. I kept waiting for you to appear, but when you did not, I went to check. The door was still locked.

"I didn't think much of it at first, so I went back to writing. Half an hour later, it opened and closed again. I set my notebook down and went to check right away. Still nothing, still locked. That time, I left the lights on in the studio. I was suddenly paranoid.

"I went to my bag and found your business card. It has your home number on it and I wanted to call you. The phones in this building don't work."

Billy shook his head. "We've never felt a need to reconnect them."

The journalist continued: "I wasn't able to get too much work done after the second incident. The third time it happened, though, I jumped and ran in. Nothing. I came back here and decided I would put on some music -- I brought my own stereo, just in case. I turned it up so that I wouldn't be able to hear the door if it opened again.

"But then the first song on the tape ended. In the silence following, I could hear other music. At first I thought it was coming from outside, and I jumped up to try and flag down whoever it might be to let me out.

"That's when I realized it was coming from inside the studio. At first, I was relieved thinking that you were here. But once I started to make my way back there, I noticed there were no lights on, even though I had left them on earlier.

"About halfway down that awful hallway, I could clearly hear the song 'Heartbeat'. But the studio was dark and I couldn't see anyone or anything. I called out, hoping to get your attention, still thinking it might be you.

"That's when the music stopped. And I could hear movement in the studio, footsteps. I flipped on the light again. There was no one else in the room.

"Then the music started again, louder. I ran to the window of the booth to see who was in there. The booth was empty. I turned and began to head out of the room. Just as I was about to step into the hallway, the lights went out and the music stopped.

"I kept moving. About halfway down the hallway, I could hear someone ... something walking in the hallway behind me. I looked back. There was no one there. I ran back to the bedroom. Only a moment later, I heard the door open and close again."

The British journalist wasn't the only one to encounter strange happenings at the old 7th Street Studio. Both Billy and Vi (among others) had heard things off and on over the years, but never anything quite as sensational as what the journalist recounted.

With a Little Help from My Friends[23]

Way back when, back before I met Ari, I was a rock star. Or at least I was pretending to be a rock star. I lived and breathed music. I played guitar for a band called The Rudiments in Albuquerque. We started as a high school garage band and eventually worked our way into three separate demo sessions at Norman Petty Studios in Clovis.

During our third session, we had been working on one song for well over four hours. Sheepishly, I admit that it had been me who was holding things up. It was a solo and for some reason there was a half-step I just kept flying right over, landing on a sharp instead of a flat note. I seem to remember we recorded that stupid line at least 20 times. Everyone else had already laid down their tracks: Jeff (our bassist) was videotaping footage for the rockumentary we were never destined to make; Stacy (our keyboardist and singer) was at ease beside Billy, our producer and engineer; Shannon (our drummer) was twirling drumsticks in the lounge. And I was still in the freakin' booth. At about midnight, we tried one more time. I still missed the half-step, but I recovered quickly. It was barely noticeable.

We rejoiced. Rather perturbed, I dropped my guitar and left the booth to hear the playback. Stacy gave me a sympathetic pat on the shoulder as I sat down

---

[23] Ibid

in the engineering room. The tape screeched softly out of the speakers as Billy rewound it.

Click! The end of the last chorus before the solo fired up. Billy cranked the volume and leaned back in his chair. We all waited, nervous. The chorus ended and slid right into the first measure of the solo.

Nothing.

Well, there was the underlying music that everyone else had recorded earlier, but no solo. Billy leaned up to the board and began to fiddle with knobs.

Nothing.

He shrugged. "Sorry," he said. "Let's try it again."

"Ugh," I said. Actually, that's not what I said (I'm not going to repeat what I really said).

Back in the booth, I had to retune my guitar. When I left earlier I had carelessly let it drop. I pulled the headphones over my ears and said belligerently into the mic beside the amp, "Crank it."

The tape rolled, the end of the chorus blared in my headphones and I closed my eyes. The next thing I knew, I was flying through the solo. It was like I was on a cloud. I was so tired and I remember feeling a bit discombobulated. Before long, the music choked off in the headphones. I set the guitar down and stood, letting the headphones rest around my neck. I looked out the window of the booth and saw all my bandmates cheering. Billy was sitting at the mixing board, a huge smile on his face.

I left the room just in time to hear the playback. It was perfect, no skipped step, no lagging time -- all perfectly fluid.

A little while later as we were heading over to the old 7th Street studio (where Buddy Holly recorded), Billy told us something very interesting. A few years back, he had been working with the Everly Brothers. They had been in a situation much like ours: As hard as they tried, they just couldn't quite get that last part to work. Finally, when they had reached the point where they were ready to settle, they played it back. As was the case with us, the track was gone. They were forced to re-record. And they did. And it was perfect.

Billy went on to tell us that this very same thing had happened not only a couple of times before, but many. In fact, he had been accused on more than one occasion of forgetting to hit the record button.

Jeff promptly pulled out his video camera. He had been filming the tape deck during my second-to-the-last take. The VU meters were highly active and the red record button for track 6 (mine) was lit. It was not a human error.

Billy's interpretation of the phenomenon is this: Norman Petty had poured his whole life into music, and even more into the studios he built. The studio where we recorded (the Mesa Theater studio) was Norman's last. It was his prize, his baby. Billy believes that Norman's spirit watches over the studio, and helps out on occasion. Considering that I've never been able to recreate that perfect half-step since that night, I tend to agree with Billy.

Ghosts have not been seen first hand here, but have been photographed. Phantoms caught on film include: a group young men who were photographed in the living quarters of the old studios (now a museum) and strange orange lights were also see in the same location. Sensitive visitors have wanted to cry for no reason.

CHAPTER NINETEEN

FARMINGTON, NEW MEXICO

The history of the Farmington area dates back over 2,000 years when Anasazi lived in "pit houses" throughout the region. They later built pueblo structures from the native sandstone rock as can be seen at Aztec and Salmon ruins, as well as many other archeological sites in the surrounding countryside.

After the Anasazi's mysterious disappearance about 1500, the area was inhabited by the Navajo, Jicarrilla Apache and the Utes into the present time. Native Americans called the area "Totah," which translates as "where three river meet," the La Plata, Animas and San Juan.

The Spanish passed through the region in the late 1700s and eventually settled in the eastern part of San Juan County in the early 1800s. It wasn't until the mid 1870s that pioneers from Animas City, Colorado began permanent settlement.

Originally called "Junction City" because of its location near the convergence of the 3 rivers, the town began to blossom into a flourishing farm and ranch economy and was incorporated in 1901. The name was later changed to Farming Town and finally, the "w" was dropped, shortening the name to Farmington.

Farmington's other historical claim to fame is that for 3 consecutive days in March of 1950, half the town's citizens reported seeing hundreds of "flying saucers" zooming through the skies between 11 am and noon.

LIONS WILDERNESS PARK
Farmington, New Mexico

Lions Wilderness Park is located outside of Farmington, New Mexico in San Juan County. There have been a number of stories about some strange sightings of a person who has been taking things from visitors to the park. This entity also has been known to make some strange and eerie noises in an attempt to scare visitors away from the park.

People who have camped in the park overnight report that they sometimes can hear the sounds of footsteps approaching them only to hear the footsteps stop very close to their camp site. Then they feel a hand touch them. However, when they turn on their lights, they report that there is no one there and no footprints to show that anyone had been there other than themselves.

Others say that very late at night they have heard screaming followed by laughs so scary that it makes their hair stand on end.

CHAPTER TWENTY

GALLUP, NEW MEXICO

Gallup's population can be traced back to 2500 BC with the settlement of the Anasazi in Canyon de Chelly. As the Anasazi population rose, so did trading in the area. By the time the Spanish Conquistadors arrived in 1540, a highly sophisticated Native American culture was thriving.

The actual city of Gallup traces its origins to the railroads and trading post entrepreneurs of the late 19th century. In 1880, while the Atchison, Topeka and Santa Fe Railroad was pushing its way slowly westward, a paymaster named David Gallup established a small company headquarters along the projected right-of-way. Rail workers soon began "going to Gallup" to collect their pay, and when the tracks were finally laid through the area in 1881, the new settlement was formally named after the paymaster.

For its first half century, the economy of the emerging town was largely supported by plentiful coal mining in the region. In fact, Gallup was for a time called "Carbon City." The town's first inhabitants were those European, Asian, Mexican and westward-seeking American workers who sought employment in the mines, as well as building the rails.

Today, Gallup serves as a major Native American trading center. The 17.5 million acre Navajo nation is home to 210,000 people and covers parts of Arizona, southern Utah and New Mexico north and west of Gallup. The Navajo capital, Window Rock, is 28 miles northwest of the city, just inside the Arizona border. There is a Navajo Museum at Window Rock worth visiting.

OLD HOUSE ON AZTEC
Gallup, New Mexico

There is an old house on Aztec where it is said that a littlie boy named Billy still romps and plays even though he died long ago. Billy met his unfortunate death while quietly playing in his room. Now it seems this little boy who died so young is to live in the closet of the front bedroom. Billy is said to be a friendly ghost who many have said enjoys playing with the children that have lived in that room.

EL RANCHO HOTEL
Gallup, NM

Formally opened December 17, 1937, The EL Rancho Hotel was built by the brother of the movie magnet, D.W. Griffith. Drawn by the many films made in the area, Ronald Reagan, Spencer Tracy, Katherine Hepburn and Kirk Douglas were among the many stars listed in the guest register. Autographed photos of the stars, Navajo Rugs & Mounted trophy animal heads adorn the magnificent two story open lobby with its circular staircase.

The El Rancho Hotel was built by Joe Massaglia in 1937 for R.E. "Griff" Griffith. Originally, Griffith came to Gallup to direct a film. He later returned to build the El Rancho Hotel. He also managed the local Chief Theater. From the 1930's to 1950's, the hotel became a temporary home for many Hollywood stars. It also became a stopping point for tourists driving on old Route 66. The hotel is now protected by the National Historic Preservation Society. This historic hotel is continually cared for by Mr. Ortega who has made it his personal hobby since its purchase.

The hotel is decorated and furnished in the Old West rustic style. It is constructed of original brick, ash tar stone, and huge wooden beams with a pitched wood shale roof. The large portico overlooks the entrance and reflects the Southern Plantation style. Entering through the solid wood doors, one views the grandeur of the lobby. The floor is brick, inlaid in a basket weave pattern, and the light fixtures are made of stamped aluminum. The stone fireplace cove is surrounded by handmade wooden staircases that spiral to the second floor balcony. The balcony encircles the lobby and displays original photos of the hotel and many autographed pictures of the Hollywood stars. Mr. Armand Ortega has recaptured the hotel's splendor and charm of yesterday.

A large number of Hollywood's most famous movies were shot in the area such as :The Bad Man, an MGM film starring Wallace Beery & Ronald Reagan in 1940; Sundown, a Wanger film starring Gene Tierney in 1941; Desert Song, starring Dennis Morgan in 1942; Song Of The Nile, starring Maria Montez & Jon Hall in 1944; Four Faces West & Colorado Territory, both starring Joel McCrea in 1947-48; Streets Of Laredo, starring William Holden & William Bendix in 1948; Rocky Mountain, starring Errol Flynn in 1950; Big Carnival, starring Kirk Douglas in 1950; Raton Pass, starring Dennis Morgan in 1951; New Mexico, starring Lew Ayres in 1950; Fort Defiance, starring Dane Clark in 1950; Fort Massacre, starring Joel McCrea in 1957; A Distant Trumpet, starring Troy Donahue & Suzanne Pleshette in 1963; The Hallelujah Trail, starring Burt Lancaster & Lee Remick in 1964.

THE GHOSTS

A number of guests as well as staff members have reported hearing disembodied footsteps and laughter on the upper floor of the lobby after hours.

Objects have been reported to have been moved about throughout various locations of the hotel by unseen hands. The mysterious opening and closing of doors has been reported in the bridal suite.

CHAPTER TWENTY-ONE

GRANTS, NEW MEXICO

The 3 Grant brothers -- Angus, Lewis and John -- were contracted to build the railroad through this region of New Mexico. As they established base camps during their work westward, the first in this region became known as Grant's Camp, then Grant's Station and eventually simply Grants.

The town grew as a farming community until 1950 when a Navajo rancher discovered uranium on Haystack Mountain, 10 miles west of town. U.S. Atomic Energy Commission contracts immediately created a mining boom in Grants for what turned out to be one of the largest uranium reserves in the world. This prosperity lasted until 1983, when a recession forced the closure of Grant's uranium mines and mills.

Although Grants was founded in the late 1870s, people had been making this region their home since the 12th century, when the Anasazi established an advanced civilization in Chaco Canyon to the north. With more than 5,000 inhabitants, Chaco included 40 underground ceremonial kivas and communal living quarters with more than 600 rooms. The Anasazi suddenly disappeared, but anthropologists trace the roots of today's Native American Pueblo Indians living throughout western New Mexico to these ancient people.

Today, Grants is a growing tourist destination favored for its fishing and boating at Bluewater and Ramah lakes, its championship golf, its proximity to Anasazi ruins and its outdoor recreation in national monuments and forests.

ECONO LODGE GRANTS
1509 E. Santa Fe Avenue
Grants, New Mexico

The Econo Lodge in Grants, New Mexico is an older three story hotel. Though no one seems to be completely certain of how it happened, this hotel has gained a certain reputation for being a very haunted place to stay.

Figure 18: The Econo Lodge in Grants, New Mexico.

I am told that though there are three floors to the facility, no one is allowed on the third floor. All of the rooms on that level are now used for storage. However, even though no one is ever allowed to be on that floor, from the swimming pool, many people have seen people looking down at them from the third floor.

A number of guests have reported hearing footsteps, the sounds of screams and the distinctive sounds of elevators going to that level. These same people have also said that when they inquired, it is revealed that the elevators do not go to the third floor. It takes a key for the elevator to go past the second floor.

Former staff members have said that they have heard that an unknown person appears in the kitchen out of nowhere. Whenever this figure mysteriously appears in the kitchen, the entire room becomes as cold as an icebox.

Other people have said that all of the stories about the hotel being haunted are fake and it started as a joke. Some have tried to confirm the incidents that have led to the hauntings, but can find no newspaper stories about the deaths. When asked, some of the local people submit that the town covered up the murders in order to not scare away tourists.

According to the story told by those who confirm that the hotel is haunted, there was a rather attractive young lady who worked as a hotel maid. She had been called to bring some towels to a guest staying on the third floor. When she arrived, however, he pulled her into the room, raped and murdered her.

Some of the staff who claim to have actually gotten to the third floor to investigate the story claim that the yellow police barrier tape is still in place on the left wing of the third floor. These same staff members also report that if you actually get to the room and enter it, that it is possible to still smell the blood and they are all adamant that the room is very cold.

According to the locals, the third floor was closed off because other guests were reported that at midnight they could hear screams of terror coming from that room and the sounds of a struggle. There are also some reports that this was not the only murder to take place on the third floor of the Econo Lodge in Grants. Some people say that the hotel is filled with evil that tends to cause the violence. Finally, there are a number of reports that if you stay on the second floor in the room directly beneath the murder room, that during the night you will hear screaming and cries for help coming from the room above.

MONTE CARLO RESTAURANT AND LOUNGE
721 West Santa Fe Avenue
Grants, New Mexico

The Monte Carlo Restaurant is an older establishment with the reputation of serving a good meal, at a good price, complete with surprisingly active spirits.

Some of this ghostly activity has been reported by the staff and some by the guests. Typical occurrences reported by the employees have been unexplainable noises that sound as if someone is walking close to them, when their eyes tell them that there is no one there.

Other staff members and guests alike have mentioned hearing nearby when there is no one there. Others have mentioned hearing faint voices that sound as if they are having an animated discussion. However, when attempts are made to find the source of the voices, the source can never be found. Still others have reported that they periodically detect the movement of someone out of the corner of their eye, but when they look directly at the spot where they saw the movement, no one is there. Then there is the spooky jukebox that starts playing all by itself. It has been checked electrically more than once and there is nothing wrong with the machine.

Figure 19: The Monte Carlo Restaurant and Lounge.

The majority of the occurrences are on the second floor of the building which originally was divided into a very nice apartment that was rented out for additional revenue. However, the apartment caught fire in 1993 was pretty well gutted before the fire was extinguished. When the repairs were done, the apartment was converted into a lounge area instead of into living quarters.

In the lounge area, there is a ghost that shakes what sounds like a key ring full of keys. Sometimes, the ghost shakes the invisible ring of keys right next to people's ears, but no one is ever seen. There are several cold spots in the lounge area, and the ceiling fan lights go on and off at will.

CHAPTER TWENTY-TWO

LA LUZ, NEW MEXICO

La Luz is a unique community of ninety-six adobe homes situated east of North Coors Road within the western edges of the Albuquerque City limits. From time to time other homes and buildings will be added to the community according to the Master Plan of Development.

In 1967, a time of "new towns" and "planned cities", La Luz was designed and developed to demonstrate an alternative to traditional Albuquerque suburban development. Ovenwest Corporation, the developer, envisioned a small new town of homes and shops, apartments and shopping centers, professional buildings and a school, which would look New Mexican yet work like a modern suburb. Residents could live close to the land and surrounded by the panorama of Rio Grande and Sandia views, yet be within city limits and within a fifteen-minute drive of downtown Albuquerque. La Luz would retain the southwestern village atmosphere with plazas and clusters of homes connected by walkways to shops and offices. The developers and the architect began to realize these ideas with several design principles to guide them.

LA LUZ CANYON
La Luz, New Mexico

This is a unique story of spirits who have returned in order to accomplish a mission. According to the story a mother and her two children were killed when their car was run off the bridge by a truck coming down from the canyon.

People say that you can experience this unusual phenomenon if you go up the canyon road to where the road divides going down to the hanging tree and stop on the bridge just before you turn onto the dirt road. Those who claim to know report that if you stop your car at this spot and wait that you will feel an unknown force push your car off the bridge.

Some who have experienced this effect wanted to see if they could find an explanation so they put baby powder on the trunk of their car. After the car was pushed off of the bridge, they got out to examine the trunk of the car and were shocked to see the handprints of children. They also reported that they could hear the faint laughter of children echoing on the breeze.

WATER TREATMENT PLANT
La Luz, New Mexico

A large portion of the water for Alamogordo, New Mexico comes from a surface collection system from Bonito Lake. The water so collected is brought to the La Luz Water Treatment Plant for processing through a pipeline primarily owned by the United States Air Force.

What few seem to know is that the Water Treatment Plant is haunted. No one is sure who or what haunts the building, but there is no doubt that it is haunted. It is reported that if you walk into the plant using only a flashlight as your illumination that the one small flashlight will light up the entire room as the light reflects off of the water and the crystals.

Those who find reason to be inside the treatment plant late at night report hearing the sounds of heavy footsteps hurrying through the deeply shadowed areas of the cavernous building. Anyone there will find themselves overcome with an eerie feeling. There are a number of cold sports that can be found as you explore the old building. Though not particularly the most desirable place to spend eternity, it would seem that many apparitions can be seen there.

CHAPTER TWENTY-THREE

LOS ALAMOS, NEW MEXICO

Los Alamos, New Mexico is a small mountain community of 18,000 people that possesses a world-wide reputation for scientific and technological development. The community features small-town living with friendly neighbors, low crime, and an excellent school system.

Twenty-five years before the Manhattan Project created the town of Los Alamos, the Pajarito Plateau was home to an elite prep school for boys, ages twelve to eighteen. The Los Alamos Ranch School combined a robust outdoor life and a carefully cultivated wilderness experience with a rigorous academic program and the structured discipline of a Boy Scout troop, perfectly mirroring the Progressive Era's quest for perfection.

There was no Christmas vacation at the Los Alamos Ranch School in the winter of 1942. Informed by Secretary of War Henry Stimson in a December 1 letter that the Army would take over the property in February 1943, Ranch school director A. J. Connell advised his students that they would have to work through the vacation to complete the school's annual curriculum.

The closing of the Ranch school was the end of school founder Ashley Pond's dream. He had come west as a boy to be reinvigorated by the thin, fresh air of New Mexico, as had many others suffering lung diseases. So successful was the cure that he tried to found a boys school near Mora, N.M., in 1904, but that version of his dream literally washed away in a flood.

Supported by automobile manufacturers from his home town, Detroit, Pond subsequently founded a dude ranch, the Pajarito Club, in Pajarito Canyon (Technical Area 18) on the eve of World War I. The Pond cabin, also known as the Dwight Young Cabin (after a lab staff member who lived there for a time), still stands and was accepted for inclusion on the State Register of Cultural Properties in 1989.

Pond planned to establish a ranch school on a nearby homestead owned by his ranch manager, H. H. Brooks, where boys might "learn by doing' in the outdoors, in a style reminiscent of Theodore Roosevelt's ideal of the vigorous life. Before leaving to join the American Red Cross in 1918, Pond bought Brooks' homestead and hired Connell, then a Santa Fe National Forest ranger, to run the school. Connell organized the school on the model of the Boy Scouts of America, consonant with Pond's vision of the outdoor life, and the scout uniform became that of the school. Its students became Troop 22 of the BSA.

Connell added a standard college preparatory curriculum to the existing routine of afternoons and weekends spent outdoors. The first headmaster was Fayette Curtis. The academic program he mapped out with Connell included English, history, mathematics, science, languages, art and music. Subsequently, teachers like Church added advanced subjects like nuclear physics, physiology and aeronautics.

Between 1920 and 1942, about 40 students between the ages of 12 and 16 attended the school annually, paying a tuition averaging $2,400, about $23,000 in today's dollars. Among the more famous graduates were Colgate; John Crosby, founder of the Santa Fe Opera; Professor Edward Hall of Northwestern University; New Mexico artist Wilson Hurley; and industrial executives like Roy Chapin of American Motors and John Reed of the Santa Fe railroad. Novelist Gore Vidal also attended the school for a short time.

The regime endured by the boys who came to the ranch school was almost as stiff as the tuition. Divided into groups according to their physical maturity, they slept in the fresh air of screened-in porches at the Big House (on the site of the present Community Center). The seniors slept at Spruce Cottage (the home just north of the historical society), the headmaster's quarters.

Students rose at 6:30 a.m., assembled for 15 minutes of calisthenics, ate breakfast at 7 a.m., made their beds, cleaned their rooms and then attended class from 7:45 a.m. until 1:15 p.m. Afternoons were spent working on the ranch or in sports activities. Work, physical development and academic achievements were all regularly reported to parents. Horseback rides, musical events, hikes, hunting expeditions, camp outs, an annual play and a Gilbert and Sullivan operetta were among the many activities at the school.

Fuller Lodge, designed by Santa Fe architect John Gaw Meem and built in 1928, served as cafeteria, infirmary, classroom building and social center where, for example, girls from Santa Fe's Brownmore Girls School might come to dance with the boys, who wore their Scouting shorts even on such occasions. The lodge was given to the school by lumberman Philo C. Fuller, the father of Edward P. Fuller, a wealthy Detroit resident who purchased the Ranch School mortgage for Pond. A sawmill was set up at the site to prepare 800 ponderosa pines personally selected by the donor and architect. The building, which remains today, is an architectural tribute to the school.

An arts and crafts building with carpentry and woodworking shops was also donated by a parent in 1934. It housed a music room and a physics and chemistry laboratory as well.

In 1940, the school reached its peak enrollment of 47 students and its physical plant was complete. The war years saw a decline in enrollment and the loss of faculty. Headmaster Lawrence S. Hitchcock was called to active service in the Army and Church succeeded him. Another teacher, Cecil Wirth, resigned because of illness. To these losses, the Army added the loss of the site, which, because of the special nature of the educational experience, could not easily be replaced.

When Connell learned that the school was to be taken over by the Army, he decided that it must close. "So much about the Los Alamos Ranch School was indigenous and appropriate only to its surroundings - the whole program, the life, the very spirit of the school developed out of its location and local tradition - that the conviction grew that this school could not be transplanted,' he told alumni.

On Jan. 21, 1943, the final diplomas given by the Los Alamos Ranch School were awarded to Collier W. Baird and Colgate of New Jersey and William Edgar Barr and Theodore Spencer Church of New Mexico.

In 1944, Connell died in Santa Fe. Later that year, Fermor Church opened a "Los Alamos School' in Taos, but it closed in 1946, ending, except in the memory of its students and staff and in the historic district of Los Alamos, the story of the Los Alamos Ranch School.

The Lodge and the Big House became social gathering places during the war, and a number of the other buildings were turned into housing for the soldiers and scientists who came to work on the Los Alamos Project. Because the school buildings were the only houses in Los Alamos with bathtubs during the war, these residences located on what are now 22 and Nectar streets were called "Bathtub Row.'

LOS ALAMOS HIGH SCHOOL
1300 Diamond Drive
Los Alamos, New Mexico

Los Alamos High School is an outstanding educational institute, fully supported by the training facilities of the Los Alamos Weapons Lab. However, though it is fully integrated in the futuristic world growing in Los Alamos, the facility is also known to be haunted.

According to both students and staff, the high school auditorium is the location of two of the most active spirits. The ghosts that haunt this part of the school are seen here more often than any other place in the school. According to those who claim to known the story, during a performance of a school play one night back in the 50's a girl fell to her death from the spiral staircase that is located above the stage. Now it is said that she returns to push unwary students off of the staircase by causing a powerful gust of cold air to blow across the spiral staircase.

Another of the ghosts that is found in the auditorium is of a girl that had a heart attack while watching a play. She was said to be sitting in the 5th seat from the left in the front row. Whenever somebody sits in this seat to watch a performance of a school play, it is said that they can feel her presence. Two of the sensations experienced are very cold air enveloping the seat as well as feeling of sadness and despair.

PEGGY SUE BRIDGE
Los Alamos, New Mexico

Near the city of Los Alamos is the remains of an old wooden bridge that connects two side of a canyon located. It is said by the locals that in the 1950s a high school student by the name of Peggy Sue that became so depressed that she went to the bridge and jumped to her death.

It is said that her ghost now lingers near the bridge and if someone walks out onto the remains of the bridge, the ghost of Peggy Sue will try to push the unwary off of the bridge. It is an old Los Alamos High School tradition to go to the bridge and brave the crossing of the bridge without being pushed to their death by the ghost of Peggy Sue.

BANDELIER NATIONAL MONUMENT
HCR-1
Box 1, Suite 15
Los Alamos, New Mexico

The Anasazi first settled in this beautiful canyon ten thousand years ago. The Tyuonui Ruins look like a miniature Machu Pichu, surrounded by green forests and mountains. The Great Kiva was a site of public religious ceremonies. Ceremonial Cave was where private initiation rituals took place. An ancient ceremonial circle, the Shrine of the Stone Lions, is sacred to nearly every tribe in the southwest. The Cochin, Hopi, Ildefonso, Santa Domingo, and Zuni Indians all believe the spirits of their ancestors can be contacted here.

THE GHOSTS

There have been stories of figures in ritual dress being seen in the canyon. Some hikers have reported hearing the faint sounds of chanting floating on the breeze.

CHAPTER TWENTY-FOUR

MADRID, NEW MEXICO

Madrid was a coal mining town from the mid 1800's through the 1940's. During World War II so many of the miners were drafted that the mine were closed and the remaining population drifted away until Madrid became an abandoned ghost town.

In the 1970's hippies, artist and outlaws began rebuilding it for their own purposes and it is alive today. The entire town has been site of numerous ghost sightings, most notably in certain houses, the old miners/town cemetery, the old church (now a house) and the surrounding arroyos. Apparitions seen have ranged from sightings of la LLorona in the arroyos, silent cowboys escorting a Spanish woman in fine dress though main street, and various ghostly forms at the cemetery. The town area was also the site of the Aztecs trade for turquoise in New Mexico / Mexico older history.

MINE SHAFT TAVERN
Madrid, NM

Opened in 1946, the Mine Shaft Tavern was purchased from the Albuquerque and Cerrillos Coal Company and restored in 1982. The business has been generally successful except for those who have an aversion to drinking their spirits in the company of spirits.

Bartenders, as well as guests have seen glasses fall off of shelves on their own and break. Some of the doors have been seen to open and swing back and forth and then close without any physical presence being nearby. Odd sounds can be heard coming from the six inch adobe walls and after closing hours objects are mysteriously moved about the building.

However, perhaps the most unsettling occurrence is when employees look in a mirror and instead of seeing their own reflections; they see that of a ghost.

CHAPTER TWENTY-FIVE

ROCIADA, NEW MEXICO

Rociada is a small town that is best known for golf and relaxation. Among the attractions are the historic Camp Davis Dude Ranch and the Pendaries Restaurant.

Camp Davis was begun in the summer of 1939 when Coach (J. "Mule") and Liz Davis took their four sons (John, Sam, Bill and Jerry) and several friends to the cool mountains at El Porvenir, New Mexico. More and more friends of the sons wanted to join the crowd for hiking, fishing and sports. Soon a larger camp was needed. In 1944 the Davises leased a camp in Upper Rociada, New Mexico. A large adobe house, dating from 1904, a recreation hall, dining hall and 8 cabins became the home for Camp Davis. In the month of June, 60 boys attended Camp, in July 60 girls, and then up to 7 families in August. This pattern continued through the late 1960s and into the 1970s. Since that time Camp has been open for families for 5 or 6 weeks a summer, as well as other groups. Bill Davis, the third of the four sons and his family carry on the tradition of providing a great retreat from summer heat at lower elevations.

PENDARIES RESTAURANT & LODGE
Pendaries Village
Rociada, New Mexico

Pendaries is a subdivision located in Rociada, New Mexico (about 30 miles northwest of Las Vegas). The main attractions include the 18 hole mountain golf course, fishing, hiking and just plain old relaxation. The subdivision has roughly 980 original lots in the subdivision. Of the original lots, approximately 100 are on the market for resale purposes. The Rociada valley and surrounding communities hold a fascinating history and several buildings constructed in the 1870's can still be seen today.

The Lodge has 18 rooms that have been freshly painted and have new carpeting. Roll-a-way beds for families are available. There are also additional accommodations available in summer homes. The full-service restaurant serves dinner daily. Breakfast and lunch may be enjoyed at the Club House near the Golf Shop. Enjoy a drink in the historic Moosehead Saloon. The Conference Center seats 80 for meetings and is also available for banquets. The restaurant, seating 100, provides the opportunity for banquets of larger groups.

Pendaries Village was established in the mid 1960's and this little subdivision has grown into a unique opportunity for outdoor enthusiasts to live and/or vacation. Just 2 hours from Albuquerque this is the perfect weekend getaway. Home to over 190 residences and a challenging 18 hole mountain golf course. You will find plenty of time (and privacy) for hiking, fishing, mountain biking and golfing.

THE GHOSTS

Many of the employees have seen an older man in the downstairs bar. No one knows his identity, but this mysterious figure will suddenly be seen standing by the bar and then he will vanish. This mysterious figure had also been seen standing outside one of the rooms in the lodge as if waiting for someone.

CHAPTER TWENTY-SIX

PHILMONT, NEW MEXICO

Once inhabited by Jicarrilla Apache and Moache Ute Indians, Philmont was the site of one of the first pioneer settlements in northeastern New Mexico. The present ranch is part of the original Beaubien and Miranda Land Grant which was granted to Carlos Beaubien and Guadalupe Miranda by the Mexican government in 1841. Beaubien's son-in-law, mountain man Lucien Maxwell, led the first settlers to the grant in 1848. With the help of his friend Kit Carson, Maxwell's settlement on the Rayado River prospered, despite frequent Indian raids and harsh wilderness conditions.

Maxwell moved his ranch north to the Cimarron River in 1857, the site of present day Cimarron. There it became a famous stop on the Santa Fe Trail, bringing American trade goods into New Mexico. Ten years after Maxwell moved to Cimarron, gold was discovered on his ranch near Baldy Mountain. For years afterward, the mountains and streams of Maxwell's Ranch swarmed with prospectors and miners.

In 1870, Maxwell sold his ranch to an English land company known as the Maxwell Land Grant and Railroad Company. After several years the land was again sold to a Dutch-based company who attempted several development schemes, but eventually sold the land in tracts for farms and ranches.

Oklahoma oilman, Waite Phillips, became interested in developing a ranch out of the old land grant in 1922. He eventually amassed over 300,000 acres of mountains and plains in a ranch he named Philmont (derived from his name and the Spanish word for mountain, "monte").

The Philmont Ranch became a showplace. Immense herds of Hereford cows and Corriedale sheep grazed its pastures. Phillips built a large Spanish Mediterranean home for his family at the Headquarters, naming it the Villa

Philmonte. He developed horse and hiking trails throughout the scenic backcountry along with elaborate fishing and hunting cabins for his family and friends.

Waite Phillips believed in sharing his wealth with people outside his family. In this spirit, he offered 35,857 acres of his ranch to the Boy Scouts of America in 1938 to serve as a national wilderness camping area. The area was named "Philturn Rockymountain Scoutcamp" (after Phillips' name and the BSA slogan, "Do a Good Turn Daily"). After observing the enthusiastic response of the first Scout campers, Phillips augmented his original gift in 1941, with an addition including his best camping land, the Villa Philmonte, and the headquarters farming and ranching operations. The second gift was made so that "many, rather than few" could enjoy his rich and beautiful land. The property, now totaling 127,395 acres was renamed "Philmont Scout Ranch".

Phillips realized that the cost for maintenance and development of the property could not and should not be derived entirely from camper fees. As an endowment he included in the gift his 23-story Philtower Building in Tulsa, Oklahoma.

In 1963, through the generosity of Norton Clapp, vice-president of the National Council of the Boy Scouts of America, another piece of the Maxwell Land Grant was purchased and added to Philmont. This was the Baldy Mountain mining area consisting of 10,098 acres.

THE HAUNTED MESA
Philmont, New Mexico

One of Louie Lamour's most famous books was entitled Haunted Mesa[24]. The mesa he described in the story is Urraca Mesa, which is found on the Philmont Scout Ranch in Philmont, New Mexico[25].

According to legend, the hauntings and other supernatural events go back to the days of the Anasazi, that mysterious civilization that once dominated New Mexico before vanishing as if it never was. This civilization has continued to be a puzzle since the day it was discovered that they had ever existed. No one knows where they came from, or when they arrived in what is now the Southeastern United States or what happened to them. There are many theories, but no facts to back up any of them.

It is believed that the end of the very civilized Anasazi came in the 12th century when something turned them into a very frightened people. With no

---

[24] Published by Bantam Books.
[25] A much more detailed account of the happenings at the haunted mesa can be found in the book Riders in the Sky: The Ghosts and Legends of Philmont Scout Ranch by Michael Connelly.

warning, it seems that they abandoned their traditional homes for fortified cliff dwellings like those found at the equally mysterious Mesa Verde in Colorado.

In these massive fortifications, this formerly happy, prosperous people lived in what appears to have been abject fear until they simply disappeared. There is no clear evidence as to what happened to those proud people, although recent archaeological finds have uncovered evidence of cannibalism and torture.

Scientists, schooled in the traditional methods of determining the fates of earlier civilizations have theorized that perhaps some of madness overcame this peaceful tribe, causing them to turn on each other. Others have believed that there was an invasion by a more powerful warring tribe like the Toltecs of Mexico which led to the ultimate end of the Anasazi. However, both of these are unproven theories. Of course, the legends of the Southwest have still another answer for what happened to the Old Ones. This answer involved the supernatural.

The legends regarding the fate of the Anasazi all revolve around a place in New Mexico known as Urraca Mesa, now a part of Philmont Scout Ranch. As mentioned by Louie Lamour in his high adventure classic Haunted Mesa, Urraca Mesa is an area notorious for its hauntings and other supernatural activity. There are stories of paranormal activities and sightings of apparitions on the mesa that extend back for many years. Even today, the mesa is taboo to the local tribes including the Utes and Jicarrilla Apaches who believe it to be the gateway to hell.

The stories about the end of the Anasazi arose over 200 years ago when the Navajo moved into the area and briefly occupied the mesa. They found ancient Anasazi petrogplyphs which led them to believe that there had once been a great battle on the site.

According to the translation of the petroglyphs found, this battle had been fought between the Lord of the Outerworld and his evil twin brother, the Lord of the Underworld. The prize they struggled for was no less than the souls of the ancient ones, the Anasazi. The battle was fierce and ended with the Lord of the Outerworld being victorious and banishing his sibling back to the nether regions, at least for the time being. In the process, however, the Anasazis were destroyed.

There is also no question that the Navajos believed the story told in the rocks. To protect the world against his return and the escape of the demons he controlled the Navajo surrounded the mesa with sacred totems and left their most powerful Shaman to guard the supposed entrance to hell.

According to the local tribes, and many visitors to the mesa, he still stands guard today, often seen bathed in a blue light and sometimes appearing in full shaman regalia or in one of his alter-egos such as a panther or a bear.

Unfortunately, according to legend, the Blue Shaman's vigil started too late to save the Anasazi people. It is said that not even his power could stop the demons from escaping their prison long enough to hunt down the Anasazi and drag their souls to hell.

This explanation has as much factual support as the theories put forth by the scientists who study the Anasazi remains. Just to be on the safe side, I would hope that the Navajo Shaman has a very long life and does not drop his guard even for a moment. If the legend is true and the demons escape again, who is to say who they will hunt down this time.

PHILMONT SCOUT CAMP
Philmont, New Mexico

Philmont Scout Ranch is the oldest of the "high-adventure bases" operated by the Boy Scouts of America, along with the Florida High Adventure Sea Base and a collection of programs in the Boundary Waters. It is one of the most renowned BSA facilities[26].

Philmont is located in the Sangre de Cristo Range of the Rocky Mountains of New Mexico. The closest town is Cimarron, New Mexico, but perhaps it is better to say that it is about 20 miles west-northwest of Springer, New Mexico, or 35 miles southwest of Raton, New Mexico. It is shaped somewhat like the letter 'I,' with the bottom section larger than the top. It is about 12 miles across (east to west) at its widest point, and about 30 miles long. There are no mountains to the south of Philmont, or to the east (indeed, part of the eastern fringe of the ranch is flatland) but the interior is quite mountainous.

The lowest elevation is 6500 feet, at the southeast corner. The highest point is the peak of Baldy Mountain (12,441 feet), on the northwest boundary. The most recognizable landmark at Philmont is the Tooth of Time (9003 feet), a granite monolith protruding 500 vertical feet from an east-west ridge. Tooth of Time Ridge, and the latitude line it sits on, marks the boundary between the central and southern sections of Philmont. The boundary between the central and northern sections is the narrowest part of the 'I'-shape, only a few miles across. U.S. Highway 64 runs through Philmont just south of this line.

Native Americans of the Jicarrilla Apache tribe and Ute tribe once inhabited Philmont. At least one Native American archaeological site exists in the northern section, and various camps seek to preserve Philmont's Native American heritage. In the mid-19th century, the Santa Fe Trail crossed the plains just southwest of Philmont. The Tooth of Time owes its name to this trail; travelers knew that once they passed it, they had only a few weeks to go until they reached Santa Fe, New Mexico. Philmont's strategic location along the trail spurred some interest in it. In 1841, Carlos Beaubien and Guadalupe Miranda obtained a large land grant from the Mexican government, including the present

---

[26] http://en.wikipedia.org/wiki/Philmont_Scout_Ranch

ranch. Soon the grant fell into the hands of Beaubien's son-in-law Lucien Maxwell, who played an important role in developing and settling it. Maxwell sold the ranch to the Maxwell Land Grant and Railroad Company, which gave up and handed it on to a Dutch development company, which decided to parcel it out to ranchers.

An old Mexican homestead was preserved on the ranch, as part of Abreu camp, for many years until it burned down, leaving only a stone fireplace and chimney. A reconstructed homestead may be seen less than a mile away at New Abreu camp. Herds of cattle, another relic of this era, graze in the numerous meadows of southeastern Philmont.

The history of mining at Philmont dates back to the years immediately after the Civil War. The story is that an Indian befriended a Union soldier, and happened to give him a shiny rock. (This contributor finds the story suspect, because any Union troops stationed in New Mexico at the time would have been involved in driving out the Native Americans.) The shiny material in the rock was found to be copper. According to the story, the soldier and two of his friends went up to investigate, and found gold. However, they could not stay and mine the gold, and by the time they returned the next year, the area was overrun by miners. Scores of gold mines were excavated in Philmont, and operated into the early 20th century. A large vein of gold is said to lie under Baldy Mountain to this day, but extracting it has not been feasible. The Contention Mine, located at Cyphers Mine camp, is open to guided tours.

The penultimate owner of Philmont was wealthy oil magnate and wilderness enthusiast Waite Phillips, who amassed a large part of the old land grant in the 1920s. Phillips built a large residence at Philmont, and called it the Villa Philmonte. He also constructed a number of hunting lodges and day-use camps. It would not have been beyond his means to bring electricity to those camps, but he decided not to. Some of these camps have been preserved, complete with wood-burning stoves, oil lamps, and other design features indicative of Phillips's often eccentric taste. (This particular contributor personally saw two of these preserved facilities, at the camps known as Fish Camp and Hunting Lodge.) Phillips used the ranch as a private game reserve, but would sometimes allow others to use it, including a few Boy Scout troops. He was so impressed with the Scouts that in 1938, he donated a significant part of it to the Boy Scouts of America. They initially named it the "Philturn Rockymountain Scoutcamp" [sic]. The word 'Philturn' comes from Waite Phillips's name, together with the "Good Turn" he did by donating the property. In 1941, Phillips added the rest of the present Philmont property, including the Villa Philmonte. To help fund the upkeep of Philmont, he threw in a large office building in Tulsa, Oklahoma. The ranch's name was changed at this time.

Philmont was run differently in the early years than it is now. Half a dozen "base camps" were constructed at strategic locations. A visiting group of Scouts would stay at one of these camps for a week, and day-hike to surrounding locations of interest. (Conventional stationary camps are usually operated in this manner, as well.) If the Scouts wanted to visit a different area, they would pack up their gear, hoist it onto donkeys, and hike to another base camp. Eventually, possibly due to the advent of modern lightweight metal-frame backpacks and other backpacking technology, the program was restructured to be backpacking-based.

Most of those who come to Philmont come for the trek, an 11-day backpacking trip. (A group of Scouts on a trek is called a crew.) Other program options include:

Cavalcades are similar to standard treks, but conducted on horseback.

Rayado Treks are twice as long as standard treks, and considerably more strenuous. Rayado crews are put together by Philmont staff, and consist of people from different parts of the country.

The Philmont Training Center offers weeklong training programs for adult leaders, and a variety of outdoor programs for trainees' families.

The Roving Outdoor Conservation School and various Trail Crew programs teach participants about ecology, conservation techniques, and trail construction methods.

Guided activities such as fishing, winter camping, and skiing, are offered throughout the year.

The area known as Base Camp is a town unto itself. It has a post office, half a dozen chapels (operating daily), two dining halls, a clinic, a store for souvenirs and sundry camping gear, housing (mainly tents) for roughly 900 staff, and tents for between 800 and 1000 trekkers. Trekkers are organized into crews of seven to twelve (usually closer to twelve than to seven), with two to four adult leaders. A contingent consists of one or more crews from the same council (see Boy Scouts of America: Organization), traveling together. Around 360 trekkers arrive at Base Camp every day of the season. When they arrive, they are assigned a ranger, a young man or woman highly skilled in backpacking. The ranger's task is to guide the crew through "processing," (basically, registration), to make sure that the trekkers actually know how to backpack, and to teach them Philmont-specific camping practices.

Crews are required to pick up a dining fly. This is a 12-foot-square tarp with two collapsible aluminum poles. Its purpose (quite contrary to the name) is to serve as a rain cover for the crew's backpacks. It is supposed to be set up as an A-frame, with two opposite sides staked down, the middle held up by the poles, and the ends open. Many crews experiment with the use of trees, hiking poles, and other devices to obtain a roomier configuration so that it can be used for crew activities such as card games. Crews may also pick up Philmont tents. These tents are also A-frame, five feet wide by seven feet long, with a rain fly. They are more difficult to set up than conventional dome tents, but very easy to break down. They have a bad reputation, which this contributor considers to be undeserved, since they are not significantly heavier than commonly used dome tents.

Crews also pick up several days' worth of Philmont food (see "Commissaries" below). Philmont also provides optional cooking supplies.

After processing, crews are loaded up onto busses and shipped off to any of several trailheads, called "turnarounds" because there is a loop in the road for the bus to turn around. The crew and its ranger are now alone.

THE GHOSTS

Having now mentioned most of the information that can be found in the literature about this Scout Camp, let us now turn our attention to those things that are only whispered about after the lights go out. It seems that the Philmont Scout Camp is also haunted.

One of the ghosts that has been seen, in addition to the spirit of the Shaman that haunts Urraca Mesa, has been that of Thomas "Black Jack" Ketchum, the only person ever hanged in Clayton, New Mexico. He was also the only man ever hanged for train robbery in the entire state, a law that was later found to be unconstitutional. But, unfortunately, this determination was a little too late for poor Black Jack.

There is a story told by a former scout about his meeting with Black Jack Ketchum while camping on the Philmont Scout Camp. He and several other scouts were backpacking through the mountains, visiting various historic sites, including an abandoned gold mine, a ghost town and one of Black Jack Ketchum's outlaw hideouts.

The outlaw hideout was a large rock overhang and the scouts thought it would be fun to camp there for the night. However, their leader insisted that they stay at a nearby-designated site. Disappointed at being refused the opportunity for they thought would be an exciting time, several of the scouts set their tents up several hundred feet away from the leader's tent, hoping they would have a chance to sneak back to the hideout later that night.

About 11:00 p.m., when the rest of the camp was fast asleep, five of the scouts gathered their sleeping bags and quietly stole back to the hideout. They set up camp under the overhang and built a fire, where they sat around talking about their trip. When the fire burned down to nothing more than red coals, the scouts settled down in their sleeping bags. The storyteller drifted off to sleep thinking about Black Jack. Suddenly, he was awakened by a noise in the bushes. He said that he felt paralyzed, unable to move and tried to call out to the others, but his throat was all knotted up.

Then he saw a cowboy, dressed all in black come running out of the bushes toward the hide out. He said the man was mostly solid but some parts of him appeared translucent. He described the man as filthy dirty, with a tattered hat, clothes from the 1800's, and terribly yellowed teeth. His face was very red, glistening with sweat, with lots of facial hair and the apparition held a revolver.

The cowboy was apparently unaware of the scout, but the boy was very scared, as much by his inability to move than by the man. As he watched, a strange fog emanated from the tree line across from a small stream and he could hear men yelling unintelligently, and then muffled gunfire.

The cowboy turned and fired his revolver six times into the trees and then ran and stood right over the scout. The cowboy was wounded in the shoulder and as he reloaded his pistol, he discharged six shell casings from his revolver that fell right on top of the boy. As the scout watched in amazement, the casings disappeared as they fell onto his sleeping bag. The cowboy then finished reloading his revolver and fired additional shots into the trees.

Suddenly, the cowboy seemed to become aware of the young scout. The expression on the cowboy's face indicated that the scout had just suddenly appeared before his eyes. The cowboy seemed to be confused and confounded, while the scout was just simply terrified. Then, the cowboy un-cocked and lowered his pistol, looked at the scout very closely, and said, "You're not supposed to be here," and then just disappeared into thin air.

Eventually, he was able to go back to sleep, but had to be shaken repeatedly by his fellow campers before waking in the morning. As the scouts broke camp, the boy told his fellow campers about the "dream," who were amused by the story. But, as the scout rolled up his sleeping bag, he found six shell casings in the dust.

Later, when they returned to base camp, the scout visited an old saloon, where a photograph of Black Jack Ketchum was displayed. The photograph was the same man that the scout had seen at the hideout.

When he told his friends, they brushed him off, as setting them up for a big hoax and the scout never told anyone about it again, but he kept the shell casings. After the scout returned home, he checked with a gun expert who said the casings were dated from sometime around 1878, but were in almost brand new condition and the gunpowder could still be smelt in them. In fact, the gunpowder was one that was used in the last century, but not today.

The scout kept the shell casings for years, but unfortunately, after he moved away from home, his mother threw them out along with several other items the boy had saved, such as comic books and baseball cards.

CHAPTER TWENTY-SEVEN

POJOAQUE, NEW MEXICO

Pojoaque is a small community located in Santa Fe County, New Mexico. The name Pojoaque means "drinking water place" or "gathering place." Studies of the area have revealed that this area was inhabited as arly as 500 A.D., however, it was not until the early 1600s that San Francisco de Pojoaque , the first Spanish Mission was founded.

Pojoaque was a major settlement and had a signifigant place in the history of the area until Don Diego de Vargas reconquered the area after the Great Pueblo Revolt of 1680. In the process of reconquering the territory, Don Diego de Vargas greatly reduced the population of Pojoaque Pueblo. Eventually, the pueblo was abandoned.

However, in 1706 five familues established their homes at Pojoaque and by 1712, the population had increaed to 79. However, the smallpox epidemic of 1890 so decimated the population that the pueblo was again abandoned.

In 1933, descendants of the original settlers once again inhabited Pojoaque and in 1936, the pueblo was recognized by the United States Government as a Tribal Reservation. Today the Pojoaque Reservation consists of over 11,000 acres of land and has over 300 members.

POJOAQUE HIGH SCHOOL
Hwys 285 & 502
Santa Fe, NM 87501

Pojoaque High School is part of the Pojoaque Valley Public School System which covers not only the schools that serve the reservation but also some located in Santa Fe. New Mexico.

According to all reports, there was a girl who was attending this school who became very depressed. In fact she was depressed to the point that she finally hung herself in the girls' locker room of the gym from a shower head.

Students and staff now report that she wanders around the gym most nights and if you go into the locker room at night you will see her body hanging from the shower.

CHAPTER TWENTY-EIGHT

RATON, NEW MEXICO

Raton is a city located in Colfax County, New Mexico. As of the 2000 census, the city had a total population of 7,282. It is the county seat of Colfax County.

THE SHULER THEATRE
Raton, New Mexico

Officially opening April 27, 1915, the Shuler Theater was cause enough to send city commissioners fleeing over the state line to Trinidad, Colorado, for safety.

Was the building of a theater a sufficient cause for such a dispute? Yes -- theater was a "hot topic" in the old days. A railroad and 40 billion tons of coal made Raton one of the fastest growing settlements in New Mexico and would later put it on a major "theater circuit". As early as the 1880s, Raton boasted a theater that attracted regular road shows. By 1882, an opera house known as the Old Rink had been erected. Serving as both opera house and a community meeting place, the Old Rink was said to have "held social sway on Second Street." The Old Rink was soon overshadowed by Hugo Seaburg's Garden Coliseum. The largest theater in New Mexico at the time, this enormous wooden theater could seat 5000 patrons, roughly the equivalent of the entire population of Raton at one time.

The coliseum burned down shortly after the turn of the century, but by that time Raton already had at least four other theaters and opera houses including the Lyric, the Grand, and the Princess. The Lyric featured a three piece orchestra to accompany its early silent movies, and the Grand continued to bring in concerts, stock companies, boxing, wrestling, and lectures, while the Princess catered to the film industry. Of these only the municipal auditorium, which eventually came to be known as The Shuler survives unto this day.

The Shuler Auditorium was the product of remarkable personal and community energy, and the person principally responsible was Dr. James Jackson Shuler, early Raton resident who twice served as mayor from 1899-1902 and 1910-1919. Dr. Shuler undertook a number of impressive projects, including the construction of a municipal auditorium. The initial plan was to build a modest city hall with $25,000 that had been voted on by the taxpayers for that purpose, but the destruction of Seaburg's coliseum left Raton without a large theater. The plan was enlarged to include an auditorium. The city fathers decided to include a fire station, extra office space, a heating plant, and a jail.

Architect William Rapp, of Trinidad, Colorado, was commissioned to design the new buildings. The interior was to conform to the classic opera house formula, including opera boxes. The interior decorations by designer F. Mayer were a rough approximation of the 18th century ornate rococo style so much in vogue in Europe during the 1800s. Early support for the construction wavered and at one point the entire city council had to flee to Trinidad to escape arrest. Despite political hardships, the cornerstone was finally laid on August 20, 1914 and was completed by 1915 at a final cost of $55,000.

When Dr. Shuler died in 1919, the city council passed the resolution:

Whereas the erection and completion of the municipal auditorium, which has been a source of such delight to the inhabitants of this city, is a monument to the forethought, idealism, zeal, and energy of the late mayor, J.J. Shuler, under whose leadership the purpose of the people was accomplished; Now, therefore, in recognition of such services, be it resolved that the said municipal auditorium be hereafter known and designated on the records of the city as the Shuler Auditorium.

The Shuler thrived during the 1920s and 1930s, but sadly enough, the Shuler fell into disrepair and by the 1950s live entertainment was rare. Many regretted the loss of the once-great opera house, but probably none more than Evelyn Shuler, the daughter of Dr. J.J. Shuler. In 1963 Miss Evelyn met Bill Fagan, founder of a touring group of actors. Out of that meeting the Kaleidoscope Players were born. The group became the state theater company of New Mexico, and took up residency in the historic Shuler Theater, attracting money for the restoration of the building. The Shuler began to be used once again as a community auditorium. Recent years have seen a variety of productions held at the Shuler including school concerts, city events, and professional theater productions.

Three of the original drop curtains survive and are still used to this day -- Ripley Park in Raton featuring the old municipal library, a Roman palace setting framed by elaborate draperies, and most significantly the original fire curtain depicting a scene from the Palisades of Cimarron against a background of American Indian motifs including swastika symbols painted on the folds of the curtain, which were an American Indian symbol of good luck.

Today Bill Fagan's international performing artists management and touring company, Double Bill Entertainments, houses its offices in the Shuler Theater, and the theater is open for tours. The Shuler can be utilized to its maximum capacity, and more people, more often, can experience the joy of viewing a performance surrounded by such grandeur. Perhaps Raton can again be on the "theater circuit".

THE GHOSTS

There are many who claim that there is no doubt that this historic theatre is most certainly haunted. Many times, those in the theater hear scraping sounds on the stage as if someone in high heels is walking across the stage.

However, it is the dressing room area that has the most unusual hauntings. The dressing area has just a curtain as a door, but it still has very different temperatures in certain areas.

In one dressing room, there is a broken mirror which ALMOST always never shows a reflection. When it does reflect something it is usually not the individual standing in front of it, but rather someone else. Others complain of feeling as if they are being watched.

CHAPTER TWENTY-NINE

ROSWELL NEW MEXICO

Roswell, New Mexico has long been known as the place where a UFO crashed in 1947. However, the Roswell area has been an important site of human habitation throughout history because of the confluence of the Spring, Hondo and Pecos rivers. Originally home to the Mescalero Apache Indians, the area was also a part of the Comanche Indian's hunting grounds.

The first known European visitor was a Spanish conquistador named Don Antonio de Espejo, who explored the Pecos Valley in 1583. In 1590 Gaspar de Castaño de Sosa led an unauthorized colonial expedition to the area from Mexico. Gaspar was arrested for his troubles and the settlement failed to materialize.

There is little documented history on the area from 1590 until the mid 1800's and the area remained largely in Indian hands for over 250 years. A settlement of crude adobe shacks at Rio Hondo is mentioned in an 1867 U.S. Government Surveyor report. This settlement is believed to have been located in the present neighborhood known as Chihuahuita. In 1866 the Goodnight-Loving Trail was established to drive cattle to market and one of the campsites on the trail was established in the Roswell area. The trail brought Anglo ranchers from Texas to the area including John Chisum and resulted in the establishment of the ranching industry in Southeastern New Mexico.

A settler named Van Smith founded the town of Rio Hondo in 1870. The town included a general store, a blacksmith shop, an adobe corral and Main Street. The first post office was established in 1873 and the town was renamed Roswell in honor of Van Smith's father.

NEW MEXICO MILITARY INSTITUTE
101 West College Boulevard
Roswell, New Mexico

The New Mexico Military Institute was established in 1891 and became a State (Territorial) School in 1893. Its purpose then and now is "for the education and training of the youth of this country with a mandate by law to be of as high a standard as like institutions in other states and territories of the United States."

New Mexico Military Institute is primarily an academic institution operating within the framework of a military environment. However, in spite of the fact that it is a school that prides itself on looking to the future, it must still deal with some holdovers from the past.

THE GHOSTS

The New Mexico Military Institute does not use the phonetic alphabet 'J' for Juliet for one of its troops for a very simple reason...it is believed to be cursed. Back in the 1800's when the school was still an all male military school in the frontier Juliet troop was on of the troops to go out and defend the school from Indians and other wild west characters. After one such excursion, no one from the Juliet troop survived.

Former students have reported that a tower with a clock was built in their honor and the letter 'J' has not been used as a unit designation since that time. However, to add another interesting dimension to this school, it is said that on some days when the sun is just right if you look up at the tower you can see faces in the rock of the boys who lost their lives defending their school looking back down at you.

I have also heard stories about shadowy figures being seen moving across the parade grounds in the early hours of the morning. There have also been stories told by former students about strange sounds and voices being heard in empty rooms.

THE PECAN FIELDS
Roswell, New Mexico

New Mexico is a state with an unusually large amount of urban legends and this next story may well all into that category. It seems to happen every Sunday during October, but if you drive down Country Club towards the pecan fields after midnight there is a little boy who runs across the street crying. If you listen you can hear the sounds of a little kid crying for help. If you call to him, he'll look over to you, but he continues his panicked run into the darkness in an attempt to escape some unseen danger. Additionally, if you look very carefully, you will see that the boy has no legs.

PUEBLO AUDITORIUM
3rd & Wyoming
Roswell Independent School District Administration Building
Roswell, New Mexico

The Pueblo Auditorium is located inside the Roswell Independent School District Administration Building. It is a rather modern structure The Auditorium is also well used as it is the home of the En Pointe Elite Dance Company. However, in spite of the activity and the relatively modern surroundings, there are still ghosts that intrude into our lives.

In the Pueblo Auditorium, there is an upstairs balcony where you can see a boy looking down at the activity going on below him. However, if you go up to the balcony, you will find that there is no one there.

CHAPTER THIRTY

RUIDOSO, NEW MEXICO

Ruidoso is a place where the Wild West was the real thing. Cattle barons, Apache warriors and Billy the Kid figured prominently in the history of the city and county.

When formed in 1869, Lincoln County accounted for one-fourth of the entire New Mexico Territory, sprawling over 29,000 square miles. It was the largest county in the United States.

Fort Stanton was built in 1859 to protect white settlers from Apaches (the fort is now a long-term care hospital and major employer in the county). Ranchers and farmers first settled on the low-lying prairies and along the Hondo River. Early tourists were attracted to the Ruidoso area because it offered a place to escape the desert heat.

The first county seat was a thriving village not far from the Bonito River called La Placita, renamed to Rio Bonito and renamed again to Lincoln to honor the president.

The county soon found itself part of Wild West history. The infamous Lincoln County War in 1878 transformed saddle hand Billy the Kid into an outlaw and folk hero.

Today, ranching still represents a vital industry in the county of the cattle barons, with 338 ranches or farms covering 1.9 million acres.

The Mescalero Apaches have turned their 460,000-acre reservation, which borders Ruidoso in Otero County, into the control center for several businesses. In 1963, the tribe took over the operation of Ski Apache Resort, a 750-acre ski area that in 1993-94 reported nearly 200,000 skier-days. The tribe also operates a casino and resort on the reservation along with a forestry products business.

With the coming of the railroad, Carrizozo became the county seat in 1909, a title it retains today, although Ruidoso is the largest town in the county. During the summer, when Ruidoso Downs Racetrack opens for a season of 68 race days, the community population swells to an estimated maximum population of about 35,000. In 1994, the track had an attendance of 236,225. The track features the world's richest quarter horse race, the All American Futurity, and also has added a casino.

Tourism and related enterprises are the cornerstones of the Ruidoso economy. Incorporated in 1945, the village is bordered by Lincoln National Forest. The beauty of the forested mountains, the mild summer weather and the ski opportunities in winter have ensured the community's popularity as a visitor's destination.

Ruidoso takes its name from the Spanish word that means noisy. It seems an appropriate choice. Settlers (both native and non-native) were inspired by the sound of the Rio Ruidoso rolling down the mountainside.

BONITA LAKE
Ruidoso, New Mexico

Bonita Lake is full of abandoned gold mines, in fact, before the flooding of the land and the forming of the lake, this area used to be a miners' paradise. When Bonita Lake was formed, the rising waters consumed an entire town which still sits abandoned beneath the lake waters.

In the camping areas around the lake you can still find many miners' carts, lanterns and other discarded items, much of it untouched. There is also a house on one part of the lake shore that many people camping in the area have reported seeing strange lights coming from as well hearing some very strange as sounds.

"I thought there were a bunch of kids goofing off" claimed one camper. "It sounded like a party with music, lots of people talking and gunfire." Later this camper discovered the only other people in the area were three adult campers and a border collie.

RUIDOSO DOWNS
Ruidoso, New Mexico

Eye witnesses report many strange activities in Hale Lake which is just outside of Ruidoso Downs. It is said that this is where a Settler, Indian dispute first took place. If you go there at night be sure to take friends. As you drive up the radio, the heater and anything electrical will not work on your car. Be prepared to stay the night.

If you drive down in the middle of the night the brakes on your car will not work. Though this is called Hale Lake, there is actually not a lake there, but rather a small pond.

Many people camping in the area have claimed to see faces in their campfires. Others have reported finding War Paint smeared on their vehicles through no culprit is ever found.

As if it is not odd enough that a number of vehicles fail their owners who enter the area after dark but then start up in the morning as if nothing is wrong there have been a lot of odd sights seen as well. Though there are no estates in the area, many report catching glimpses of illuminated Gates. Still others report seeing a man wearing all leather on horseback who seems intent on running out in front of their cars. However, even though many have thought that they ran over this man, when they look back they see him sitting on his horse staring after them.

However, in spite of all of the odd reports made by people who have tried to camp in the area, probably the weirdest part of this all are the bizarre dreams that everyone who camps around the lake reports having.

CHAPTER THIRTY-ONE

WATROUS, NEW MEXICO

Samuel B. Watrous was born in Connecticut, orphaned while still young and was sent to live with an uncle. Not happy having to rise early, do chores before breakfast and labor all day long, he left and joined a wagon train and headed for Taos, New Mexico. While there, he clerked at a store but soon caught the urge to try his luck at mining. He headed for San Pedro but found mining not to his liking and decided to earn his living as a storekeeper and farmer.

Watrous acquired some land in 1846 to start a farming and mercantile business. Over the years, the farm and business affairs of Watrous flourished and he became a respected member of the community. In 1879, it was learned the Santa Fe Railroad would build through the settlement. Watrous promptly donated land for the right-of-way, station and yards. When finished, he was totally surprised to the see the name WATROUS on the new station's name board. Railroad officials said it was the least they could do for such a public-spirited citizen of the community.

Today, the community that was known as Watrous is a ghost town.

THE RANCH
Watrous, New Mexico

There is an old ranch house near the community of Watrous that was once used as a relay station for the riders of the famous "Pony Express" during the 1800's. Even though the Pony Express is no more, apparently, there are still spirits of some of those riders who still continue to carry out their duties.

Residents of the house have reported waking to the sounds of a shot gun blast in the room in which they are sleeping even though they are sure that there is no one else in the house.

The residents of this old home have also seen a lady and a man in a horse drawn wagon riding over the hill near the house. However, when those that live there race up the hill after the couple, the field on the other side is empty. The couple vanishes as mysteriously as they came.

There are also cold spots near the fireplace even when there is a roaring fire burning on the hearth.

CHAPTER THIRTY-TWO

TRUTH OR CONSEQUENCES, NEW MEXICO

Truth or Consequences, population about 7500, is located on Interstate Highway 25 in the Rio Grande valley some 150 miles south of Albuquerque and 75 miles north of Las Cruces. Originally, the location was called Palomas Springs or Las Palomas after the palomas (doves) which frequented the cottonwood trees along the river. In 1914, the name, marked by the local post office, was changed to Hot Springs. (A village a few miles south is still called Las Palomas.)

By the 1940's, the name of the community was about to change again, a response this time to a publicity stunt by Ralph Edwards, the host of the popular long-running radio show called Truth or Consequences. Edwards had offered nationwide publicity to any city that would change its name to "Truth or Consequences." In a vote in 1950, a majority of the citizens of Hot Springs elected to answer Edwards' challenge, overriding the protests of some residents. In another vote, in 1964, an even larger majority chose to keep the name.

Truth or Consequences – "T or C" to most New Mexicans – lies just upstream from Elephant Butte Dam and the lake which makes the region an attraction to snowbirds, tourists and recreation seekers. It is bracketed by the Fra Cristóbal and Caballo ranges on the east and the Black Range on the west. As county seat, T or C serves agricultural and ranching interest.

Before Euro American settlers gave names to the location where T or C now stands, Native Americans bathed in the hot springs. Evidence of their presence can be seen near Ralph Edwards Park in rock outcrops which bear deep mortars once used by Indian women for grinding seeds into flour. Apaches were said to have used the springs for the curative powers. T or C's Geronimo Springs Museum honors T or C's prehistoric past.

The first Spanish colonist, Juan de Onate, passed through the area in 1598. Spanish-speaking people began to settle there by the middle of the 1800's. After the Civil War, the U. S. government established forts and maintained troops in the region, trying to make it safe for miners, ranchers and farmers flooding into New Mexico Territory and facing incessant Apache raids. The army forced several bands in the region, including the Warm Springs Apaches, onto reservations.

One of the most colorful characters was Lozen, an Apache woman said to have ridden as a warrior with her brother, Victorio, and later, with Geronimo himself. According to accounts, she fell in love with a Confederate deserter who had been sheltered by the Apaches. When a wagon train came along headed for California's gold fields, he left, breaking Lozen's heart. She never married, devoting herself instead to using her unusual powers to sense danger and heal her people.

T or C changed from a quiet health resort in 1916, when the Elephant Butte Dam was completed. About five miles south of T or C, the dam was built to contain flood waters and release it for irrigation along 200 miles of the lower Rio Grande valley. The dam created the largest lake in New Mexico. When the reservoir is filled to capacity, water backs up for 45 miles and creates some 200 miles of shoreline. The reservoir and Elephant Butte State Park are the destinations of boaters, wind surfers and fishermen from all over New Mexico and west Texas. On some holiday weekends, as many as 100,000 people enjoy the lake.

T or C is still known for its hot mineral baths, which are open year around. The relaxing and healing attributes of the baths are combined with a full course of related services, including Swedish massage, energy therapy, reflexology and ayurvedic science. Several lodges offer bed and mineral bath for the cost of a room. Renovations are under way for some of the older facilities. One facility under renovation, with a French touch, will be called the Sierra Grande Lodge, easily be the swankiest in T or C. The owners hope to draw customers from across the country and Europe to enjoy French cuisine and other amenities.

THE HOSPITAL
800 E. 9th Street
Truth or Consequences, New Mexico

Ask any hospital employee that has worked at Sierra Vista Hospital for any length of time, especially if they worked a night shift and they will tell you about a paranormal experience they have had. Unexplained events have become so common that staff almost expect something odd to happen.

This is an old hospital built in the early 1950's and as a result there tends to be a lot of sightings. Nurses will tell you that they will hear the sound of a baby crying a day before a baby will be delivered. There have been numerous times night shift staff will see ghosts moving about the floor out of the corner of their eye only to disappear when they turn to get a better look. Beds have raised and lowered by themselves without anyone at the helm operating the bed. Linen closet doors would open on their own as one would pass by.

When the hospital first opened nuns operated it and would cook brownies for the patients. The nuns are long gone and do not work in the hospital any more, however there have been several sightings of nuns wearing traditional habits cooking in the little kitchen area in the hall on the second floor.

It is also said that once in a while the smell of brownies cooking can be detected, but investigation will reveal that no one is cooking brownies!

A new hospital is scheduled to be built soon.

CHAPTER THIRTY-THREE

MESILLA, NEW MEXICO

Old Mesilla, also called La Mesilla, is a century-and-a-half year old adobe village in the Rio Grande valley just west of Las Cruces, New Mexico. At one time it was even the county seat for Dona Ana County. I believe they must like the old plaza and gazebo, the San Albino church's stained glass windows, the antiques, the Southwestern craft and fashion shops, the art galleries, the well-stocked regional book store, the restaurants, the local tavern and that house of dietary sin, the J. Eric Chocolatier store.

This ancient town lies beside the historic Camino Real, or Royal Road, which connected Mexico's capitols with Santa Fe for almost three centuries, from 1598 to 1881. Spanish and, later, Mexican and Anglo colonist and freight caravans camped in the vicinity, watered livestock in the nearby river, grazed the animals in the surrounding grassy bottomlands, cooked and sang and slept and sometimes fought around evening fires, and, in the later days, watched warily for Mescalero Apaches.

Mesilla became permanently part of the United States in the mid 1800's, after the United States appropriated western Texas and the Southwest – a region roughly the size of Western Europe – in the course of the Mexican/American War and its aftermath. Mesilla, one of the most important settlements in the new territory, serviced Camino Real freight caravans, fought the Mescalero, supplied the U. S. Army's nearby Fort Fillmore, entertained Butterfield and San Antonio-to-San Diego stage coach passengers, endured Union and Confederate occupations, and served as territorial capitol.

After the Civil War, Mesilla emerged as the commercial, transportation and social center for the region. It attracted legends like Kit Carson and Pancho Villa, promoters like Albert Fountain, gunfighters like Sheriff Pat Garrett and outlaw Billy the Kid, and hustlers like future Langtry, Texas, judge Roy Bean. It staged fandangos (dances), bullfights, cockfights, theater and some pretty entertaining gunfights.

Mesilla lost its place in the sun in 1881, when the railroad bypassed the village in favor of nearby Las Cruces. Mesilla became the perfect place for a community of ghosts.

THE GHOSTS

THE FOUNTAIN THEATER
Mesilla, New Mexico

The Fountain Theater is believed to be haunted by the spirit of a long-dead, frustrated actress. The theater is located just off the southeast corner of the plaza, on the site where the Confederates set up their regional military command during the Civil War.

The Albert Fountain family built the theater on the site as a vaudeville house in 1905. It now serves as a motion picture theater, showing independent, art, classic and foreign films. Unlike a typical theater, the Fountain Theater has rickety wooden seats, café tables and chairs, and historical wall murals. It offers patrons not only popcorn, soft drinks and candy, but coffee and pastries and the occassional "spirit" as well.

LA POSTA DE MESILLA RESTAURANT
Mesilla, New Mexico

La Posta, as it is generally referred to be locals, is one of the oldest structures in Mesilla and an entry on the national register of historic buildings, is a good place for ghosts. During its long history it has served as a way station for Butterfield's stagecoach line, which failed; a business building for Sam and Roy Bean's short-haul freighting and passenger service, which failed; and a lodge known as the Corn Exchange Hotel, which welcomes such illustrious guests as Kit Carson, Pancho Villa and other famous people stayed and where the owner died of the plague.

THE GHOSTS

It has long been said that the La Posta de Mesilla Restaurant is haunted. Employees talk about the ghosts smashing glasses, moving chairs, opening and closing doors, throwing clocks, chilling the air, exuding sulfur smells, shoving customers. Sometimes, they even scare the dickens out of the caged parrots at the restaurant's entrance.

GALLERI AZUL
Mesilla, New Mexico

The building that now houses the Galleri Azul was once the home of one of the earliest Jewish families in the area. There are a number of stories that the ghost of a child who died in one of the back bedrooms of this home a long time ago still haunts the scene of his death.

THE DOUBLE EAGLE RESTAURANT
Mesilla, New Mexico

The Double Eagle is not only a first class restaurant, but it is also said to be the home of the most famous ghosts in Old Mesilla. The Restaurant is named for the 1850's era 20-dollar gold coin, the "Double Eagle," which had the image of the national bird stamped on each side. Originally the territorial-style home of the wealthy Maese family, who owned an import/export business, the Double Eagle has also served as the governor's headquarters and as a military hospital during the Civil War occupation of Mesilla.

The historic old building has always exuded a Victorian-era elegance, which the restaurant embodies to this day. Built around a courtyard, the Double Eagle is a reminder of a more elegant time long gone, but not forgotten. It is possible to forget ones troubles while sitting within its darkly paneled walls and pressed tin/gold leaf ceilings burnished with age, shimmering with elegant nineteenth century French chandeliers, ornate mirrors and antiques. History is all around you at the Double Eagle.

Double Eagle Entry

Upon passing through the post-Civil War, 1,000-pound cast iron and gilded gates, patrons are surrounded by a vast assortment of antiques. The divider separating the entry and the Imperial Bar has two rolled-glass panels etched with water lilies and cattails, framed with oak-turned columns and spindle fretwork. The large cherry and walnut German cupboard is in the style of Empire Revival and has a French polished veneer finish with a pullout serving tray. The 12-foot gold-leafed pier mirror is carved with a shell and acanthus leaf pattern. A shadowbox protecting the ornate solid gold-framed print of a reclining "Dame with Pussy" is American, circa 1930, numbered 902 and signed V. Curws.

Imperial Bar

The 30-foot hand-carved oak and walnut Eastlake style bar is framed with four Corinthian columns in gold leaf. The detail of the back bar is illuminated by two Imperial French floral Corones: each five feet tall, with 23 lighted brass flowers, 10 of which have blue Lalique crystal rosette shades. The antique brass foot rail was originally from the Billy the Kid Saloon. Hanging above the bar are two magnificent classic French Baccarat chandeliers, measuring seven feet by three feet.

The large museum-quality pastel, "A Nude Woman with Her Dog," by Georges Lefevre, is in the Rubenesque style from France, circa 1910. The long silk screen of the "Girl Carrying Flowers" and the oil painting of the young "Woman in Green Playing Tambourine" are of Turkish influence, circa 1905-1920. "The Selling of the Slave Girl," signed by A. Salazar in 1916, has been in the owner's family collection since 1923. The pastel of a "Young Girl Embracing Her Mother" is European and a Greek revival style.

The Louis XV-style mirror is of hand-carved walnut in a floral and laffice design. The ceiling in this room and many of the other rooms is highly decorative pressed tin, accented with 18 karat gold.

Lew Wallace Room

The room to the right of the main entry is named after Territorial Governor Lew Wallace, who was the author of the novel "Ben Hur." He denied Billy the Kid's plea for a pardon, which led to the "Kid's" jailbreak from the Lincoln County Courthouse. This room and the adjacent owner's office are part of the original structure.

The furniture bears Victorian and Eastlake influence. The major oil painting on the south wall, "Sea Nymphs on Rocks," is from the famed Hudson River School and is signed by W. L. Judson, circa 1910. The Flemish oil painting of a street scene is signed by Wilfred Jentin, circa 1880. The large oval oil painting of "Lewis and Clark's Discovery of the West" is very unusual. The goddess "Diana," signed by F. Bauer, is circa 1910. The 1857 map of New Mexico and Arizona shows Mesilla as the capital of Arizona, with both Territories extending to California.

Gadsden Patio

The Gadsden Patio commemorates the Gadsden Purchase, which was signed on the Mesilla Plaza. In 1849, one year after the Mexican-American War ended, gold was discovered in California. Jefferson Davis, Secretary of State under President Franklin Pierce, appealed to the President for the exclusive right to extend his Southern Railroad Company to California. The only passable route, because of mountains to the north, crossed the Rio Grande River near Mesilla, which belonged to Mexico at the time.

Secretary Davis persuaded President Pierce to recall James Gadsden, Ambassador to England. Gadsden lived in Mesilla for the next three years negotiating the purchase of the land extending from the Rio Grande to California. On Dec. 30, 1853, the Mexican Flag was lowered and the 32-star American Flag was raised, declaring this land to be part of the United States.

The signed Gadsden Purchase, a fifteen-million-dollar agreement, was then sent to the two Congresses for ratification in the summer of 1854. It is believed that Mexican President Santa Ana had his soldiers ambush the courier, stealing the fifteen-million-dollar draft.

The seven-foot carved stone fountain is surrounded by Areca Palms, Springerie Ferns and Bougainvillea trailing from the cathedraled atrium. Four marble statues of women are from the Greek and Roman Revival periods and are late 19th century. The alabaster bust on the east wall shows a female wearing a bronze gladiator helmet, circa 1900. The Sequoia redwood architectural medallion is a large piece of Victorian ginger bread from the Gump Mansion in San Francisco.

The three Library of Congress archive proofs of the Gadsden Purchase -- the only known copies in New Mexico -- are mounted in circa 1850 ornate nickel silver frames. A rare 1849 map of "The Frontiers of Utah and New Mexico" depicts the Gadsden Purchase area of southern New Mexico, including Mesilla. A pair of gilded bronze torches, with frosted crystal flame shades, lights the entrance to the Maxmilian Dining Room.

Porfirio Diaz Salon

The entry to Peppers Restaurant, a vista to Southwestern Dining, was named for the President of Mexico (1876-1911). The cowhide-covered Empire sofa and snakeskin-covered Grecian Revival chairs are outstanding pieces of Southwestern decor. The wrought iron chandelier is an especially fine piece of Spanish Toledo work and is complimented by the Mesilla blacksmith gates. The window into the Juarez Room was an original doorway with hand-hewn lintel, now much too low to use for a door. The turquoise lizard-covered Queen Anne chairs and ebony tables accent the Southwest Dining decor of pottery duck, fish ladies and hand-carved pigs. The Indian pottery and graphic motifs painted on

210\SPIRITS OF THE BORDER

the floors and French doors are examples of award-winning designs by Karen Wood.

Benito Room

Mexico revolted against Spain and won the 1821 Revolution, claiming most of western America. Texans' battle with General Santa Ana at the Alamo in 1836 was one of the many subsequent disagreements between the United States and Mexico. In 1846, the United States declared War on Mexico. The U.S. won, and in 1848 signed the Treaty of Guadalupe Hidalgo, which ended the War. From this treaty, more than half of the Republic of Mexico was deeded to the United States, including the present states of California, Arizona, New Mexico, Texas, Utah and Nevada.

The International Boundary was established 12 miles north of present Las Cruces. The new border placed Mesilla in Mexico and the large town of Dona Aña in the United States. Wanting to remain Mexican citizens, many of the residents of Doña Ana moved to Mesilla, doubling the population overnight.

Named President of Mexico in 1857, Benito Juarez led the Liberal Mexicans in La Reforma against the French-supported regime of Maximillian. This room's ceiling is of original vigas crossed with latillas, which in some areas are covered with plaster. The New Mexico colonial chairs were copied from a 350-year-old museum piece and are hand-carved. The Mexican folk art pieces decorating the Juarez Room represent the release of bad dreams and evil thoughts. This symbolism and humor still cause these fifteen hand painted clay pieces to be highly sought by collectors.

Carlotta Salon

Folklore enhances the hidden Carlotta Salon. In the 1850's, the restaurant was the home of an affluent Mexican family who hired a maid. The family had a teenage son who fell in love with this maid, much to the distress of his mother, who had much better things planned for her son.

Love persisted, however, and his mother came home one afternoon to find the two lovers entwined. Enraged at what she saw, the mother grabbed a pair of scissors from the chest of drawers and stabbed the maid to death. In the process, the mother mistakenly stabbed her son, as he stepped to save his lover.

It is said that the ghosts of the young lovers inhabit the Carlotta Salon to this day. The ghosts make their presence known in many ways. Even though modern motion detectors are armed at night, broken glasses and tipped-over chairs are found by morning. There are two upholstered Victorian arm chairs in the room that are rarely used. The cut velvet fabric, however, is worn in the shape of human bodies, one larger than the other, but both small by today's standards.

The Carlotta Salon was named for Marie Charlotte, daughter of the King of Belgium, who was born in 1840 and died in 1927. She was the wife of

Maximillian, Archduke of Austria, and the Empress of Mexico from 1864 to 1867. An oil portrait of her holding her small white Maltese dog dominates the room. The two oval portraits of Señor and Señora Maese, the owners of the home, are of the type frequently commissioned by families of that era. The heavy glided brass and cut crystal lamp once lighted the boudoir or famed red-light madam 'Silver City Millie."

A framed Las Cruces Sun News article of the "Young Lover Ghosts" and a photograph believed to be depicting the presence of the ghost lovers are displayed in the salon.

Maximillian Room

Ferdinand Maximillian Joseph, Archduke of Austria, was made Emperor of Mexico in 1864 by Napoleon III, who hoped to establish a French satellite in the Western Hemisphere. The opposition of the Liberal Mexicans, U. S. protests and political troubles in France led Napoleon to abandon Maximillian. After the withdrawal of the French, Belgian and Austrian forces, Maximillian was captured and shot by Mexican leader Benito Juarez.

The room's three Baccarat crystal chandeliers, measuring three feet wide and seven feet tall, are in the classic French shape with 18 brass arms containing more than 1,000 hand-cut lead crystals. They are beautiful and add luster to the 18- and 24-karat gold pressed-metal, awe-inspiring ceiling. The magnificent ceiling was painstakingly leafed by hand with six-inch squares of gold. The music balcony has an 18-karat gold-leafed brass railing cast in the lyre pattern with wrought gilded spandrels. The imposing balcony support structure of California Sequoia giant redwood is hand-carved black Bear heads and acanthus leaves gilded in 18-karat gold.

The stained-glass panels over the double doors are in the Greek Revival style of Tiffany, with scrolls and ribbons surrounding the enameled center medallion. The 11 gold leaf French pier mirrors, are ornately carved in the Greek Revival style. It is most unusual to find a collection of this size.

The draperies are a French documentary stripe in silk damask. The huge portrait of King George is in the Louis XIV style. He is dressed in a long robe of ermine with black tails, traditionally worn only by royalty. It is very rare to find a collection of antique Queen Anne chairs of this magnitude. The five round tables are fine antiques from the Victorian, Eastlake and Greek Revival periods.

Isabella Ballroom

Queen Isabella sold her jewels to finance Columbus' voyage of discovery to the New World. Don Cristóbal Colon de Carvajal, of Madrid, Spain, the direct descendant of Christopher Columbus, was honored in the Isabella

Ballroom in 1992, at a Grand Banquet commemorating the 500th anniversary of Columbus' voyage to America.

A large, full-length oil painting of a young girl in red with a doll is an important example of primitive American art, circa 1830. If you look closely, the mother's face is painted on the doll, which was a common technique for traveling artists of the time. An equal to this painting can be found only in museums. The portraits of James Gadsden and Mexican General Manuel Diaz, the authors of the Gadsden Purchase, hang on either side of the French doors. The portraits of a woman with a lace cap, a lady with flowers in her hair and a lady with a lace collar are of the Philadelphia or Baltimore School, circa 180.

The Mexican-colonial oil painting of the Virgin de Guadalupe, the patron saint of Mexico, with three angels above the flames of Hades, is circa 1800's. "The Mediterranean Harbor" scene and the "Sailing Ships at Sunset" are European 19th century. The oil portrait of a young girl in a blue dress is a European primitive.

The very valuable 17th-century Italian Corinthian columns lintel imposed by dental and bead molding, acanthus leaves and flowers, have a weathered-gray gilt finish. The rare, early 19th-century round mirror is framed in 18-karat gold-leafed bead and point molding.

THE GHOSTS

The most famous haunting comes from a doomed love affair. La Senora Carlota Maese, haughty, snobbish, consumed with ambition, flaunted her family's wealth, power and prestige in the community. She planned for her eldest son, Armando, to marry into the aristocracy of Mexico City. "La Senora Maese tiene las estrellas en los ojos," said the women of the village. "Mrs. Maese has stars in her eyes."

Young Armando, however, had cast his eye on a different star, a beautiful teenage servant girl, Inez, whose long black shock of hair hung to her waist. All Mesilla whispered of young couple's love, their "secret" rendezvous.

La Senora learned of the tryst. Infuriated, she discharged Inez, ordered her to stay away from the home and Armando. You must remember, she said to Armando, your station in life, the reputation of your family, the aristocracy of Mexico.

Soon afterward, La Senora left town but returned earlier than anticipated from her trip. She discovered the young couple embraced in Armando's bedroom, at the southwest corner of the courtyard. Insane with rage, she stumbled from the room, out into the courtyard. Her hand fell on a pair of stiletto-like scissors. On a rampage, she flew back into the room, slashing with the scissors. "No, Mama, no!!!" screamed Armando. She stabbed young Inez in the breast. Wildly, she struck again, this time stabbing her son, who had tried to shield his love. Inez died cradled in Armando's arms, his kisses on her lips, his hands stroking her long black hair. Armando himself died three days later. From that moment until her death, La Senora Carlota Maese never spoke another word. The spirits of Armando and Inez never left the room, now a gracious and cozy dining room called the Carlota Salon. They still whisper each other's name. Inez' perfume mysteriously fills the air. The two light candles, leaving them burning on the dining table. Mischievously, they sometimes move furniture or shatter wine glasses. They rest in a pair of overstuffed chairs at the corners, leaving the arms and seat cushions slightly worn.

Armando and Inez have their room at the Double Eagle, but a poltergeist has the run of the rest of the place, especially the long, heavy, carved wood bar, which is illuminated with sparkling chandeliers. He – I presume that the poltergeist is a "he," this sounds just like one of us "he's" – flings carving knives across the kitchen floor, rakes wine glasses from shelves, slides dishes across diners' tables, slams doors in empty rooms, shoves furniture from appointed places, mimics voices of employees, and whispers the names of patrons. Cali Tellez, a retired county sheriff's deputy and a good friend, said he responded several times when burglar alarms went off in the Double Eagle. One night, he said, he and other deputies found knives and cooking utensils scattered all across the kitchen floor.

PEPPERS CAFÉ
Mesilla, New Mexico

Peppers is a Santa Fe-style Southwestern Cafe established within the Double Eagle Restaurant. Peppers was developed in 1986 by owner C. W. Ritter in response to customers' requests. With the large number of tourists visiting Mesilla in casual clothes, Ritter realized some people felt they were not dressed properly to enjoy elegance of the Double Eagle.

To meet these demands, Ritter stripped a section of the large building back to the basics -- adobe walls and wooden slat flooring. Even a section of the original layered roof of cottonwood vigas (tree trunks), latillas (branches) and bark was uncovered. From this original base, he constructed a less formal eatery for the many customers that flock to Mesilla.

Perhaps also uncovered during this time frame was the spirit that sometime appears to startled diners. It is a man who one moment is there and the next moment he is gone.

BILLY THE KID GIFT SHOP
Mesilla, New Mexico

At the southeast corner of the plaza, can be found the Billy the Kid Gift Shop. The building that houses this interesting establishment was once the Mesilla courthouse and jail. It was in this historic old building in 1881 that a jury convicted Billy the Kid of ambushing and killing Sheriff William Brady up in Lincoln, New Mexico, and within these same four walls that Judge Warren Bristol sentenced Billy to "be hanged by the neck until his body is dead."

There are some who claim that the spirit of Billy the Kid moves items around inside the gift shop that bares his name. A few former employees also claim to have caught a glimpse of someone in western wear who seems to merge with the walls when attempts are made to corner him.

EL PATIO CANTINA
Mesilla, New Mexico

On the southwest corner of the plaza is found the El Patio Cantina, site of another business once operated by Sam and Roy Bean in the 1850s and 1860s, This was thought to be an especially good spot for a business since it was immediately next to the Butterfield stagecoach line's regional offices, now the El Patio Restaurant.

Sam was the county sheriff but he also ran several businesses in Mesilla. Roy, wanted for stabbing a man in California, had turned up in Mesilla broke and bedraggled, and gone to work for Sam. Sheriff Bean left town for a few days on business, leaving Roy in charge of the El Patio Cantina. Roy knew that Mesilla's citizens kept valuables in the cantina's safe, one of the few in the community. When Sheriff Bean returned to Mesilla, he found little brother Roy had cleaned out the town's safe and fled for Texas. He would eventually land in Langtry, Texas, proclaiming himself judge and the Law West of the Pecos.

There are stories of unexplained sounds and voices that seem to come fro the shadows that whisper your name.

OLD MESILLA CEMETERY
Mesilla, New Mexico

South of the plaza, lays the village cemetery. According to legend here can be found La Llorona, the Weeping Woman, one of the most famed ghosts of Mexico and the Hispanic Southwest, It is said that this specter haunts the Mesilla Cemetery, sometimes scarring the bejesus out of school kids who run among the graves at night on a dare.

GRIGGS HOUSE
Mesilla, New Mexico

In 1850, the Mesilla Civil Colony Land Grant was established by the Mexican government to give settlers in Mesilla land ownership. The grant was later honored by the United States Government. The Civil Colony Land Grant was established to govern the entire town and to distribute the common lands. Father Ramon Ortiz was the Commissioner of Lands in 1851 and in 1853, Guadalupe Miranda filled the office. The Civil Colony Grant Board does not exist today. The Town of Mesilla was incorporated in 1861. In 1882, the year after the railroad was constructed; Mesilla lost its position as the county seat, which it had held since 1855. The county seat was transferred to Las Cruces. In 1958, Mesilla became re-incorporated and became governed by a mayor and Board of Trustees.

The wrangle of politics caused a situation unlike any other known, for the residents of La Mesilla took their politics as seriously as Texas regarded cattle and the branding iron. The fight between the Republicans and the Democrats was called "battle of the bands." It began in August, 1861 and spread with astounding rapidity. Citizens were thrown into confusion. Many, panic stricken with the sudden outbreak, took up arms, or ran in every direction seeking safety for their families.

The Republicans gathered at the house of Johnny Lemon; the Democrats met in the Plaza where they listened to Padre Gallegos and other loyal Democrats warn them of the fearful fiends that would ravage and devastate the village.

General Gregg arrived with a full detachment of armed-to-the-teeth soldiers from Fort McRae after Washington had been informed of impending trouble between the two factions. They camped in those lands cut by erosion into odd shaped hills with a few level places near the prairie lands for several days. The temperature was hot enough to melt ball bearings. Perhaps their presence avoided trouble. In any case, when it became evident that matters would be settled without gunplay, the General took his troops and galloped back to Fort McRae.

No sooner had the troops disappeared over the horizon than danger hung over La Mesilla like a vast funeral pall. The Democrats decided to antagonize their inhospitable neighbors by marching their band around the Plaza singing a song they knew would irritate the Republicans. The words were sung to the tune of Marching Though Georgia.

The Republicans retaliated by lining up their own band, led by Antonio Garcia playing heartily on his "flica" horn. They marched around the Plaza in one direction while the Democrats marched in the opposing direction, playing and singing just a loudly as their enemies. When they met at the end of the Plaza, the result was as volatile as a lighted match thrown into a can of gasoline.

The riot started with shouts of insults and curses and eventually erupted into flashes of sabers and revolvers but before the sun set over this new and growing town, ten men lay dead in the streets, their wives and children rendered homeless without a bread winner. The dusty street in front of Grigg's store was strewn with forty bleeding, wounded men. One individual lost his eyesight during the skirmish. Another had to have a leg amputated when gangrene set in and threatened his life.

Thinking fast, Old Man Griggs sent one of his clerks galloping hell-bent-for-leather on his fine Kentucky gelding, to overtake General Gregg and his troops. The general and his troops galloped the hard-packed soil back to La Mesilla with breakneck speed, but the damage had already been done.

A detachment of troops was left in town to discourage any further outbreak and the town quieted down. The dead were buried. Families rendered destitute depended on the charity of their neighbors. Both Republicans and Democrats suffered; none escaped without experiencing a loss of some kind.

La Mesilla was in the third judicial district and no judge was appointed to the bench at this time; so no one on either side was ever tried for murder.

Among La Mesilla's eminent visitors was Lew Wallace, whose greatest fame actually came from his novel, Ben Hur, which he wrote while governor of the Territory of New Mexico. Another was Kit Carson, famous Indian Scout and guide. Carson was a familiar sight on the dusty streets of La Mesilla where he carved his name on a tree that was carelessly cut down by a thoughtless resident and used for firewood. It is said that Carson ate regularly in the old La Posta Inn, a thick-walled fortress against rampaging Indians.

The house was built in the early 1800's and is now used as a storage area for honey which is produced near the house.

THE GHOSTS

Several sightings of the apparition of Old Mrs. Griggs have been reported in the front bathroom of the house. Here a young woman saw her reflected in the mirror while she was cleaning up the area. Footsteps and unusual odors are often encountered in the kitchen area. Sounds of objects being moved about are also common.

CHAPTER THIRTY-FOUR

EAGLES NEST, NEW MEXICO

Eagles Nest is located in the Moreno Valley in the midst of the beautiful Sangre de Cristo Mountains. Nestled between the states two highest peaks - Baldy Mountain (12,441 feet) and Wheeler Peek (13,161 feet), it sits at the junction of US Hwy 64 and State Hwy 38. High above sea level, at 8,300 feet, the village rests on the western slope of Baldy Mountain, an area rich in Gold Rush history.

Before the miners, the area was called home by the Ute and Jicarrilla Apache Indians who roamed the area in search of game and golden feathers for ceremonial worship. When Elizabethtown, just 5 and 1/2 miles north, was in its heyday, the Eagle Nest area was utilized mostly for ranching and farming.

In 1873 Charles and Frank Springer founded the CS Ranch on the banks of the Cimarron River and in 1907 they applied for a permit to build the Eagle Nest Dam. It was almost 10 years before the Springers could hire the engineering firm of Bartlett and Ranney of San Antonio, Texas to design and build the dam. Finally, in 1916 construction on the dam was begun and was completed in 1918 to store the surplus waters of the Cimarron River for power plants, mining and irrigation. Most of the labor for building the dam was provided by the Taos Pueblo Indians. The largest privately constructed dam in the United States, the concrete structure is 400 feet wide, stands 140 feet above the river bed, and is 9.5 feet thick at its crest and 45.2 feet thick at its base. Supposedly, eagles built nests on the sides of the new dam and that's how it got its name.

The Eagle Nest Dam, completed in 1918, is the largest privately constructed dam in the United States. The dam created the Eagle Nest Lake which varies between 1,500 and 3,000 surface acres, depending upon weather cycles. Surrounded by rolling pasture and stunning mountains, the fishermen began to arrive when the lake was stocked with trout. Along with the fishermen, entrepreneurs also arrived, building businesses and transforming the quiet farming community into a tourist mecca, providing entertainment to the visiting cowboys, fishermen and other tourists.

One of the biggest industries was cutting and selling ice from the lake. T.D. Neal hired men to drive out upon the lake and cut block ice that was stored in ice houses filled with sawdust. Jobs were scarce in the area and many families survived the winters by ice cutting and trapping.

In the 1920's illegal gambling was introduced to the area. Eagle Nest became a popular spot along the road from Santa Fe to Raton where politicians and other travelers attended the horse races. A favorite stop over for the dignitaries, they were said to have caused quite a ruckus with their gambling, drinking and dancing.

In 1927, Walter Gant, an oilman from Oklahoma hired a business man by the name of William B. Tyer to oversee the construction of the grandest resort that Eagle Nest had ever seen -- the Eagle Nest Lodge. Bill Tyer lived in a cabin on the Gant property and oversaw the many details of building the luxurious lodge. When it was completed, Bill Tyer stayed on to manage the Eagle Nest Lodge, which featured 12 rooms, a lounge, a restaurant, horseback riding, fishing, and hunting expeditions for the many travelers who stopped to enjoy its magnificent view of Eagle Nest Lake. Considered the finest lodge for miles, it soon expanded to include a guest annex that featured five studio units with their own bathrooms and kitchenettes. They also connected the main building to the Casa Loma via a walkway/lounge they called the Loafer's Lounge.

The local saloons heartedly welcomed the travelers, rolling slot machines out upon the boardwalk early in the morning to entice the gamblers. Judge Neblett, for whom the Colin Neblett Wildlife Area is named, was a frequent visitor, as well as several governors. Though gambling was illegal, it was obviously overlooked by the politicians. In fact, it has been said by several of the locals, that when illegal gambling was first introduced to Eagle Nest in the 1920s, that the local Sheriff owned many of the slot machines in Eagle Nest, Red River and Colfax County. However, since we first published this story in the summer of 2003, we have since heard from Jerry Ficklin, a local historian and writer, who once lived in Eagle Nest and spent many summers there between the years of 1945 and 1960, that this "tidbit" is nothing more than a legend with no documented support.

The El Monte Hotel (now the Laguna Vista), as well as Doughbelly's Cafe (now the building that houses Julio's,) The Gold Pan, and the Eagle Nest Lodge offered roulette and gaming tables, as well as slot machines. Slot machines were also found in many of the stores.

Eagle Nest was in its heyday during the 1930's, with disputes often resulting in shots fired back and forth across Main Street. Reportedly one saloon owner, along the road that travels north from Eagle Nest to Idlewild, was known to provide free wine to those who came through its doors. The free pouring wine would inevitably lead to fights and discord among the rowdy customers, which the saloon "advertised" as free entertainment.

THE LAGUNA VISTA SALOON
Eagles Nest, New Mexico

Locals call the Laguna Vista Saloon, built in 1898, the "Guney". The El Monte, as it was originally called, was allegedly built with stolen railroad ties, which are still visible in some of the rooms. A would-be innkeeper transported the petrified railroad ties from Ute Park to Elizabethtown for two summers, but when he returned after the winter, the railroad ties were missing and a new hotel had been built in Therma, which later changed its name to Eagle Nest. Behind the original saloon were a 17-foot deep hand dug well and several icehouses.

The El Monte was one of the busiest saloons in the 1920's and 30's when the politicians stopped over on their way to the horse races in Raton, New Mexico to partake of the many roulette, gaming tables and slot machines offered in the saloons, inns, and businesses of Eagle Nest. It was sometime during this period that the El Monte's name was changed to the Laguna Vista Lodge and was operated by a couple named Gene and Pearl Wilson. At this time, the Wilsons often had to protect their gambling profits when transporting them from the saloon to their living quarters, by arming themselves with guns.

In the early 1950's, Bob and Edith Sullivan purchased the property from the Wilson's, leasing the restaurant to Walter Ragsdales, who operated it for several years. As Eagle Nest Lake's popularity began to grow with the tourists, the Sullivan's advertised for college girls to help staff the lodge, restaurant, and saloon, as the small village of Eagle Nest could not provide the staffing needed for the popular tourist destination*. In 1964, the "new" hotel was built next to the original hotel for additional guests.

In 1971, Bert Clemens bought the property from the Sullivans and continues to operate it to this day. Bob and Edith Sullivan's son, Robert, stayed on in Eagle Nest for many years and was honored for his 25+ years as fire chief, councilor and mayor. Edith Sullivan, who operated the Laguna Vista for some twenty years, was honored as the Grand Marshall of the July 4th parade in 2003. Unfortunately, Mrs. Sullivan passed away on May 19, 2004.

So, does this old hotel and saloon have ghostly visitors similar to those at the St James Hotel in Cimarron, New Mexico, just a few miles down the road? Mr. Clemens says "yes," though he has never personally encountered them. At one point, a psychic visited the property who counted at least 22 spirits lingering around the place. One employee reported to Mr. Clemens, that while she was in the kitchen she heard the vacuum running in the dining room, but when she went to investigate no one was there and the vacuum was sitting still and silent.

The current manager, Jim, also indicates that eerie things happen, such as the piano in the dining room sometimes plays when no one is there, and a dining table chair is pulled up next to the piano. The staff will replace the chair next to one of the dining tables only to find it later back in front of the piano again.

Customers and staff have reported that a woman in dance-hall dress often appears, and then vanishes toward the site of the hidden staircase. This spirit is said be that of a woman on her honeymoon with her husband, enjoying a stay at the hotel. Her husband ventured out one day to go hunting and never returned. The distraught young woman was left stuck and destitute and was said to have become a saloon girl in order to provide for herself. Supposedly, it is her spirit that lingers at the hotel in search of her long lost husband.

An old staircase, which led from the Hotel Lobby to the upstairs rooms, has been boarded up. Most often the Ghost of Guney disappears at the site where this staircase used to be.

In talking with a former employee of the Laguna Vista, Kristi Dukes, who was a cook in the restaurant in 1999, she stated that she encountered several spooky visits from a spirit that is said to have once been a saloon girl in the old lodge. According to Kristi, both her and her mother Jane, who also worked in the restaurant, would often encounter these visits whenever the music they were listening to in the kitchen was anything other than classic rock or country music.

When Kristi, who often liked to listen to Rap, would change the music, strange things would occur. On one such occasion a marble rolling pin was thrown at Kristi, on other occasions pots and pans would fall off of the walls. Once, when odd things were happening, Jane asked Kristi to turn off the music but when she switched the stereo to the "off" position, the music continued to play. She then unplugged the stereo and, though it had no batteries, the music played on. Frightened, the two left at the end of the evening only to return the following day to a silent stereo.

The Laguna Vista Restaurant Dining Room.

It is in this room, which was once the hotel lobby that held the hidden staircase to the upstairs rooms, that the ghost is most often encountered. The spookiest story actually occurred when Kristi brought her daughter Rayni, who was 2 years old at the time, to work one day. She had placed little jingle bells on her daughter's shoes so that she could keep track of her while she was working. Suddenly, Rayni walked into the kitchen very gently and slowly. Kristi said she looked very odd and when she asked Rayni what was wrong, Rayni replied, "the lady told me to stop making noise". When Kristi asked Rayni where the lady was, Rayni led her mother into the dining room and pointed at "someone" saying "that lady." Kristi saw no one but Rayni insisted that her mother remove the bells from her shoes.

The locals say that the hotel caught fire about twenty years ago and closed, and that's about all they say. There's no doubt that the old hotel caught fire, because there are obvious signs of fire damage in two different locations at the old hotel. But, the question remains -- when?

And, was the fire the cause of the closing? At least one person has said that a later fire was started in a second location, probably by vagrants living in the old lodge. But, still neither fire has succeeded in demolishing this once wonderful luxury resort.

Just outside the front door, the lake beckoned the guests for fishing and boating, and to the right, are the remains of a man-made pool and a garden, as well as what appears to be stables. Several outbuildings are housed on the property, including private cabins and a caretaker's home.

So, what happened to this place? No one seems to know though it is said that when questioned on resident said that both his mother and aunt worked there, but they would not talk about what happened. However, at least one person from Angel Fire speculated that the place had become somewhat of a speakeasy with all manner of vices including gambling and prostitution and that was the reason the locals were reluctant to talk about it. However, this is just rumor and speculation with no basis in fact from anyone associated with the old lodge.

JULIO'S RESTAURANT
Eagles Nest, New Mexico

Another spirit is said to reside at Julio's across the street. Now a restaurant, Julio's was once another popular gambling spot in Early Eagle Nest days. Supposedly, a woman resided next door to Julio's who was said to dislike men. Stories abound about pots and pans being thrown about in the restaurant and items are often moved from one place to another. Men appear to be her favorite target, as she plays pranks on many of them that come through what was once her front door.

CHAPTER THIRTY-FIVE

WHITE OAKS, NEW MEXICO

White Oaks was a boom town as a direct result of the gold and coal found in the surrounding mountains. The dramatic rise from a tent-city to a bustling, thriving, territorial New Mexican town of 2,500 almost overnight is a prime indication of man's attraction to gold. The fact that White Oaks was located in the middle of nowhere did not prevent hordes of prospectors, businessmen, and an occasional outlaw from making his way into the area that became the richest in New Mexico. All told, the mines of White Oaks yielded more pure gold than any other in the United States. Still, this could not prevent the eventual "petering out" of the gold supply, which, coupled with the lack of a railroad spur, spelled doom for White Oaks. These facts alone drove the inhabitants from the town they had created and loved, but they never erased their memories, a fact that makes White Oaks remain alive in the memories of many to this day.

The area around White Oaks is a tough climate. Though game was abundant the ground is both dry and unforgiving. The small stream, located two and a half miles from the actual town site, gave the name to the community because of the abundance of white oak trees on its banks. This is the only surface water available in the area, making thirst a constant danger.

The area was first known to the Piros Indians, who made use of the large numbers of antelope and deer. The Piros were eventually forced to surrender the location to the Apaches, who were semi-nomadic in their lifestyle. Like the Piros before, the Apaches found the area abundant with game.

The first European contact in the area was by members of Don Juan de Onate's expedition, who arrived in search of food in the late 1500'S. They gave the land the title of Mal Pais because of the lack of water and the abundance of lava rock.

Though Onate moved on further north to establish the first Spanish colony in New Mexico, many of his expedition found the area around White Oaks promising. By the 1600's, inhabitants of Spanish-Indian descent lived out on the Mal Pais country, grazing their herds in the White Oaks area. Despite the apparent lack of water, the local sheepherders managed to maintain enough for their flocks. Forced into the higher location because of the raiding Comanches and Apaches, the sheepherders found the area cooler, safer, and abundant with grass. The Apaches apparently followed the herders into the mountains, however, and they were forced to eventually move away from the site. The large black rocks gave sufficient protection to the attacking Indians and made life difficult even for the toughest herder.

Elevated 6,500 feet above sea level, the small valley is surrounded to the north by Lone Mountain, to the east by Mt. Patos, and the south by Carrizozo Mountain. To the west lies Baxter Mountain, smallest in elevation, but greatest in yieldings, for from its sides came the huge finds of gold. The mountains are sparsely covered with various trees consisting of juniper, cedar, pinon, and, in the higher elevations, White pine, which is suitable for timber.

As is common for most of the Southwest, there are two rainy seasons in the White Oaks area. The first is the main summer season, during which the rains are short and very powerful, dropping floods in a matter a minutes. The second is the winter season, of which the rains last longer and are generally much gentler in their nature.

As remote as this area of the Southwest may be, it has always managed to keep its inhabitants happy. The wild game, the cool breezes that swoop down from the mountains and the security offered from the surrounding plains make the site of White Oaks a prime location. Long before the American prospectors moved into the area, local New Mexicans had managed to survive plagues, severe drought, Apaches, Kiowas, Comanches, and poverty. To them, gold was just another part of the Mal Pais country.

Gold was apparently found in the nearby mountains by the 1800's, though no mining efforts were conducted by the locals. The local natives were eager to find just enough 'free gold' to perhaps purchase some new sheep or a bottle. Whatever the case, the secret of gold was kept quiet. The area of what was to become White Oaks was only mentioned in the local cantinas and that in passing. The Mal Pais country thus maintained its secret until a California '49er stopped in San Antonio, New Mexico, and overheard a conversation of 'free gold' in the area. His hearing of "gold in them thar hills" changed the face of New Mexico.

THE DISCOVERY OF GOLD...

A native of Missouri, John J. Baxter had been luckless on the coast and remembered New Mexico. Knowing enough Spanish to understand the locals, Baxter made his way to the area. There, after combing around the gulches and arroyos, he found some of this 'free gold'. The year was 1878, and the beginning of the White Oaks legend had begun.

Baxter was unable to keep his discovery quiet, however, for by 1879, the word had spread to Jack Winters and John E. Wilson, both of whom were panning Baxter Gulch, as it was now known. The two commenced to hard work, every morning transporting the water necessary to wash the dirt on the backs of mules from the spring two and a half miles away. Then, in the evening, they would pack in all of the pay dirt possible back to their cabin located at White Oaks Spring. This was done all summer, the men finding enough nuggets to make their efforts worthwhile. Still, no vein had yet been discovered. The arrival of a certain Tom Wilson would change all that.

Reportedly a fugitive from Texas justice, Wilson was accepted into the partnership. Working the head of Baxter Gulch, he came upon the sudden discovery of a vein while taking a rest. Sitting down on a boulder to eat his lunch, Wilson's eye was suddenly caught by the glistening of crystals in a nearby rock. Striking the stone with his pick, he picked up the slivers and returned to camp, showing his partners his find. Immediately they returned to the site, digging and exposing the vein. This was the basis for the famous Homestake Mine.

Tom Wilson, apparently afraid of news of gold getting to the authorities, sold his share to Jack Winters for a couple of silver dollars, two ounces of gold dust ($38.00), and a pistol, then left for parts unknown. No matter, the first great vein was found at White Oaks.

John E. Wilson and his partner Jack Winters set out to make good their newly found vein. The Homestake Claim, 1,500 feet long by 600 feet wide, was split between the two men, Wilson taking the south half, Winters the north. Named the North Homestake and the South Homestake, the two claims brought about the customary gold-rush to the area. Within a short amount of time, all of Baxter Mountain and most of nearby Lone Mountain were covered with claims. White Oaks was beginning to grow.

FROM ISOLATION TO PROSPERITY...

At the time of the discovery of the Homestake White Oaks, which was officially founded on August 15, 1879, was a long way from anywhere. The main line of travel through New Mexico was south from Las Vegas and Santa Fe to El Paso via the Rio Grande. The nearest post office was ninety miles to the west in San Antonio. The Homestake find changed all this for in late 1879 the camp, now growing into a small town, applied for a post office. The petition was granted and a mail contract was awarded to the National Mail Company.

Morris B. Parker's family was amongst the new wave of 'miners' hoping to strike it rich at White Oaks during the summer of 1882. Coming from all over the country, people flocked to the small valley, claiming whatever areas they could in hope of finding that one special spot. Parker's family relocated from St. Louis in what he describes as a 'new start." His father, Erasmus Wells Parker, had managed to purchase the South Homestake in 1881, yet knowing almost nothing about mining. Returning to St. Louis, Parker gathered his family, convinced his wife of the opportunities, and headed for White Oaks in 1882.

After making the trip to Las Vegas by train, the family of five had to make the last 175 miles to White Oaks by buggy. This was no easy feat for the toughest of families, for there was the constant threat of Indian attack, dehydration, or simply getting lost. Luckily for the Parkers, they did not meet up with any Indians and made the journey to their new home with relative ease.

Once in the town, which numbered around 500 inhabitants in 1882, the Parkers set about 'fixing-up' their two-room cabin, made entirely from wood, with a flat, mud roof. This was the common house for the average family, for White Oaks was still in its 'infant' stages as a boomtown in 1882. The main street, White Oaks Avenue, ran through the middle of the town. Trees were quickly planted on both sides of it to provide both shade and beauty. The town had grown from the mining camp into a small tent town and from there into a shantytown. After the sudden population boom of 1880-1882, the town went from a so-called hog town into the final stage of a beautiful, little mountain paradise.

With a strong population apparently here to stay, Jonathan H. Wise organized the town's first newspaper, the White Oaks Golden Era, which was handed out in December 1880. By 1882, Starr's Opera House was completed as well as an attempt to start another newspaper called the White Oaks Scorpion, but this one never made it off the ground. Stores, saloons, a school, even a town hall were soon built, adding to the growing town. J. Howe Watts laid out the entire town and was named surveyor. Arthur Lampson was named the first postmaster.

Supply prices were generally higher than elsewhere in New Mexico, but nobody seemed to care for everyone was waiting their chance to strike it rich. Flour was six dollars for a hundred pounds, butter for fifty cents a pound, canned fruits for sixty cents a can. Drinking water was still cheap, at forty cents a barrel, for it was also being used for panning, which was in the general interest of the entire town.

The town hall, constructed in 1882, measured 24 x 48 square feet. This building was to be the focal point for most town activities. Church, Sunday school, day school, dances, political meetings, plays, and just about everything else happened at the town hall in the early days of White Oaks. Lyman Hood held the first services for the new church in early 1884. He was paid the salary of $75 a month, most of which was raised by church members.

The early and rapid growth of White Oaks called for a stage line to cover the ninety miles between it and San Antonio. At first biweekly, then daily, a stage line, was organized to transport the newcomers across the barren Mal Pais country to the secluded valley of White Oaks. During these 'infant' stages of the town, every day held moments of fun, tragedy, and most of all, disappointment. The influx of people to White Oaks was a motley bunch, consisting of the serious miner down to the violent outlaw. Good men and bad, all gold-hungry, visited the streets and hoped to find their luck in the hills of Baxter Mountain.

While all these newcomers were in town, money was in great circulation. Local storeowners found themselves hard pressed to keep up with the supply demands. The money that gave them stability more than made up for any misgivings, however. All in all though, times were tough in White Oaks, and getting tougher.

The gold found along Baxter Gulch had long been exhausted and no other significant find had yet been discovered. Not until 1885, almost six years after the initial discovery, would another significant find be found. Most of the money spent on the South Homestake, including that of Morris Parker's father, had been lost in the mine's failure to yield large amounts of gold. Still, this long period of nonproduction may have been a blessing in disguise for White Oaks.

With the lack of gold being found in the mountains, the undesirable people eventually left town. Only the determined citizens remained, believing that fate was bound to change and give them the success they longed for and deserved. Before the times changed, however, White Oaks had to endure the visits from an unwanted bunch of ruffians, mainly one notorious William H. Bonney.

DEALING WITH THE KID...

The nearest town to White Oaks was Lincoln. Located forty miles to the east, it was not only the county seat but the scene of a recent merchant war that had produced the name of William H. Bonney, alias 'The Kid".ʻIn 1880-1881, the Lincoln County War rocked the small community of just over 350 residents, throwing the entire New Mexico Territory into an uproar.

It was from this turmoil of open gun fighting that William Bonney emerged. Young of age and fast with a gun, he was best known for his thieving of horses and cattle in New Mexico, which he sold in the Texas Panhandle and vice-versa. After the Regulators, to which the Kid belonged, disbanded, he remained on the warpath against the murderers of his former employer, John Henry Tunstall.

White Oaks was more often than not a stop the Kid made on his way to and from Texas. Whiteman's corral, an unloading place for new prospectors anxious for a night on the town before heading up into the hills, was frequented by the Kid and his partners. Probably more than one newcomer sipped Ws cup with the likes of Bonney.

White Oaks, in the early days, was a typical Western town as far as the inhabitants went. Rough, hardcore men and women flocked to the numerous hog town businesses to perform the nightly ritual of shooting up the evening sky. Gamblers, horse and cattle thieves, and gunslingers made up the daily excitement in White Oaks in the early years. During the years of 1881-1883, when the Kid and his confreres made things exceedingly lively and the prostitutes were numerous, White Oaks was a dangerous place to be.

Indeed, the presence of Bonney stirred things up in more ways than one. After selling Thomas Cooper fifty-four head of cattle for $10 each in June 1880, Bonney left the White Oaks vicinity with a bunch of horses. Though never caught for this theft, his impact was already being felt on the pocketbooks of local businessmen. This was the beginning of a wild-goose chase for Bonney, which netted nothing in the end.

The people of White Oaks, though small in number, were mostly law-abiding citizens, and did not want their town to become a haven for the likes of Bonney. Like the Parkers, most of the White Oaks population had come from the east and were much more 'settled'. While White Oaks would tolerate the normal saloon, gambling hall, and other means of evening entertainment, the citizens were determined to prevent outlaws and thieves from taking up under their roofs. As a result, the town was never very hospitable towards the Kid.

Though Bonney and his buddies found the White Oaks area prime pickings as far as stealing went, the citizens were always on the lookout. On November 15, 1880, the Kid and some of his cohorts stole eight fine horses from the Alexander Grzelachowski ranch and headed towards White Oaks. On the way, they stopped at the ranch of Jim Greathouse and sold four of the group to him. Grzelachowski was able to retrieve all but one of the horses from parties in White Oaks who had bought them from the stables of West & Sam Dedrick, who were known to 'assist' the Kid in his dealings.

On the night of November 22, another theft was attempted near White Oaks, this time at the home of John B. Bells, who owned some of the finest horses in the area. The following morning, Bells reported to the deputy sheriff, William H. Hudgens that the Kid was in the area at Blake's Saw Mill, near town. On this information, Hudgens quickly summoned a posse and lost no time in heading for Blake's Saw Mill. On their way, the posse encountered Mose Dedrick, brother of Sam, and William J. Lamper, who were heading towards White Oaks. Both men were known accomplices of the Kid and had curiously left town around the same time as the posse. Suspecting that the two men had recently come from a rendezvous with the Kid, Hudgens arrested them both. Pushing on, the posse stumbled upon the outlaw camp, startling the gunfighters.

A hot gunfight ensued, and both the Kid and Ws cohort, Billy Wilson, lost their horses. The outlaws fled into the hills, scattering as they ran. Searching the camp, the posse discovered canned goods, the Dedrick brothers' overcoats, and other items of interest that had obviously come from White Oaks that morning. The posse then returned to town, empty-handed.

The next evening, apparently in a spirit of daring, the Kid and two of his partners, 'Arkansas' Dave Rudabaugh and Wilson, returned to White Oaks, riding up the main street in the moonlight. Spotting Deputy Sheriff James Redman, a member of the posse, standing in front of the Hudgens store, Rudabaugh, just for kicks, took a shot at him. Though it missed, Redman ran for cover. Suddenly, a crowd of thirty to forty men, armed with rifles and pistols, rushed onto White Oaks Avenue, startled by the shot of Rudabaugh. The outlaws quickly turned to their heels and left town.

Having had enough of the Kid and his menacing tactics, White Oaks decided to end the problem once-and-for-all. Another posse was organized to hunt the outlaw down and finish him off. Consisting of around twelve to fourteen men under the direction of Deputy Sheriff James Carlyle, the posse made for the ranch of Jim Greathouse, another accomplice of the Kid's, located about forty miles from town on the Las Vegas road.

Traveling through a heavy snow, the posse arrived at the ranch around three in the morning and immediately erected breastworks within firing range of the house. After taking the German cook, Joseph Steck, hostage, the posse was able to confirm that the three outlaws were indeed inside. Surrounding the house, the posse then demanded the surrender of the outlaws, promising them no harm. The outlaws, fearing lynch-mob justice, refused. Carlyle then wrote a note to Bonney, demanding his surrender. Steck was sent to deliver the note to the outlaws, who laughed with the Kid at the idea of surrender. Steck was forced to relay messages between the two parties, the last being one from Bonney inviting the posse leader inside to discuss terms. Carlyle at first refused, but after Jim Greathouse put himself as hostage for Carlyle's safety while he was inside, the deputy agreed and fell into the trap.

Hour after hour passed as evening came, then late night and still no resolve of the issue. Around midnight, events came to a boil. The posse from White Oaks grew suspicious about the happenings of their leader and called out that they were going to storm the house. Just then a crash came through a window and a man came tumbling out. Shots ripped the air and after hearing the dying man's yell, the posse realized that they had killed Carlyle. With this accident, the posse abandoned the siege. As soon as the outlaws saw this, they left the house for the open range.

Jim Greathouse had managed to slip away during the shooting and spent the night at a nearby ranch. He returned the next morning along with his cook, Steck, to find Carlyle frozen stiff where he had fallen. His body was covered with a blanket and returned to White Oaks, after which the posse returned to the house and promptly burned it down.

Greathouse, upset by the destruction of his property, called upon the Las Vegas Gazette and entered a recital of his losses. The Gazette, in reply to Ws story, printed Greathouse's version of the encounter: Jim Greathouse, owner of the ranch where the brush between the White Oaks boys and members of 'the Kid's' gang recently took place, is in Las Vegas. He reports that his ranch was burned during the affair and that he lost $2,000 by the conflagration, including ranch property and general merchandise. He disclaims any thought of harboring desperadoes and says the fact that they were there is wholly due to their demanding accommodations.

As we understand the case, he does not know positively who burned his ranch, but presumes that it was done as an act of retribution by the Oaks party to avenge the death of Jim Carlyle, one of their number, who was shot down by 'the Kid." Bonney apparently read the Gazette and issued a reply, though not directly to the paper, but to Governor Lew Wallace in Santa Fe. In his letter, Bonney states his reason for being in the White Oaks area was to see Judge Leonard, who had his "case in hand." He also denied any sort of gang under his rule and that Carlyle was shot by his own posse when he attempted to jump through a window fearing that his posse was going to attack. Bonney closed by placing the blame for all of the violence on the propaganda of John Chisum, the cattle king of New Mexico.

Governor Wallace calmly replied to the Kid's plea with a posting of a $500 reward for his capture. Obviously the rest of the territory, like White Oaks, was tired of the menace of William H. Bonney. The Gazette praised Wallace's move, but asked that the amount be raised to $5,000. Only this type of action and price would drive the Kid from the territory.

After the Greathouse affair, the residents of White Oaks became determined that no foothold, of any sort, was to be allowed within the vicinity of the town for any member of the Kid's gang. The killing of Carlyle, though not actually the Kid's doing, placed a heavy shadow over his image and made his career take a different angle. Carlyle had been a very popular man in White Oaks and his death was a big reason for the eventual hunting down of Bonney in Ft. Sumner by Pat Garrett. Though the incident at the Greathouse ranch was destined to make the Kid into a legend, White Oaks demonstrated that it was not going to be a town that tolerated lawlessness. White Oaks had its deal of frustration because of Bonney and his cohorts, but the town was on the verge of another experience like never before recorded in New Mexican history.

THE 'GOLDEN' DAYS...

By 1885 White Oaks had assumed the semblance of a real town. Surviving the early difficulties of Billy the Kid and the failure of any significant strikes, the town settled down to the face the future. Streets and cross streets had been surveyed and laid out. Store buildings, made from stone as well as wood, were constructed along White Oaks Avenue. The early-day boomtown atmosphere, with its wild saloons, wide-open gambling, and guns and knives had virtually disappeared. The residents were all law-abiding, eager to make progress and willing to face the future. There were at least three young lawyers: John Y. Hewitt, H. B. Fergusson, and George Barber. Doctors, bankers, businessmen of all types found their way to White Oaks after 1885.

A second town hall was built which served mostly as an athletic club for boxing, wrestling, gymnastics, and for musicals. A two-story brick school building was built on the north side of the valley. It had four rooms and served au grades from kindergarten through accredited college-entrance courses. Upon entrance into the school, the room on the left was for grades one through four, the room to the right for five through eight. Up the stairs, the room to the left was for nine through twelve and to the right the kindergarten, for it had a good heat source. The view from the school was commanding, for one could see the entire town from the upstairs window.

The school, because of the recent increase in revenue, was just one of many new buildings being built after 1885. All of the additions were the result of gold being mined successfully once again from Baxter Mountain.

Gold fever resurged in White Oaks during 1885. The success of the North Homestake mine paid off for James A. Sigafus and Frank Lloyd, the mine manager. The mine had three shafts measuring 600, 700, and 800 feet in depth. Steady profit was managed from the gold veins inside the shafts. All told, the North Homestake was the second largest yielding mine in White Oaks.

The South Homestake, meanwhile, was once again at work. Morris Parker's family suddenly found new revenue in their hands from the mine's two shafts measuring 500 and 1,066 feet, respectively. Production was booming when disaster struck in the form of fire. On July 1, 1891, a candle was left burning on an oil-soaked shelf in the hoist room of the main shaft. Only two men were on shift, both of whom lost their lives in the blaze. The entire mine was rendered useless until repairs could be made, if ever. Because of the cost, this was never attempted.

Instead of rebuilding the old shaft, focus was turned to another area in the mine known as the North Shaft, which was producing good ore. This shaft was making enough money to offset the disaster in the main shaft, though the owners of the South Homestake had to be careful just how far they permitted their workers to pursue this angle. The reason for this is the vein that the North Shaft was working in ran from the North Homestake mine as well. The dividing line between the two mines was becoming very close as the two mines worked towards one another.

The work suddenly became quite slow, though the work was pressed on, hoping that the vein would reappear. The problem was that the line between the North and South Homestakes was very near, so near that the workers could hear one another in the opposite mines. Morris Parker's father grew more and more apprehensive with each day, feeling that the vein was all on the side of the North Homestake. Within twenty-five feet from the dividing line between the two mines, the vein was relocated. With this find, one of the richest pockets of gold ever found in the mines of White Oaks was discovered.

Joe Grieshaber, the Parker's foreman, blasted two 'shots' into the pocket. A short, fat German man, he was determined to see just what the discovery could possibly yield. It was impossible to go in the North Shaft after blasting for some time because of the lack of any kind of artificial ventilation, which prevented the dust and debris from settling. Still, Grieshaber was determined to see exactly what his blasts had done to the pocket.

Sneaking back to the mine that night with young Morris Parker at his side, Grieshaber made the descent into the shaft and though the lighting was only from candles, the two saw plenty.

'The sight that met our eyes was like a jewelry shop. Clean, bright, shining gold! Big blotches, leaf and wire gold. Coarse and fine, too, and a lot of it!' they later reported.

Filling their sacks with samples, the two men slept in the mine that night, taking their findings to town the next morning. After having the gold tested and checked out, the total in cash for one night's work was an astonishing $18,000! When the time came for the mine to finally shut down, the South Homestake was the third best producing mine in White Oaks.

From that time on, the two Homestakes progressed normally and well. For ten years the two mines continued production, and White Oaks prospered as a result. Homes were popping up everywhere and new ranches began to cover the outlying areas around town. White Oaks realized that the time would come when the veins would become exhausted, but that fact didn't seem to bother the town during the fever of the 'golden days'. By 1890, the town's population had grown to more than 2,000, a remarkable achievement in such a short amount of time.

The largest and richest find, was yet to come, however. Though the location for the Old Abe mine was first located in 1879, shortly after that Homestake claim by Winters, no significant production ever came from the area until years later. The original three owners failed to see any future in the claim, so they opened up the area for bidders in 1883. In January 1884, John Y. Hewitt, H. B. Fergusson, and William Watson located two claims near the former Abraham Lincoln, called the White Oaks and the Robert E. Lee. Lawyers, all three, had their practices in town, but spent much of their time working the claims they had set on Baxter Mountain.

The eventual site for the Old Abe as it came to be called was very near to the North Homestake, meaning that miners were riding over the shallow covering of the richest vein in New Mexico for years. For eleven years, nothing much was done to make good on the claims of the three attorneys. During the fall of 1890, the owners made a deal with the owners of the South Homestake for some assessment of their samples. The samples were taken by none other than Joe Grieshaber and Morris Parker, and the results were more than satisfactory. Twice as much gold was found in the samples as had been expected.

That same fall, Watson and his nephew, Watt Hoyle, worked below all previous work and sank a ten foot hole. As the values of their efforts increased almost daily, the hole became deeper. Twenty feet, then thirty until the pile of dirt surrounding the hole was too huge to continue with this method of digging. The mill at the South Homestake was then borrowed for the grinding of the ore from the Old Abe, for production at the earlier mine was at a low. The mill produced successful gold, the likes of which had never been seen before in White Oaks. Mr. Rolla Wells, president and principal owner of the South Homestake, offered $300,000 for the Old Abe, but the three lawyer partners felt that they were on to something big and promptly turned down his offer. A deal was then worked out with the owners of the North Homestake as well, for use of their mill. Production, by 1890, had virtually ceased for the two Homestakes, and the Old Abe was the only reason for the two not to shut down operations completely.

White Oaks had been facing the possibility of a bleak and apprehensive21 future until the discovery of the Old Abe. Life sprang up once again, for money was now flowing into the local businesses like never before because the Old Abe, unlike the other mines on Baxter Mountain, was owned entirely by local men. No outside investors of any sort were involved with the mines yieldings, meaning more revenue for White Oaks. The mine employed large numbers of men and they reaped in the benefits as well. New faces appeared on the streets, the town took on a look of prosperity as never before, and the population reached its peak around 2,500.

As with previous large findings, new buildings were built, including a two-story bank. Named the Exchange Bank, it was located on White Oaks Avenue, just like all the other buildings of importance. Watt Hoyle, as a result of greed and love, decided to construct a 'superior' residence. The result of his efforts and spending was a two-story brick home, complete with a viewing balcony on top. The story goes that he was building it for his prospective bride and when she wrote him that she was not coming to White Oaks, he walked up to the North Homestake and leaped to his death. In actuality, Hoyle never finished the inside but did live in the home with his older brother and his wife. The home became known as 'Hoyle's folly". While all of this complacency and prosperity was going on, another disaster struck the town for the second time. This fire, the greatest in the town's history, struck the Old Abe on March 9, 1895. A kerosene lamp exploded in the hoist house, sending flammable liquid all over the wooden frames of the mine. The place was turned into a mass of fire, killing nine of the twenty men who were working underground at the time. The men were below the surface, almost 800 feet down.

When the station tender noticed the disaster on hand, he quickly summoned to his fellow miners and they began the long climb towards safety up the vertical shaft. Climbing up a vertical ladder is not easy, even under normal circumstances. With the pressures of depleting oxygen and sheer exhaustion, it's a wonder that eleven men were able to make it out at all.

It took the townspeople two days to extinguish the flames. In a heroic effort, White Oaks, both men and women, fought against the terrible fire with all of the strength and water they could muster. Tents were set up outside the mine for the weary as well as coffee and meals. Most men, however, refused to stop their efforts, for there were friends trapped inside. All of the town efforts went for nothing as the nine bodies were carried out one by one after the flames were extinguished. It was a heavy and sad day for White Oaks.

The funeral was a particularly sad event. The entire town was present, overflowing the church. "Nine coffins, side by side, filled the width of the church. After the music and the service, the bodies of the young men, active and full of life a few days before; now blackened, scorched, some of them unrecognizable, were carried out one by one and placed in open wagons and led to the cemetery."

The graves had been prepared beforehand, the fresh dirt lying alongside the open holes. There was a brief prayer at each one, and then the coffins were lowered into the earth, the 'headstone' being nothing more than pieces of wood.

Each grave, though containing a well-known and loved man, was unmarked; no name, cause of death, or dates inscribed. As one can imagine, the next few weeks were filled with grief and readjustment for many in White Oaks.

After making some necessary repairs and adding extra safety precautions, tile Old Abe was hard at work once again, producing the finest form of gold known to man-untarnished. Most of the world's gold does not come from high-grade specimens, but rather from mines of low gold content, which may contain as little as half an ounce of gold per ton. Gold is also often nothing more than a by-product of the smelting of copper, lead, and silver ores. The mines at White Oaks, however, produced magnificent specimens of pure, bright yellow gold. 100 percent pure, the gold was heavy and coarse; produced from the tight seams of the earth. The mines of White Oaks were undoubtedly able to produce some of the best gold ever seen by man.

The Old Abe mine was the richest mine in White Oaks without question. At one time the mine employed forty workers yielding between forty-five to fifty tons of gold per day! Though the last mine in operation, it was the biggest and best of them all. The only working shaft was 1,350 feet deep, making it one of the deepest dry mine shafts in the world. The mine continued to produce gold until just after the turn of the century, when it, like the Homestakes, became 'worked-out'.

Other mines of significant importance were the Lady Godiva and the Little Mack, in which Robert Leslie worked. The veins in both of these mines were small, and produced little compared with the other mines mentioned. All told, the mines of White Oaks yielded around $20 million dollars worth of gold and other minerals. The North Homestake was the first mine to cease operations, followed a couple of years later by the South Homestake. Though some 'clean-up' was done producing minor finds, the mills were shutdown for good. As the mining petered out, the town began to fade. By the early 1900's, White Oaks was a far cry from what it had been just 10 years before. Its last hope was the railroad, which had to pass through White Oaks and bring permanent prosperity.

DEPENDING ON THE RAIL...

Long before the decline of White Oaks, the thought of running a rail spur through the town had been in many minds. The soaring cost involved in the transport the vast amounts of gold from the mines by wagon was driving the owners of the mines crazy. As early as 1882, rumors persisted of such an undertaking. As things ended up, White Oaks was simply passed by because of the bungling of some of its leading citizens. White Oaks might have been a bustling town today if the railroad and built a spur into the town.

The idea for a rail spur lay with the cost of transportation by wagon from the mines to the nearest railroad depot, at that time in San Antonio, ninety miles away. El Paso, Texas was a growing metropolis and it badly needed fuel such as coal, timber, and of course the minerals coming from the White Oaks' mines, for its expanding population. White Oaks, barely three years old at this time, needed a spur in which it could transport the gold and other minerals cheaper and safer than by wagon. The amount of time between shipments could be cut down tremendously as well. With the n-Lines of Organ, New Mexico, on the way as well, the project seemed to be only a matter of time from turning into a reality.

El Paso newspapers joined in on the clamor for the prospect of a new railroad. The rail was to be named the El Paso and White Oaks Railroad Company. The general opinion was that a literal empire lay in the building. This rail would not only join the city of El Paso with the gold mines of White Oaks, but would have depots at Organ and other ranches as well. All that was needed was a builder. Morris Locke seemed to be that man, though he did not actually begin any construction until 1889. Starting from El Paso, Locke managed to lay ten miles of rail costing him $170,000.

Progress was very slow because of opposition from the Southern Pacific and the Santa Fe Railroads, which had just moved into Roswell, New Mexico, only eighty miles from White Oaks. Locke soon found the task too stressful and he sold the venture to Jay Gould, who bought it for $50,000. Gould, much like Locke, found the task and terrain too difficult and the project was abandoned. Seeing the location of White Oaks as being too high and rough for his expenses, Gould left the rail, and White Oaks, behind.

It was not until Charles B. Eddy, who visited White Oaks many times before 1900 and became convinced that the coal, gold, and other minerals found there could be warranted some kind of a line, that serious efforts were made to build a railroad to the town. Calling it the White Oaks & Kansas City Railroad, the title made the local headlines. Wanting to connect White Oaks to a nearby city, Eddy proposed running a line from El Paso, which was eagerly accepted. Posting $10,000 with the El Paso City Council on September 20, 1897, Eddy promised to begin actual construction within ninety days.

What Eddy was also banking on were the Salado coal fields at Capitan and the vast timber resources on the Sacramento plateau, for these brought additional tonnage to the railroad. Hoping that capitalists would aid Wm in the funding of these resources, Eddy built the railroad from El Paso to Alamogordo, a town that arose because of just such a venture. Then disaster struck in the form of a major setback in the Salado coalfields, causing Eddy to panic. Seeing this 'certain' promise fail him, Eddy lost faith in the gold mines of White Oaks, choosing to run his line away from the low mountains and create a stopping point at White Oaks junction (Carrizozo, New Mexico) instead. This destination was reached on August 3, 1899, but the people of White Oaks soon realized that the dreams of having a railroad running through their town were becoming bleak. There was one final hope for White Oaks in the form of having a spur run from White Oaks Junction near the end of town, but the egos of the leading citizens got in the way. The original survey called for White Oaks as an objective. The railroad requested that 'the town provide a right-of-way, free of charge, along a proposed route which would at least affect buildings in existence. It asked for a flat, vacant acreage near the west edge of town for depot site, shops, and sidings, and a cash bonus of $50,000."

Town meetings were held and the requests were approved at first, but then opposition arose. Though the railroad countered the opposition by canceling the cash bonus, the leading citizens refused to compromise and expressed their determination not to spend a dollar. Their attitude was indicated in their slogan: "Regardless of what we do, the road necessarily must pass through White Oaks. It is the shortest, easiest, and cheapest route available. There is no other way."

The problem was that there was another way, finding a second route north of Lone Mountain where the summit was even lower than at White Oaks. Even after actual construction began on the alternate route, the dissenters persisted in their claims: "White Oaks, with its manifold advantages, does not need a railroad." When the Old Abe mine declined at the turn of the century, there was nothing left to support the town. Though the mistake was realized, it was far too late. Thus the people of White Oaks, by their own stubbornness and lack of foresight, were closely associated with the oblivion of their town. The railroad was built all right-just not through White Oaks. This fact, perhaps more than the exhaustion of the mines, spelled the end for the town.

FADEOUT...

If destiny had placed itself only twelve miles to the east of Carrizozo, New Mexico, in the mountains of White Oaks, everyone would be calling the town the best in New Mexico. Instead, White Oaks is a ghost town.

The fadeout of the town came after the railroad decided to run around White Oaks, instead of through it in 1900. After this was realized, many people simply left town leaving only the determined ones behind. As White Oaks slowly decayed, the railroad steamed on by, just twelve miles away.

The burial grounds of most ghost towns are much like the ruins near them. Cedarvale cemetery is very different, for the best part of the once active and prosperous town of White Oaks now lies there at rest. The names are mostly of just the locals, but there are some who deserve more attention. Among these names are William McDonald, who became the first governor of New Mexico after the territory achieved statehood and Mrs. Susan McSween Barber, the wife of Alexander McSween and lone survivor of the Lincoln County War as far as the 'big' names go. She was known as the "Cattle Queen of New Mexico" and married George Barber in 1880. Never 'cleared' of the gossip that surrounded her after the war, Susan McSween presided over a range that numbered over five thousand head. Finally, in 1902, she sold out and moved to White Oaks, where she died in 1931 at the age of eighty-six.

The place is a monument for all to see, for the graves are not neglected. Dave Jackson, who arrived in White Oaks in 1897, tended to the cemetery until his death in 1963. Though deaf and 'broken down' because of the years spent working in the mines, Jackson felt that he belonged to his duty of maintaining the Cedarvale cemetery. 'So many of my friends are here that I took it upon myself to maintain the cemetery."

White Oaks, much like the gold that came from nearby Baxter Mountain, was a flash as far as time goes. Still, it made such an impact upon the southwest that it lives today. Its citizens, though forced to leave for one reason or another, kept the memories of their town alive in their hearts. Unlike many other ghost towns, White Oaks left behind people who cared for their town, even in its demise. The legend of White Oaks lives on in the stones, the ruins, and the old timers, like Robert Leslie, who return to speak of the wonderful times spent amongst the streets of the town. 'It was a sad day when we all were forced to move because of no other option. The town had simply vanished." White Oaks had produced some of the world's finest gold and if it were not for a stubborn few, it might still be alive today[27]

SCHOOLHOUSE
White Oaks, New Mexico

Taken this context, the history of White Oaks makes a little more sense. It helps explain why, in a town with an opera house, three churches, drama clubs, a newspaper, literary societies and a beautiful brick schoolhouse drunkenness, killings and visits from Billy the Kid and other desperados were common, especially in the early years. And if the darker side of a town could somehow manifest itself physically, that must surely explain the debaucherous suburb, appropriately named Hogtown that grew up outside White Oaks. White Oaks had the churches and drama clubs; Hogtown had the saloons and whorehouses.

Continuing, let's say that a railroad is being built nearby, and the good side of White Oaks sees in it an opportunity to connect with the outside world, but the bad side sees only a chance to make money. So unfortunately, the bad side holds out for a tremendous sum for right-of-way rights and the railroad bypasses White Oaks and goes to Carrizozo instead. Without the railroad White Oaks (and Hogtown with it) slowly faded away.

Does this mean that the evil side of White Oaks won out? Maybe, evil did when then, but the victory was only temporary, because the good side is clearly in evidence now. Just visit once and you'll be convinced this is one of the most stately and beautiful places in New Mexico. Not one but two elegant Victorian mansions, the wonderful school building, and a solemn and ultimately very touching graveyard named Cedarvale are some of the high points.

---

[27] http://www.whiteoaksnewmexico.com/History/indetail.html

HOYLE'S CASTLE
White Oaks, New Mexico

In White Oaks is an abandoned house is a poignant reminder of a lost love. In the 1880's, Andy Hoyle built the brick mansion for his mail order bride, a woman he had fallen in love with after she answered his ad in an eastern newspaper. But after she arrived something went wrong.

Within a few weeks, she boarded a stagecoach and headed back to her home on the east coast. Andy was crushed by her departure. One day, he simply disappeared, leaving his mansion abandoned. However, some say his ghost haunts the lonely old building, waiting for his promised love to return.

CHAPTER THIRTY-SIX

ESCONDIDA, NEW MEXICO

NEW MEXICO STATE TB SANITARIUM,
Escondida, New Mexico

The New Mexico State TB Sanitarium was built by the Civilian Conservation Corps and opened its doors in 1932. It originally had 50 beds but was expanded to eventually have 1,200 beds. Several structures comprise the location. Originally the site looked like the spokes of a half of a wagon wheel, when viewed from the air.

The most predominant today are the dorms, where patients were housed. All together there were 9 wards for patients. The main hospital is now hidden back behind the NM State police headquarters. This building had an explosion proof operating room with glass block windows. There was also a kitchen, dining facility and a recreation hall where 16mm films were shown to staff and patients.

In the early years the hospital did well. Service was described as outstanding by patients and staff alike. However, that would eventually change.

By October 1952 many unfavorable reports about the hospital had been reported. Alva Simpson, in a letter to the state governor, claimed that the biggest problem was that patients released from the sanitarium had to be treated for improper nutrition and lack of sanitation. The facility was closed shortly afterwards.

The old hospital was converted and became a battery manufacturing plant named Eagle Pitcher. This factory operated for many years before being closed down.

Today, this historic old facility is abandoned, with piles of trash in most of the buildings. There is a bottle dump just west of the main site where there are mounds of old medicine bottles. The New Mexico State Police have also used the area as a shooting range, so spent brass from rounds fired by officers can be found around the dump area as well.

The area has changed greatly over the years. The major change is a road that now runs through the site. The New Mexico State Police have also built a regional headquarters near the old hospital.

THE GHOSTS

People have reported seeing glowing balls of light moving about the ruins of the sanitarium after dark. Unusual noises, to include, screams and shouts have also been heard coming from the old dorm buildings.

CHAPTER THIRTY-SEVEN

CANADIAN RIVER, NEW MEXICO

The Canadian River is a very long, major U.S. waterway that flows from its headwaters in the Sangre de Cristo Mountains in far southern Colorado border near Raton Pass, down through east central New Mexico, then east across the Texas Panhandle into Oklahoma, where it drains a sizeable portion of that state before reaching its confluence with the Arkansas River just west of Fort Smith, Arkansas.

Starting as a narrow river in New Mexico, the Canadian gains in size after entering Oklahoma, and becomes a waterway that, in places, is more than a mile wide. In New Mexico, the river has a navigable flow that is usually limited to years of above normal rainfall in the desert between Raton and Tucumcari. Its major tributaries include the Vermejo, Ute, Mora, Conchas and Cimarron Rivers, most of which offer paddlers really great whitewater runs when they flow.

The geology of the Canadian River includes granite cliffs and canyons hear the headwaters and a deep sandstone canyon with historical ancient ruins between the Cornudo Hills to the west and the Kiowa National Grasslands to the east. Golden and bald eagles can be seen soaring high over the river valley, but few signs of civilization will be found along the river and its tributaries.

PENITENTE CHAPEL RUINS
Canadian River Canyon, New Mexico

Los Hermanos Penitentes (The Penitent Brothers) is an ancient society of flagellants existing among the Spanish of New Mexico and Colorado. The Hermanos Penitentes are a society of individuals, who, to atone for their sins, practice penance's which consist principally of flagellation, carrying heavy crosses, binding the body to a cross, and tying the limbs to hinder the circulation of the blood. These practices have prevailed in Colorado and New Mexico since the beginning of the nineteenth century.

Up to the year 1890, they were public; at present they are secret, though not strictly. The Hermanos Penitentes are men; in the latter half of the nineteenth century they admitted women and children into separate organizations, which, however, were never numerous. The society had no general organization or supreme authority. Each fraternity is local and independent with its own officers. The chief officer, hermano mayor (elder brother), has absolute authority, and as a rule holds office during life. The other officers are the like as those of most secret societies: chaplain, sergeant-at-arms, etc. The ceremony of the initiation, which takes place during Holy Week, is simple, excepting the final test.

The candidate is escorted to the morada (abode), the home, or council house, by two or more Penitentes where, after a series of questions and answers consisting in the main of prayer he is admitted. He then undergoes various humiliations. First, he washes the feet of all present, kneeling before each; then he recites a long prayer, asking pardon for any offense he may have given. If any one present has been offended by the candidate, he lashes the offender on the bare back. Then comes the last and crucial test: four or six incisions, in the shape of a cross, are made just below the shoulders of the candidate with a piece of flint.

Flagellation, formerly practiced in the streets and in the churches, is now, since the American occupation, confined generally to the morada and performed with a short whip (disciplina), made from the leaf of the amole weed. Fifty years ago the Hermanos Penitentes would issue from their morada (in some places as Taos, N. M., three hundred strong), stripped to the waist and scourging themselves, led by the acompanadores (escorts), and preceded by a few Penitentes dragging heavy crosses (maderos); the procession was accompanied by a throng, singing Christian hymns. A wooden wagon (el carro de la muerte) bore a figure representing death and pointing forward an arrow with stretched bow. This procession went through the streets to the church, where the Penitentes prayed, continued their scourgings, returned in procession to the morada.

Other modes of self castigation were often resorted to; on Good Friday it was the custom to bind one of the brethren to a cross, as in a crucifixion. At present no "crucifixions" take place, though previous to 1896 they were annual in many places in New Mexico and Colorado. The Penitentes now confine themselves to secret flagellation and occasional visits to churches at night. Flagellation is also practiced at the death of a Penitente or of a relative. The corpse is taken to the morada and kept there for a few hours; flagellation takes place at the morada and during the procession to and from the same.

The practice known as flagellation was introduced into Latin America during the sixteenth and seventeenth centuries, though no actual records are found of any organized flagellant societies there until comparatively recent times. In some localities of Mexico, Central, and South America, flagellant organizations, more or less public in their practices, existed until very recently, and still exist in a few isolated places. All these later organizations were regulated and controlled by Leo XIII.

The origin of the New Mexican flagellants or Hermànos penitentes is uncertain, but they seem to have been an outgrowth of the Third Order of St. Francis, introduced by Franciscans in the seventeenth century. Their practices consisted principally in flagellation, without incisions and with no loss of blood, carrying small crosses, and marching in processions with bare feet to visit the churches and join in long prayers. The barbarous customs of the New Mexico Penitents are of a much later origin. The New Mexican flagellants call their society, "Los hermanos penitentes de la tercer orden de San Francisco," and we know that when the last organization came into prominence in the early part of the nineteenth century, the older organization no longer existed in New Mexico.

When their practices reached their worst stage (about 1850-90), the attention of the Church was directed towards them. The society was then very strong among all classes and the ecclesiastical authorities decided to use leniency. In a circular letter to the Penitentes of New Mexico and Colorado in 1886, Archbishop Salpointe of Santa Fe ordered them in the name of the Church to abolish flagellation, and the carrying of the heavy crosses, and sent to the different hermanos mayores copies of the rules of the Third Order of St. Francis, advising them to reorganize in accordance therewith. His letter and orders were unheeded.

He then ordered all the parish priests to see the Penitentes personally and induce them to follow his instructions, but they accomplished nothing. To make matters worse, a Protestant paper, "La hermandad", was published at Pueblo, Colorado, in 1889, which incited the Penitents to resist the Church and follow their own practices. Archbishop Salpointe, in a circular letter of 1889, then ordered the Penitentes to disband. As a result the society, though not abolished, was very much weakened, and its further growth prevented. In spite of the fact that the Catholic Church drove the brotherhood underground in the 1880's,

Penitentes were a powerful influence in the communities of the San Luis Valley until about 1920. Although the Penitentes were politically active, their real power resulted from the responsible roles they fulfilled in their communities. They took care of spiritual functions, provided charity and watched over the economic needs of people in their communities. Widows, for example, received contributions of food, firewood, and money if necessary. Orphans were adopted. The sick received care. The members' roles were clearly defined and dutifully accepted.

By the late 1940's, when the Catholic Church lifted its ban on participation in the brotherhood, membership had fallen off dramatically. Then, in the 1960's and 1970's, activity resumed. However, most of the members were middle-aged or elderly men whose activities consisted of meeting for prayers during Holy Week and walking in occasional processions. By the 1990's only about a half dozen active moradas existed in the valley and membership had become vastly reduced. The old adobe moradas, once so mysterious and steeped in spirituality, toppled inward.

Although life has clearly changed in the valley, anyone that understands the valley and its people will tell of the influence of the Penitentes. While there may only be a few remaining in the brotherhood today, the community traditions and practices established by members in the past remain a part of the foundation of Hispanic culture in the valley today.

THE GHOSTS

The ruins of a Penitente chapel stand on the northern edge of the Canadian river canyon, some 40 miles east of Wagon Mound New Mexico. It has been reported that shadowy figures have been seen darting across trees and rocks.

Unnerving feelings can be easily sensed that seem to emulate from the area near the old chapel and sometimes disembodied voices chanting and what sounds like the cracking of a whip are heard.

I have never been able to find anyone who spent the night out there.

CHAPTER THIRTY-EIGHT

CIMARRON, NEW MEXICO

The first pioneers to visit the Cimarron country were the Anasazi, the Ancient Ones. The best known of these are Folsom Man, discovered in 1926 in the Des Moines, New Mexico area and the Ponil People, evidenced by the site of Indian Writing on Philmont Scout Ranch.

Spanish Conquistadors visited the Cimarron area looking for the lost "City of Gold" but found only Native American peoples and their homes. Jicarrilla Apaches and Moache Utes roamed the hills and mountains around Cimarron. These peoples hunted buffalo, deer, elk, and grew some crops; with Ute Park being their favorite campsite. Mountain men followed the beaver and other animals, making Taos the center for southwest fur trading. Names like the Bent brothers, Ceran St. Vrain, Kit Carson and Uncle Dick Wootton appear in the history of this area.

Colonizer and landowner, Charles Beaubien partnered with Guadalupe Miranda to obtain a large land grant from the Mexican government and proceeded to settle in the Rayado area, south of Cimarron. They met with constant opposition to settle this area in the early years. However, their later settlements did well, particularly when Kit Carson and Lucien Maxwell joined them. In 1849, brother-in-law Jesus Abreu joined the settlement.

Their walled compound continued to ward off Indian attacks for several years, while their crops and livestock herds flourished. In 1857, Lucien Maxwell moved his family to the Cimarron River after purchasing Miranda's share of the grant. During the time that Maxwell lived on the Cimarron, an Indian Agency was located there with the gristmill providing flour and grains, which were sold to the Indians.

In 1866, gold was found on Maxwell's land, on the Baldy Mountain Mine site. Later other mines such as the French Henry, the Aztec, and the Montezuma were established. Maxwell allowed miners on his land for a portion of the proceeds. Also, he allowed families to settle on his grant for a portion of the cattle or crops that they raised. In 1869, Maxwell sold the large grant to a group of Englishmen. The Colfax County War occurred when the Englishmen did not wish anyone to occupy the land without full payment and the local pioneer settlers did not agree with this! The war resulted in several shootings and murders.

In the 1870s cattle ranching had developed into a hard but profitable business in the Cimarron area. The development of the Eagle Nest Dam provided irrigation for the farmers living at the foot of the Sangre de Cristos. The railroad's entrance into Colfax County in 1906 allowed logging to become another profitable industry in the area. A train called the Swastika Route briefly traveled from Cimarron to Ute Park. Along with logging came the development of lumber mills in the area to process the wood; most of which was made into railroad ties. During the early 1920s was a boom time for Cimarron and it was during this time that "New Town" was developed. In the early part of the 20th century, mining made a brief come back in the mountains and hills around Cimarron.

By 1941, however, the Baldy and Aztec mines closed for good. The coal town of Dawson closed forever in 1951, erasing itself from the map but not from the hearts of the people who lived there. During the 30s, 40s and 50s until present day, ranching has played a major role in the Cimarron and Colfax County area. Today you will still see many working cowboys in and around Cimarron.

In 1922, the Maverick Club was organized by 50 prominent citizens of Cimarron. The purpose of the club involved social, civic and educational objectives. They used the term "Maverick" to denote the group of "strays" who felt they did not fit the mold of the typical service groups in the area. Besides, they weren't sure if they could be branded by others' rules. There were no membership dues, and once a man joined, he was a Maverick for life.

On July 4, 1923, the newly formed club sponsored its first rodeo for the community. It has become an annual event held continuously for more than seven decades. The Maverick Club also participates in charitable activities and hosts an annual Ladies Night Dinner and Dance for the wives and girlfriends of Maverick Club members.

ST. JAMES HOTEL
Cimarron, New Mexico

The St. James Hotel began life as a small saloon in 1873. The two story hotel has been in continual operation since it was added to the saloon in 1880.

Entering the St. James Hotel in Cimarron, New Mexico is like stepping back in time. The hallways of the guest area are decorated with deep red carpets, and red brocade wallpaper. The small ventilation windows above the doors are hand painted in different western scenes. Antiques, most original to the hotel, abound. Such wonderful pieces as 5 ft tall iron candelabra lamps, vintage chairs, a pump organ, even a roulette table that used to be in the gambling area of the original saloon, are scattered throughout the hallways. On the walls are framed photos of the famous guests the hotel once catered to.

The rooms are all named after former guests. For instance, repeat customers such as Buffalo Bill Cody, Jesse James, and Zane Gray, often chose to stay in the same room each time they visited. These rooms they were partial to now bear their names.

Figure 20: The St. James Hotel.

The history of this old hotel is equally as fascinating. In 1862, upon the recommendation of Ulysses S Grant, President Lincoln appointed a young Frenchman named Henry (formerly Henri) Lambert as his personal chef, a position Lambert held until that fateful day in 1865.

After Lincoln's assassination, Henry made his way west in search of gold. However, instead of discovering gold, he discovered he could make a very good living cooking for the miners in a small New Mexico boom town called Elizabethtown (E-Town). While passing through E-town, Lucien Maxwell, land baron of New Mexico Territory, had the opportunity to taste Henry Lambert's cooking. Lucien was so impressed he offered Lambert a job cooking for him in nearby Cimarron (Spanish for "wild" or "unbroken").

Henry accepted the offer and moved to Cimarron. In 1872, while still working for Lucien Maxwell, Henry began building Lambert's Saloon and Billiard Hall. It wasn't long before Lambert's Saloon became wildly popular, catering to the cowboys, traders, miners, frontiersman, and many others traveling this last leg of the Santa Fe Trail.

The Saloon did so well, in fact, that in 1880 Henri added 30 guest rooms and the St. James Hotel was born. The hotel, considered at the time to be one of the most elegant, luxurious hotels west of the Mississippi, soon became as popular as the saloon itself.

Before long the hotel guest registry read like a who's who of the Old West;

- Jesse James stayed there often, always in room 14 and always signing the registry with his alias, RH Howard

- Buffalo Bill Cody met Annie Oakley in Cimarron and they both stayed in the hotel while planning and rehearsing their Wild West Show. They took an entire village of Indians from the Cimarron area with them when they took the show on the road
- Wyatt Earp, his brother Morgan, and their wives spent 3 nights at the St. James on their way to Tombstone. After leaving the hotel they made their way to the small town of Las Vegas, NM (about 30 miles southeast of Cimarron) where they met, and became friends with, a gentleman named J.J. "Doc" Holliday
- Zane Grey penned his novel "Fighting Caravans" while staying at the hotel
- Lew Wallace, Governor of New Mexico Territory, wrote part of Ben Hur there.

Other famous, and infamous, guests included Doc Holliday, Billy the Kid, Bat Masterson, Kit Carson, Clay Allison, and Pat Garret. Probably the most famous unknown person to stay at the hotel was Bob Ford. Doesn't ring a bell? Bob Ford's claim to fame was that he killed Jesse James.

Not surprisingly, with this combination of guests, the hotel boasts a violent history. At least 26 men were killed in gunfights at the hotel. The ceiling of the Saloon (currently the dining room) still has 22 original bullet holes in it. Luckily, when Henry built the hotel he had the foresight to add 3 feet of hard wood above the tin ceiling of the saloon to keep stray bullets from penetrating the floor of the upstairs guest rooms!

As times changed, railroads began taking the place of horse and buggy, mining and ranching became less profitable, and Cimarron's popularity begin to dwindle. Eventually, the once popular and elegant St. James Hotel fell into disrepair. Through the years it went largely uninhabited and passed from owner to owner until the mid 1980's when the beautiful old hotel was purchased and restored to its former luxury.

Today, the hotel is once again a hotel, but, much to its credit, it is far from being modern. There are no phones, no radios, and no televisions. Almost all of the furniture is original to the hotel, from the antique chandeliers, to the beds and dressers in the guest rooms. A stay at today's St. James Hotel is eerily similar to a stay during the heyday of the Wild West

THE GHOSTS

. The second floor of the hotel is the most active, with stories of cold spots and the smell of cigar smoke lingering in the halls. (Smoking is not allowed in the hotel.) A prior manager said that "you never see them, but you do feel and hear them." Another report from a former owner, states that she walked into the dining room and saw a pleasant-looking cowboy standing behind her in the mirror at the bar. The spiritual activity of the hotel has been featured on the popular television shows Unsolved Mysteries and A Current Affair.

Room 18

As the story goes, one night in 1881, the owner of the St. James was playing cards with some men in the 2nd floor card room. It was getting late, the men had imbibed a fair amount of whiskey, and the stakes were high. So high that, confidant he would win, the owner bet the hotel. However, a guest of the hotel, Mr. Thomas James (TJ) Wright also felt he had a winning hand and stayed in the game when all the others folded. When all bets were made and the cards were shown, TJ proved victorious. Satisfied with his win, TJ decided to retire for the night. As he made his way down the hall and began to turn the corner towards his room he was shot from behind. TJ continued on to his room, room 18, shut the door and slowly bled to death.

Perhaps the death of Thomas James Wright's was so traumatic that his spirit still remains locked in time. Whatever may be the reason, Room 18 is considered the most haunted room in the hotel. The room is considered so haunted, in fact, that nobody is allowed to enter the room, much less sleep in it. It is said that residing in the room is TJ's very angry, malevolent presence. The employees of the hotel say that no one is allowed in the room because whenever anyone goes in something bad happens in the hotel.

One former owner said she was pushed down while in the room and, on another occasion, saw a ball of angry orange light floating in the upper corner. The room holds only a bed frame without a mattress, a coat rack, a rocking chair and bureau which has been made a shrine to the Old West. Sitting atop the bureau is a Jack Daniels bottle, a basin and pitcher, a hand of cards, an Ace Copenhagen tin, and several shot glasses. On the wall is a bad painting of a half-naked woman.

Others have said that the real reason that the management will not let anyone sleep in Room 18 is that there has been more than the average number of mysterious deaths in the room.

For those of a doubting frame of mind, there was a Thomas James Wright born in New Mexico in 1859 and one of the old guest registries does show that a TJ Wright stayed in the hotel several nights in 1881.

The Mary Lambert Room

Another spirit is believed to be that of Mary Lambert, wife of Henry Lambert, the man who built the St. James Hotel. She lived many years in the hotel, gave birth to her children there, watched at least 2 of her babies die there, and eventually, in December of 1926, died there herself. The people that work at the hotel call her the protector. They firmly believe her presence is still there and they believe she watches out for the hotel and the people in it.

It is said that you can often smell Mary's perfume when her presence is near, and many staff members, previous owners, and guests swear they have indeed smelled it. It is also said that if you are staying in her room and you leave the window open she will tap on it incessantly until you close it. On other occasions, a milky transparent woman can be seen in the hallways.

The Kate Lambert Room

The employees of The St. James are given the option of living in the hotel. One of the employees, a young lady, decided to stay in the hotel and was given the Kate Lambert Room which is the last room on the right at the end of the 2nd floor family wing. The room is directly across from the Mary Lambert room, and directly next to room 18.

The young lady has said the almost as son as she began to stay in the room, she had problem sleeping. Many times every night she would awaken, although there was nothing specific, such as a noise, that would explain her being awakened. Due to her lack of sleep, she was usually exhausted the next day.

Because of the hotel's history, ghost hunters and psychics often visit the hotel, so she asked one of the psychics to come to her room. The psychic told her that the spirit of TJ was trying to posses her. However, on the plus side, the spirit of Mary Lambert was protecting her from TJ.

The psychic told the tired young lady that it was this nightly spectral battle was what kept waking her up. The young employee liked the room in which she was staying very much and certainly did not want to move. However, the psychic told her that if she stayed in the room, eventually the spirit of TJ would eventually succeed and posses her. Just to be on the safe side, the young lady moved to another room and found that she slept soundly each night, no longer waking up in the early hours of the morning.

Non-Specific Hauntings

In addition to the well known spirits haunting the St. James, employees have reported that many non-specific hauntings occur on a daily basis. There are cold spots, things are constantly falling off of walls and shelves and the computer and phone at the front desk behave erratically. Cameras and video equipment often break or don't work correctly

The dining room, which used to be the main saloon, still houses the original mirrored bar. Many guests have reported seeing the reflection of a cowboy sitting at one of the tables only to look around and discover there is no one else in the room.

Hanging above the 2nd floor landing is a large crystal chandelier. During restoration, one of the previous owners discovered that every time she would turn it off before leaving, it would be on again by the time she got to the parking area. This happened repeatedly, even though there was no one in the hotel. Since they were in the process of restoration she thought maybe it was an electrical problem, but the electricians found nothing that could account for the light coming on by itself. Now the staff just leaves the ornate chandelier burning 24hrs a day.

One employee who was working the front desk reported that he very clearly heard a high pitched shriek coming from the far corner of the lobby. Looking up from his work, he was dumbfounded to see absolutely no one on that side of the room. Quickly looking around, his eyes rested on three other guests mingling at the other side of the lobby, apparently having not heard the loud scream, they were completely unphased.

The Annex

Apparently, the original hotel is not the only place with strange happenings. In the 1980's a modern 10 room annex was built onto the hotel. The rooms in the annex have all the amenities, including phones and cable TV.

It is said that there has been unexplained activity in the annex. According to one employee there were two girls staying in one of the room in the annex who had an unusual experience.

It seems that one of the girls was taking a shower when the other girl opened the bathroom door. The girl in the shower yelled for her friend to close the door and let her finish her shower. The door shut, but a few minutes later it opened again. By the time the girl got out of the shower this had happened 3 or 4 times. Angry, the wet girl wrapped a towel around her and stormed out of the bathroom prepared to yell at her friend for continuing to open and shut the door. To her surprise, her friend was not in the room. She finally talked to her friend, the girl that had been in the shower discovered that whoever or whatever had been opening and closing the shower door, it was not her friend as she had not even been in the room at the time.

There is also another, though, friendly, spirit known to inhabit this old hotel. The owners have dubbed this spirit the "little imp", as it likes to torment new employees in the kitchen and dining room. Described as a small man with a pockmarked face, the little imp has been known to burst glasses, re-light candles, and move objects in front of nervous new hires.

CHAPTER THIRTY-NINE

THE HAUNTED HIGHWAY
HIGHWAY 666

The number 666 have always been known as the Devil's number, but for some reason this was the number assigned a stretch of highway that starts in Taos, New Mexico and crosses four states until it terminates in Salt Lake City, Utah. Route 666 is a lonely, deserted stretch of road with a long history of accidents and apparitions.

Because of the so-called bad luck along this stretch of road, state highway officials in all four states have been asked at one time or another to change the name of this highway. The only state to respond to this demand until just recently, was Arizona. Because a lot of Arizona motorists complained the highway running through their state is now named Highway 191. Also disgruntled, a man from Indiana wrote one of his U.S. Senators, asking why New Mexico didn't change their section of the highway's name. In each case and state (except in Arizona) the demands were tabled. Eventually, however, quite a bit of this highway has become Highway 191, even in Utah.

Originally named in 1926, it was the sixth branch of the now defunct Route 66, and therefore became Route 666. Most of the highway now will be named Highway 191.

However, people still don't like having to drive on a road that refers to the antichrist and still remember that it once had such a name. There are a large number of stories about this highway that certainly stretch the credibility of anyone. According to one story that has been told by a number of people who routinely drove this deserted stretch of highway there have been several brushes with what appears to a phantom truck.

According to one young man, he was on his way to Gallop one evening and the highway was deserted except for himself. Then suddenly, in his rear view mirror he saw a truck that looked like it was on fire heading straight for him, right down the middle of the highway. The truck was going so fast that sparks were flying up off the wheels and flames were coming from the smokestack of the big eighteen wheeler.

The sight if this wheeled monster scared the young man so badly that he pulled way off the road and walked 20 feet or so out into the desert away from his car and waited for the truck to pass him. By the young man's estimate, the truck had to be going at least 130 miles an hour. He then got back into his car and continued on.

In addition to the mad trucker that has been seen a number of times, there are also stories about big black phantom automobiles that race along the road at high speed, as well as packs of demon dogs that have been seen on this highway. The dogs always attack at night with the flashing of yellow eyes and sharp teeth; shredding the tires of those silly enough to stop along this highway at night. There are also stories about one or two individuals who were daring enough to get out of their cars at night along this stretch. Both are said to have disappeared.

Then there is a beautiful, young and frail girl in a long nightgown that roams the road. People see her walking along the side of the road, all alone in the dark out in the middle of nowhere. They stop to help her but as they approach the young lady, she instantly vanishes.

There are many other tales of people who either disappear along this route or suddenly appear out of nowhere. There are even tales of the same person, disappearing at one point along the highway and then reappearing at another location miles away, without having any recollection of where they have been or what they have been doing.

There are also a number of stories told by Native Americans of unwanted passengers appearing in the backseat of the car along several deserted stretches of New Mexico highway, but especially along Highway 666. It seems that skin walkers or evil-minded Medicine Men, can shape shift into various animals such as crows, coyotes, or wolves and appear out of nowhere in front of your car on the highway.

This occurrence, in and of itself, can cause unexplained accidents along the road. However, this is usually a warning of things to come and can happen several times before the evil shaman decides to appear in the backseat of unsuspecting motorist's car. So it is advised that several people ride in the same car along this stretch of highway so the evil skin walker has nowhere to sit. This may work and it may not, for the skin walker can play all sorts of tricks on the eyes, being able to shape shift as he or she does. So it is also good advice not to be driving all night or to be very tired, as this is when the skin walkers are on the prowl stealing souls for themselves.

"Drive Route 666 at night, and you drive at your own risk," the signs should say. Even in the daytime some of the long, deserted stretches are enough to frighten drivers, or at least put them to sleep, which is just as dangerous as seeing anything. Take a lot of people with you and don't leave any space for unwanted passengers who just might decide to appear in your backseat. Pull off the road if a huge diesel truck comes barring down on you from either direction.

Don't be curious to see if there is a driver in that single car passing you in the night. Don't look for lights floating in the sky. Hope you don't see any young girls in white dresses. Never stop if you spot something peculiar and don't pick up hitchhikers. Lastly, if demon dogs approach you in the night, just keep driving.

CHAPTER FORTY

LAS VEGAS, NEW MEXICO

A century and a half ago, travelers who reached Las Vegas on the long Santa Fe Trail journey could stop at a spring-fed well for a drink and to water their teams. The same well, dug by settlers around 1840, now restored, it is the nation's oldest surviving well along the Santa Fe Trail. The well, or Hays Springs Well as it is sometimes called, is located at 2213 Hot Springs Blvd. Visitors today toss coins into the historic wishing well - a water source that, in the 1930s, granted residents wishes for relief from a crushing drought. In the grip of the Dust Bowl era, the Rio Gallinas and virtually every well in Las Vegas went dry. The 6" x 17" shale bowl well, fed by seven springs, remained the community's only constant source of water and saved the people from drought. The well has a depth of just under 4 feet and maintains a year-round temperature of 50 degrees.

THE PLAZA HOTEL
Las Vegas, NM

Byron T. Mills was 3 prominent Las Vegas attorney and abstracter who owned the Plaza Hotel during most of the first half of this century. He arrived in Las Vegas in 1852, just after the landmark hotel was completed, and took over ownership of the property some 36 years later. According to the January, 1945 issue of New Mexico Magazine, Mills was beginning to dismantle the hotel and sell its furniture in anticipation of demolishing the three-story structure. The article neglected to explain his motives, but devoted considerable space to Mills' knowledgeable discourse on the hotel's history. Mills was even quoted as saying, "I almost feel guilty [about the demolition]. It certainly is an old landmark."

For reasons unknown today, Mills never followed through with his plan. Some speculate a disembodied "Byron T." haunts the hotel today out of a sense of guilt while others believe he remains because he loved the hotel more than he claimed in life. A third faction suggests the historic hotel's resident ghost simply enjoys the company of others, especially women, which may explain both the reported presence of a man coupled with the sudden scent of perfume.

THE GHOSTS

A number of the stories of hauntings seem to come from room 310. More than one lady traveling alone has reported the presence of a man in their room. Almost everyone would agree that the spirit of Mills has a special fondness for women who are alone in their rooms and traveling salesmen.

One particular salesman had checked into his room on the third floor, dropped his bags, and went directly to the bathroom. When he got out he noticed the door's dead bolt was locked. That's funny, he thought I don't remember locking the door. He then undressed for his shower, carefully putting his money under his clothes, neatly piled next to the sink. When he got out of the shower, he was startled to find his money now on top of his clothes!

Another employee who was staying in one of the third floor rooms for a time tells that she was awakened in the early morning hours by a door opening and footsteps across the room. Then she felt someone sit on the bed. She sat up, and saw nothing. She tried to go back to sleep, but until 5:00 am, when her husband finally returned, she heard Byron pacing back and forth across the room.

Other employees report smelling cigar smoke in the bar, and hearing heavy boots walking when there was no one there.

The hotel bar was also the scene of another of Byron's pranks. According to one story, there were a couple of devout Catholics, who after church one Good Friday, decided to go to the bar for drinks. They were sitting on the patio, feeling a little guilty to be spending that holy day in such a frivolous way, when a drop of blood fell out of nowhere, landing on a white tablecloth. They fled in horror, and have not indulged in liquor on Good Friday again.

CHAPTER FORTY-ONE

CUBA, NEW MEXICO

The area currently called Cuba has a long and interesting history. Native Americans have occupied the area near the village for hundreds of years. In the 1700's Spanish ranchers and farmers settled the area. There are many large ranches and farms in Cuba and the surrounding areas. Cattle, sheep, and goats are the primary livestock raised. There are several stories that explain how Cuba got its name. One story claims that the name came from the Spanish word for water tank/trough, Cubeta Cuba was once surrounded by a great deal of water. Another popular story claims that the name came from soldiers who had visited the island of Cuba and felt the landscape resembled that of the island.

The Cuba area is known for its wildlife and beautiful views. Cuba, and indeed all of New Mexico, is known for its spectacular sunsets. If one were to look at the nearby mountains during a particularly good evening they would think they were afire from the red glow of the setting sun. Cuba is also an ideal area for hunting, or wildlife spotting. Herds of elk and deer roam the nearby foothills, and the Jicarilla Reservation. The high number of large private ranches in the Cuba and Lindrith areas combined with high deer and elk population attracts hunters from all over the world.

The village of Cuba has a population less than 1000. However, it serves an area with a population approaching 5,000. It is also a favorite stop for travelers on NM 44/US 550, a major highway connecting central New Mexico with the Four Corners region.

The village is at the base of the Nacimiento Mountain Range and at the edge of the Navajo Reservation, Jicarilla Reservation and the Jemez Pueblo.

REED CANYON
Cuba, New Mexico

Trail Creek in this peaceful canyon is a deserted area haunted by the ghosts of settlers moving west after the Civil War. The sounds of whips and wagon wheels rolling over the steep hills sometimes last for hours. Barking dogs, crying babies, laughing children, and busy people shouting commands at one another are heard along the trail. Sheepherders, tree cutters, and campers have all heard the preternatural sounds. Reed Canyon is named after a man who built a stone cabin in the mountains and charged outlaws a high price to hide out there. Reed died in 1900, but the ruins of his house remains. Ojitos Mesa in the canyon area is a location of frequent reports. This area of many passing wagon trains is where you can still hear the sounds of travelers. Barking dogs, rumbling wagons, horses, children, and shouting voices are often heard. Ojitos Mesa is where many of the reports originate.

CHAPTER FORTY-TWO

ESPANOLA, NEW MEXICO

Espanola, New Mexico is a small town, with very little for people to do in the evening after their work day is done. Perhaps there is a reason. Consider the following story told by someone who lived in this quiet village for a short while.

I was living in Espanola, New Mexico for about two months. If you have ever been there you would know that there is not much to do but gamble. A friend and I asked the lady that I lived with where we could go play pool. She told us of a place down the street so we went! It was a pizza place with arcade game and 3 pool tables in the back.

As soon as we walked in I had a weird feeling, but I brushed it off. I figured that it was just because I had never been there before. We started to play pool, and I was on my game from the get go. I couldn't have lost if you had paid me. After about the third or forth game I went to the restroom.

The hallway was very dark and as soon as I got into the bathroom I felt like I wasn't alone. I didn't waste any time, and got out of there. I told my friend, and shortly there after he used the restroom. When he came out he said "Let's go." I asked him why and he told me that he had gotten the same feeling.

We decided to stay, and after a while I heard this guy talking who I thought worked there. I went up to him and asked if there was a spirit that he knew of in the building. He asked me why and I told him that I just felt something weird! He told me that there were a couple of ghosts, to which I asked if they were friendly. He said "Sometimes..."

From there he told me about how his family had built the building, and it used to be a banquet hall. They closed it, and years later his father had decided to open it back up. They had just gotten it all cleaned up and ready to open, and his father went to do some finishing touches. He came back to the house white and shaking. The family asked what had happened and he told them that he was getting ready to leave and he glanced up at a religious painting on the wall. He said that it looked like someone had cut it. He got up on a chair to get a closer look and said that it looked like claw marks. He looked closer and it disappeared.

The family went down to the restaurant and when they walked in they saw it too, and it disappeared again. The guy told me that there had only been a few people that had ever said anything, or felt anything. All I can tell you is whatever was in that building was not friendly. After that we would go to Santa Fe to play pool!

CHAPTER FORTY-THREE

WHITE SANDS, NEW MEXICO

White Sands National Monument is the world's largest outcropping of pure gypsum. The area is surrounded by the missile range and is about 30 miles northeast of WSMR headquarters. It lies just north US Highway 70 about 15 miles west of Alamogordo, 54 miles east of Las Cruces and slightly less than 100 miles from El Paso.

The monument consists of approximately 176,000 acres of pure white gypsum "sand" that shifts continually from one high dune to make another. The glaring white area is almost bare of vegetation. However, many species of plants have adapted to this unusual habitat, and through the gradual extension of roots and stalks, have avoided being buried by the drifting sand. A variety of plants fringe the edge of the park where they grow in weird shapes and forms.

Found also in the 275 square-mile tract are several species of reptiles and rodents that have adapted to their strange environment by developing a bleached white protective coloration.

As the years pass the moving sand bares relics of the past. Among items brought to the surface in the past was an ancient two-wheel cart believed to be an early Spanish carreta.

This isolated area was made a national monument in 1933 and named White Sands National Monument. It was from this national monument that White Sands Missile Range took its name in 1945. In fact, only 50 percent of the white dunes are protected in the monument. The other half are on the missile range east of the Space Harbor.

ALKALI FLATS,
White Sands, New Mexico

Alkali Flats is in the eastern foothills of the San Andres Mountains in the Great White Sands area. This entire area is known for unexplained happenings. Tracks of giant 'humanoid creatures' were found there in 1931. The thirteen prints measured sixteen to twenty-two inches long and eight to twelve inches wide. The stride was about five feet with a separation width of two feet.

The prints were about 2.5 inches deep in 1931, but by 1974, they stood 1.5 inches ABOVE ground. The surrounding soil had eroded away AROUND the compacted footprints, leaving eerie pedestals of alien footprints. By 1981, the prints stood over two inches high. Archeologists consider the unexplainable footprints to be at least ten thousand years old.

Even given the great age of these unusual tracks there have been reports of strange creatures seen roaming the area and very few of the locals will venture into some parts of the Great White Sands area even in the daylight.

CHAPTER FORTY-FOUR

CLOUDCROFT, NEW MEXICO

One hundred years ago, the railroad was completed between Alamogordo, New Mexico and El Paso, Texas. The railroad's owners were intrigued by the majestic mountains to the East of Alamogordo and soon sent a survey party to the summit. They discovered untouched wilderness -- a wonderland of wildlife, plants, and trees. They were also impressed with the way the clouds blanketed the ground because at 9,000 feet above sea-level, Cloudcroft was literally in the clouds. The name Cloudcroft is a term related to an English description of a clearing covered in clouds.

Soon after, an excursion train was established to the top of the mountain and the village of Cloudcroft was born. For the first half of Cloudcroft's existence, the train was the only means of travel to the village (except possibly by pack mule). In the mid-1940s, the first highway to the village was opened -- taking away much of the train's logging and excursion business. The train discontinued service to the village in 1948.

THE LODGE
Cloudcroft, New Mexico

The Lodge was originally constructed in the rustic mountain community of Cloudcroft, New Mexico in 1899, by the Alamogordo & Sacramento Mountain Railway. It was owned and operated by the railroad and intended to be a resort for workers who were the by-product of the railway's search for timber.

The hotel was immediately successful- it's breathtaking location in the lushly wooded Sacramento Mountains offered a welcome cool retreat to literally thousands of heat-punished Texans (New Mexico, Oklahoma, and Arizona were not yet states at this time). An article published in the Albuquerque Journal-Democrat near the completion of the Lodge in 1899 stated, "This beautiful building will be known as Cloudcroft Lodge and its interior will be furnished with a lavish hand, yet in keeping with the character of the place. Fireplaces, with wide, hungry mouths, will sparkle, crackle and dart forth welcome tongues of flame to hundreds of merry guests, who will find new pleasure in life during the long, sultry summer."

In 1908 the El Paso & Southwestern Railroad System- the Lodge's new owner- advertised that the hotel, restaurant, dancing pavilion, tennis court, golf links, bowling alley, billiard parlor, burro trips and children's playground were accessible for "weekend rates of $3.00 round trip," and that Lodge rates were "$12.50 and up" per week.

On June 13th 1909, a raging fire blazed through the Lodge, utterly destroying it. By 1911, the Lodge was completely rebuilt and reopened on its current site, and its appearance has remained virtually the same since then- a historic, timeless gem suspended in time. Over the long, distinguished history of the Lodge, it has played host to numerous famous folk- including Pancho Villa, Gilbert Roland, Judy Garland and Clark Gable (in fact the last two carved their names into the wall of the Lodge's Tower, where they can still be seen to this day). But by far the most infamous guest of all at the Lodge is the specter of Rebecca.

THE GHOSTS

Rebecca has become one of the most famous ghosts in New Mexico. The lovely young lady was a chambermaid at the Lodge who reputedly disappeared from the premises sometime in the 1920's/30's. They claim that this restless wraith has made her presence known here ever since her death.

Rebecca was said to be a gorgeous red-haired chambermaid who worked

Figure 21: This is believed to be a photo of Rebecca.

and lived at the Lodge in the 1920's/30's. Similar to her fellow Lodge employees, she lived in the employee's rooms, which were located in the basement at the time. She was by all means a very friendly and flirtatious young lady, and unforgettably lovely.

There was some rumor that Rebecca moonlighted as a prostitute, although no proof of this claim existed. Whatever the case, according to the story, Rebecca's jealous lumberjack boyfriend caught her in the arms of another man at the Lodge (possibly in Room 101, aka the Governor's Suite) and became enraged. Shortly after, Rebecca disappeared from the Lodge, never to be seen again. Well, not alive, anyway. Because soon after her disappearance people began to report having some very strange, even ghostly, experiences...

Over the years, there have been many sightings of an auburn haired apparition floating through the halls, a vision seen by both employees and guests alike. One guest heard scraping sounds in the hallway late one night and opened the door to see a red-haired woman in a 30's style night dress rearranging flowers in a vase on top of an antique chest.

Another guest was shocked when he went to take a shower, only to find a "vaporous female" reclining in his bathtub. There have also been reports of objects such as watches, ashtrays, and silverware sliding across surfaces untouched... doors opening and closing on their own... lights and other appliances turning on and off by themselves... furniture moved inexplicably... and even faucets turning on and toilets flushing for no apparent reason.

But perhaps one of the strangest events happened one Halloween night, when a man dressed in a tuxedo came into the Lodge's dining room and sat alone at an intimate, two-chaired table. He ordered two dinners and two glasses of wine. Everyone in the room watched closely as the man ate his meal and carried on a conversation with someone who wasn't there. No one ever saw anyone sit with the man or even go near him, yet at the end of his meal, both wineglasses and both plates were empty.

Rebecca's manifestations are many. One of her favorite "hangouts" is the Red Dog Saloon- an old-west style saloon with rough-hewn walls and Southwest decorum- which is located in the basement, where the employee's showers used to be. This is a very active spot as the lights go off and on untouched. Even more mysteriously, 1930's-era poker chips have been mysteriously found in the middle of a floor which had been clear only minutes before. Ashtrays move by themselves and flames appear in the fireplace with no logs or other source of fuel.

Lodge patrons have called the front desk to complain about the loud music coming from the saloon at times when the saloon was empty and wasn't even open. Others have reported seeing an apparition of a twirling woman has been reportedly seen on the dance floor. One bartender claimed to have seen the reflection of a beautiful red-haired woman wearing a long dress in the mirror behind the bar- yet the woman wasn't there when the bartender turned around to look at her.

Another paranormal hotspot seems to be found in the "Tower"... a three-story structure that stands tall above the Lodge itself. The Tower is kept locked, with two levels of small sitting rooms with windows that yield a panoramic view of the lush mountains. Some have reported feeling cold spots and a "presence" in the Tower, and the third floor- which is where the locked door leading to the Tower can be found- is reportedly very paranormally active as well.

Additionally, there is also said to be a lot of activity surrounding Room 101, the Governor's Suite. Some have theorized that Rebecca carried on her "trysts" in this room and was perhaps even caught in the act there by her lumberjack boyfriend one fateful day. Whatever the connection, the Lodge staff has gotten calls from Room 101 where no one is on the other end, even when no one is in the room at the time. Despite having a modern, computerized phone system, the phone calls from Room 101 persist.

The light in the ceiling fan just outside of Room 101 is also said to turn off and on at will. A former housekeeper claimed that after making up a bed, she would come back only to find an indentation as if someone had just laid or sat there. She also said that guest's shoes would mysteriously move a few rooms down from where they were supposed to be. It would seem that even in spectral form Rebecca is a very fun-loving and mischievous spirit.

To this day, employees and guests alike are still reporting strange and mysterious encounters at the Lodge. There have been a number of reports that the toilets in the ladies room had been flushing by themselves earlier that very day. Whether you believe in Rebecca or not, the Lodge is still an amazing, unique place with a ton of fascinating history. The forest scenery and mountain views are heavenly, and the Lodge itself is a graceful and timeless treat lavishly furnished with the Victorian and country lodge decor of a bygone era. There is even a fabulous restaurant called- what else?- Rebecca's

CHAPTER FORTY-FIVE

DAWSON, NEW MEXICO

The town of Dawson, New Mexico is a forgotten spot on the map with an unforgettable history. In 1869, John Barkley Dawson came to the Vermejo Valley looking for a place to homestead. He found it 5 1/2 miles upstream from the little settlement of Colfax and paid $3,700 to owner Lucien B. Maxwell for the deed, finalizing the verbal deal with a handshake[28].

After settling on his land, Dawson was somewhat surprised to find coal on his property. Scraping chunks of coal from the surface of his farm land, he burned it in his stove rather than using wood. At first, his neighbors thought he was a little crazy, but out of curiosity, several asked for samples and were pleased at the results, so much so that Dawson began to sell the coal to his neighbors.

In 1870 Lucien B. Maxwell sold his interest in the Maxwell Land Grant. The property was quickly sold two more times over the next two years and in 1872 it was in the hands of a Dutch Firm who was aggressively looking for ways to exploit the resources of the grant. The grant owners immediately attempted to extract rents from many of the squatters living on the grant; however, they often had no way of knowing who was a legal owner and who was not.

---

[28] http://www.legendsofamerica.com/HC-Dawson1.html

When they found out that the Dawson land was heavily laced with coal, they wanted to develop the vein and attempted to evict Dawson. Dawson was ready to fight to protect his land, whether it be in court or with guns, but reason prevailed and Dawson finally consented to settling the matter in the courts. Dawson admitted that his transaction with Maxwell in 1869 was purely verbal; stating that a promise and a handshake was the way Maxwell had always done business.

Dawson hired an attorney and the case was tried in the fall of 1893 when the court found in Dawson's favor. The court held that the Land Grant Company could not prove that Dawson did not own the land and the mineral rights and to Dawson's surprise and the Land Grant Company's chagrin, the courts further found that Dawson had not bought the 1,000 acres that he had thought, but rather 20,000 acres.

Dawson and his partner, Charles Springer, ranched the land until 1901, when he sold most of the land to the Dawson Fuel Company for $400,000. He retained 1200 acres for himself and continued to ranch.

The Dawson Fuel Co. was founded with the help of Charles B. Eddy of El Paso, Texas, a railroad promoter. A 137-mile-long railroad was built from the mine to Tucumcari, New Mexico linking the spot with the Rock Island Lines. By August 1, 1901, a crew of fifty miners was ready to work. A sawmill was busy turning out lumber for houses, coke ovens were smoking and by the end of that first year, Dawson was well on the way to becoming a city and the center of the largest coal mining operation in New Mexico. Later, the company built a hundred cottages for 500 more people and erected additional coke ovens. Off to a quick start, the town was prosperous and growing.

Tragedy struck the first of many blows to the new community on September 14, 1903 when fire broke out in the No. 1 Mine, followed by several explosions. With the grace of God, 500 miners escaped. The men worked for a week to control the fire and when it was over three were dead.

By 1905, 124 coke ovens were belching fire and the town was thriving with about 2000 residents. By this time the settlement boasted a post office, a liquor store, a mercantile, a school, a newspaper and a large hotel.

In 1906 the Phelps Dodge Corporation bought the Dawson mines and, sparing no expense, determined to make Dawson a model city and the ideal company town. The company built spacious homes for its miners, supplied with water from the company's water system. They also built a four-story brick building which housed the Phelps Dodge Mercantile Department Store which sold virtually anything the townsfolk might need -- food, clothing, shoes, hardware, furniture, drugs, jewelry, baked goods and ice from its own plant. A modern hospital was built which maintained a staff of five doctors and was complete with a laboratory, surgery and x-ray equipment. For their leisure time, the miners enjoyed the use of the company built movie theater, swimming pool, bowling alley, baseball park, pool hall, golf course, lodge hall, and even an opera house. Phelps Dodge also supported two churches, one Catholic and one

Protestant. Children attended either the Central Elementary School in downtown Dawson or the Douglas Elementary School on Capitan Hill. A large high school building was built that eventually employed 40 teachers and their athletic teams won many state championships. The company also built a steam-powered electric plant, which powered not only Dawson, but also the nearby towns of Walsenburg, Colorado, and Raton. Providing good-paying jobs for the residents, the extra features of the company town helped keep the employment stable and under the new management Dawson's population grew quickly to 3,500.

The residents were well aware that mining was a dangerous business -- the best of coal mines being squalid, hot, dark holes permeated with black dust. Even if the miners escaped the constant dangers of cave-ins and explosions, their life expectancy was sharply reduced by "black lung" and other affects of the sooty mine air. From time to time a miner would fall into a pit or die in the collapse of a seam, and the company built cemetery slowly began to fill.

In 1913, Stag Canyon No 2 Mine at Dawson, New Mexico was the 2nd worst coal mining disaster in U.S. History, claiming 263 lives.

Dawson became a mecca for miners from all over the world with immigrants arriving from Italy, China, Poland, Germany, Greece, Britain, Finland, Sweden, and Mexico. The miners worked together to dig the coal that fueled an area equal to 1/6 of the United States and Dawson grew into a company town of about 9,000.

The Phelps Dodge Company strove to make the mines as safe as possible. They did such a good job with Stag Canyon Mine No. 2 that it attracted the eyes of coal-mining experts who, in 1913, described it as "the highest achievement in modern equipment and safety appliances that exists in the world." The New Mexico Inspector of Mines completed two days of inspection of the Dawson pits on October 20, 1913 and reported that Stag Canyon Mine No. 2 was totally "free from traces of gas, and in splendid general condition."

Yet, Dawson was doomed to suffer a series of tragedies that shadowed its history to the end. During this period of abundance and prosperity Dawson suffered its worst catastrophe on Wednesday, October 22, 1913,only two days after the mine's inspection. The morning dawned bright and clear and 284 miners reported to work at Stag Canyon Mine No. 2. Work went on as usual until a little after three p.m. when the mine was rocked by a huge explosion that sent a tongue of fire 100 feet out of the tunnel mouth shaking the homes in Dawson two miles away.

Relief and disaster crews were rushed from neighboring towns. Phelps Dodge sent a trainload of doctors, nurses and medical supplies up from El Paso and striking miners in Colorado ceased picketing and offered to form rescue teams. Working around the clock, rows of bodies were brought to the surface. The distraught wives and family members clogged and impeded the operations around the mouth of the mine.

Only 23 of the 286 men working in the mine were found alive. Two of the rescuers were themselves killed by falling boulders in the shaft. Mass funerals were conducted for the victims and row upon row of graves dug, making it necessary to extend the cemetery far up the hill. The cemetery was marked by white iron crosses and the burials continued for weeks. It was the second worst mine disaster of the century.

Investigators determined that the explosion had been caused by an overcharged blast in a dusty pillar section of the mine. Dynamite, not a permitted explosive, was being used. The Bureau of Mines allowed certain types of explosives, but blasting was to be conducted only when all miners were evacuated and water sprays were to be used to settle the coal dust. These rules had obviously been ignored.

Safety measures were heavily increased after the disastrous explosion and subsequent accidents were comparatively minor with few fatalities. The mining continued and in 1918, the Dawson mines reached their peak production of over four million tons of coal.

But tragedy hit Dawson again on February 8, 1923, at about 2:20 PM, in Stag Canyon Mine No. 1. When a mine train jumped its track, it hit the supporting timbers of the tunnel mouth, and ignited coal dust in the mine. There were 123 men in the mine at the time. Many women who lost husbands in the earlier disaster waited anxiously for their sons to appear out of the smoke. Early the next morning two miners who had been in an isolated section of the mine walked out. They were the only survivors. The cemetery was extended once again and more white crosses took their place in the cemetery.

After the clean up, Dawson continued to thrive for almost three decades, with sons following their fathers into the mines. But gradually railroads began to convert to diesel-electric locomotives, while natural gas and heating oil replaced coal as the fuel to heat homes. There was a brief resurgence of mining during World War II, but after that, it was clear coal was a fuel of the past. On April 30, 1950 the mine was shut down. The announcement meant the death of the company town. Phelps Dodge sold the whole town, buildings and all, to a salvage company in Phoenix. The giant coal washer was shipped piece by piece to Kentucky and several houses were moved out and relocated. The company safe ended up in the Phelps Dodge headquarters in Bisbee, Arizona, where it is still displayed at the mining museum. Over the next dozens of years, ranchers operating Phelps Dodge's "Diamond D" ranch occupied the few dwellings remaining.

Over 350 white iron crosses in the Dawson Cemetery mark the graves of those who perished in the mining disasters. The cemetery, a deeply moving site, is now the only part of Dawson still open to the visitor. These silent sentinels, some with individual names and some unmarked, are poignant reminders of the tragic deaths of the victims, and, more importantly, their lives.

For a while, Dawson had been truly forgotten by New Mexico until two brothers went on a metal detecting expedition in 1991. Dale and Lloyd Christian were shocked when they saw the uncared for and abandoned cemetery. When

Dale Christian returned home to Albuquerque he petitioned the New Mexico State Historic Preservation Division to place the cemetery on the National Register of Historic Places.

The New Mexico Office of Cultural Affairs was unaware that the cemetery even existed and asked Christian to provide measurements of the site. Not only did he provide the measurements, but he also provided pictures and an accounting of the number of graves and pictures. The Office of Cultural Affairs was amazed and although very few cemeteries are placed on the National Register, the Dawson Cemetery was added on April 9, 1992.

Now the site is again part of a working ranch, just as it was prior to 1901. Every two years former residents hold a picnic on the site of their former town on Labor Day weekend. And on Memorial Day, many visit the cemetery where their relatives still lie buried.

THE GHOSTS

Today, the cemetery is the main thing to see at Dawson and this is the area of the most hauntings.

Many swear that the cemetery of this old silver boomtown is haunted by the ghosts of miners killed in cave-ins. As stated above, two separate mining disasters killed most of the men in Dawson and then the town was abandoned at the turn of the century. However, the spirits of those that died in the disasters are still very much present in this old town as it is said that the light from their bright carbide lights can be seen hovering above their graves at night.

CHAPTER FORTY-SIX

COLFAX, NEW MEXICO

Colfax was a small community located in Colfax County along New Mexico's border with southeast Colorado. Colfax County is very diverse in geography and industry. Plains and ranch land cover expanses of land near Springer and Miami. In the northernmost portion of the county, Raton is the gateway to Colorado. Along the Colorado border lays Valle Vidal, a national forest unit with summer fishing and recreation activities. Traveling west along Hwy 64, visitors pass through the old western town of Cimarron, home to Philmont Scout Ranch. Further west is the Cimarron Canyon with breathtaking scenery, opening at the pass to a spectacular view of Eagle Nest Lake and the Moreno Valley. In the southwestern corner of the county, Angel Fire boasts a growing ski resort only 30 minutes east of Taos.

THE GHOSTS

Today not much is left of Colfax except the spirits who still appear where this town once stood.

The Weeping Lady of Colfax is the apparition of a woman who appears in the back row of the combination church and schoolhouse here. Her spirit still grieves for her young son, who died of an unknown illness in the late 1800's. Inconsolable grief killed the mother within a few months of her son's death. Reported phenomena include sounds of sobbing, the cries of a young boy and unseen footsteps are heard in the church/schoolhouse. On occasion, the mother appears as a ball of light that floats and wanders through the abandoned town.

The lights of other spirits can be seen floating above graves in the old cemetery.

CHAPTER FORTY-SEVEN

CORRALES, NEW MEXICO

The Village of Corrales is a small, oasis of calm located within a large, fast-growing metropolitan area. The village is bordered on the east by the Rio Grande and, across the river, by the Sandia Indian Reservation. To the south is the City of Albuquerque while to the west and north is the City of Rio Rancho. The greater metropolitan area of Albuquerque numbers well over a half million people, but the population of Corrales is about 7300 who work to retain a rural lifestyle.

Prehistoric sites indicate the Corrales Valley has been occupied as early as 500 A.D. when the ancestors of the present-day Indian Pueblos derived sustenance from the fertile valley. Subsequent populations, including Hispanic, European and American families, settled here to raise grapes, apples, and livestock.

Today, Corrales is distinguished by its broad green pastures and orchards, its rich historic and artistic character, and of course the sounds and scents of roosters, cows, horses and sheep. To cross the borders into Corrales is to step into another time and place where the stresses of twenty-first century life give way to the grace and pace of another era.

RANCHO DE CORRALES RESTAURANT
Corrales, New Mexico

Formerly known as the Territorial House, this ancient hacienda was built in 1801 by Diego Montoya. Though now a very well known restaurant, this old building has seen a lot of hatred and death within its adobe walls.

A bloody shoot out between members of the Emberto family took place here in 1898. It started when the son killed his father's mistress. The father then shot and murdered his wife, blaming her for prompting the murder. In the ensuing gun battle, the father was also killed. The Embertos were buried on the property and their inflamed passions are felt to this day.

THE GHOSTS

Employees and many customers of the Rancho De Corrales Restaurant are aware of a strange presence that haunts the old section of the building. Reported activity includes items moving on their own, disembodied voices and the apparition of a woman in 1800s era clothing.

There is also the apparition of a man sitting in a rocking chair that has been spotted on several occasions in the banquet room. This room also has moving cold spots, candles light themselves and chairs are moved about in various odd configurations. Other areas of reported phenomena include the north dining rooms and the bar.

CHAPTER FORTY-EIGHT

SOCORRO, NEW MEXICO

When Onate's expedition reached the Socorro Pueblo, it was in sad shape after crossing the waterless Jornada de Muerto. The Teypanas, the natives of Socorro Pueblo helped the Spanish survive. For 100 years after Oñate's expedition passed in 1598, Socorro became a way station on El Camino Real – the Royal Road – which led from El Paso del Norte to Santa Fe and the Spanish-claimed territories to the north. During the 1600's, the Spanish built four missions among the Piro Pueblos, including one in Socorro. Spanish families surrounded the mission, farming and raising livestock on land given them as large land grants.

In 1680, when the Pueblo Revolt broke out in northern New Mexico, driving the Spanish colonists out of New Mexico Territory, the Teypanas left also, establishing a new community farther south. Nothing remains of the pueblo which offered succor to the Oñate expedition. Socorro was not re-settled until 1816.

In 1821, Mexico won its independence from Spain. The New Mexico Territory received this news belatedly and celebrated with a show of enthusiasm. For many years, however, New Mexico was a neglected appendage to the new nation of Mexico. Life in Socorro remained the same hard-scrabble frontier effort it had always been. The farmers and stockmen were beleaguered by Indian raids, disease and, when crops failed, hunger.

The citizens of Socorro County became Americans in 1841, when General Stephen Watts Kearny entered Santa Fe and occupied the territory in the name of the United States. In 1854, Fort Craig was built south of Socorro to protect the area against Apache and Navajo raids and to protect the northern end of El Camino Real. With the outbreak of the Civil War, the fort remained a Union Army Post. Today, the remains of the fort are open to visitors from dawn to dusk, seven days a week. The site has interpretive signs and a campsite. In this harsh terrain, a sensitive tourist will gain a new appreciation of the hardiness of the early settlers.

With the coming of the railroad in the 1880's, miners, merchants and cattlemen arrived in Socorro County from the eastern states. Mines in the area added to the importance of the town. Smelters opened. Socorro had a grain mill and a brewery. California mission-style homes were built among the adobe buildings of the boom town.

World War II increased activity in Socorro County, and an incident of historical importance to most New Mexicans occurred in San Antonio. Frank Chavez opened a small restaurant in his store and created the first chile hamburger at the Owl Bar and Café. Word-of-mouth says these are the best hamburgers in New Mexico, and knowledgeable travelers on Interstate 25 adjust their schedules in order to reach San Antonio and the restaurant at lunch time.

Another event during World War II – momentous to the entire world – was the first atomic blast, in 1945 at the Trinity Site east of Socorro. A large piece of steel from the experiment rests in the downtown plaza of Socorro. The site is now a monument, open for public tours twice a year.

The acclaim accorded to New Mexico Tech for its advances in mining, engineering, geology and other sciences has drawn major research facilities to the area. In addition to serving as the headquarters for the National Radio Astronomy Observatory's Very Large Array, the campus provides a home for the lightning research facility of Langmuir Lab. Tech's golf course is on the list of ten best public courses in New Mexico.

VAL VERDE HOTEL
Socorro, New Mexico

Built in 1915, the Val Verde is not as large as other hostelries in New Mexico, but from a stand point of beauty and convenience, she stands without a peer. It contains sixty guest rooms, a commodious dining room, a kitchen, a spacious lobby and writing rooms. With the exception of a few "grander" suites, the rooms share two common bathrooms located on the second floor. Each room is equipped with its own shower.

In present times the rooms are rented out as apartments, with two of the old rooms composing one apartment. The kitchen and dining room were converted to a restaurant while the old lobby is now a bar. Inside the building, one stair case leads to the upper floor. This door is locked so access to the second floor is by two fire escapes located at the rear of the building. These are also the stairs that the tenants use for access to their apartments.

THE GHOSTS

Figure 22: The front of the Valverde Hotel.

A great deal of activity takes place in the stairs leading to the second floor. Randomly flashing lights and small orbs (called globules) can be seen whisking about with Infrared cameras. The activity only seems to take place when a live band is playing, and even then only if it is "earth based" music with such instruments as violins and harmonicas. Perhaps sound vibrations somehow summons the spirits from where they normally reside.

Others have said that the spirit of an unidentified woman has also been seen on the stairs and landing. Though efforts have been made to identify this unknown figure, to date no one has been able to give her a name.

During its long history, a total of 10 people have died in various locations within the hotel. Five of these deaths were thought to be suicides.

I

PART III

MILITARY GHOSTS

CHAPTER FORTY-NINE

FORT CRAIG, NEW MEXICO
Black Mesa, New Mexico

Fort Craig was one of a number of military posts built prior to the Civil

Figure 23: One of the Ruined Walls at Fort Craig.

War to protect the settlers from marauding Indians. It also came to prominence during the abortive Confederate invasion of New Mexico. When the eleven states seceded from the Union in 1861 and formed the Confederate States of America. The Confederacy was desperately short of raw materials for war production. Those materials had to be imported from abroad and often paid for in gold. Gold and seaports became very important to the South.

The Confederacy was very much aware that California and the Western part of North America held both seaports and gold, and the South wanted them. A plan was devised to allow the Confederacy to both achieve the means to purchase raw materials and also to cut the government of the United States off from its western territories. In the summer of 1861, the 2nd Texas Regiment, Mounted Rifles, led by Lt. Col. John Baylor seized control of the Mesilla Valley (near present day Las Cruces) and declared New Mexico a Confederate territory. In the winter of 1861 a Confederate brigade invaded New Mexico with the hope of fulfilling the South's ambitions in the west.

The brigade was commanded by General Henry H. Sibley, formerly of the United States Army. It was comprised of three regiments of cavalry - the 4th, 5th, and 7th Texas Mounted Volunteers - and independent battery of artillery, totaling almost 3000 men and at least 18 cannons.

Opposing the Sibley Brigade were a few companies of the 5th and 7th US Infantry, a few companies of the 2nd Cavalry, a battalion of the 3rd Cavalry, a few batteries of artillery, one company of Colorado Volunteers, several regiments of New Mexico Volunteers, and some untrained militia. The overall commander of the U.S. forces was Col. Edward Canby.

The first battle of the campaign was south of Socorro, near Ft. Craig, at Val Verde ford. The Texans drove the Federal forces from the field and captured a battery of cannons in the savage encounter that saw the only documented use of lancers in the War Between the States.

Canby retreated into Ft. Craig though, and Sibley could not get him out. The Texans lost many supply wagons to a surprise cavalry charge by the New Mexico Volunteers. Short on supplies, Sibley chose to bypass Ft. Craig and continue north toward Albuquerque.

Albuquerque was occupied on March 2, 1862 and Santa Fe five days later. The Confederates were critically short of food and other supplies, and needed the Federal stores at Ft. Union on the Santa Fe Trail north of Las Vegas. At Ft. Union there were about 1300 Federal troops, including several companies of Regulars and New Mexico Volunteers, but mainly the newly organized 1st Colorado Volunteers, known as "Pike's Peakers". The 1st Colorado had arrived at Ft. Union after a Herculean effort, including a march through a blizzard. The fort and its troops were commanded by Col. John Slough. Slough's orders from Canby were to protect Ft. Union at all costs, but not to start a major battle. Slough thought the best place from which to defend Ft. Union was on the road to Santa Fe, so he started down the road toward Glorietta Pass.

On the 26th of March, a force of about 400 Confederates under the command of Maj. Charles Pyron was scouting the western end of Glorietta Pass, called Apache Canyon. They came around a bend and ran into Slough's advanced party of about 415 men under the command of Maj. Chivington. Chivington attacked at once and drove the Confederates down the canyon in a wild running fight and captured dozens of Texans. Fearing the entire Confederate brigade was nearby he halted his men and withdrew to Kozlowski's Ranch near Pecos. Maj. Pyron fell back to "wood and water", two critical items in New Mexico during the early spring and sent for help. His courier found Lt. Col. William Scurry at Galisteo, just going into camp with two battalions of the brigade. Within minutes Scurry put his men on the road to Apache Canyon. An all night march through bitter cold brought them to Pyron's position about dawn. The Texans prepared for a Federal Assault and waited throughout the 27th.

At Kozlowski's, Slough and Chivington decided on their plan of attack. Slough would take about 2/3rd of the troops' including all the artillery, down the pass toward Santa Fe. Chivington would take his battalion of 113, guided by Lt. Col. J. Francisco Chaves of the New Mexico Volunteers over the shoulder of Glorietta Mesa and fall upon the Confederate flank. The plan was set in motion on the morning of the 28th.

Scurry had decided not to wait at Apache Canyon. He started almost all of his force, including Pyron's men, eastward through the pass. He left his supply wagons with a small guard at Johnson's Ranch at the junction of Glorietta pass and Apache Canyon. Around mid morning he hit Slough's lead elements near Pigeon's Ranch, located on the Santa Fe Trail. Scurry deployed his men in a long line and set his artillery up on a low hill. Slough did the same though his line was shorter than Scurry's since Scurry's force had over 300 men more than Slough.

Scurry's battalions attacked with great vigor but were met with equal vigor by the Coloradoans. Slough's position was not strong, but the attack was stopped long enough to give his men time to fall back to a better one. Slough tried to send men to his right around Scurry's flank but a detachment of Texans met his men head on and stopped them. Scurry kept pressure on Slough's line while organizing his own force in a three pronged assault. Late in the afternoon the Confederates attacked Slough's entire front driving in the flanks and threatening the center. The outnumbered Federal infantry held the Texans at bay long enough for the artillery to pull back to a third line. Scurry's men pursued, but were exhausted from the six hour battle. Slough soon abandoned this line leaving the Confederates in undisputed possession of the field.

While all this was going on at Pigeon's Ranch Chivington had completely missed Scurry's flank falling instead on the Confederate supply train parked at Apache Canyon. Lightly guarded the train was captured and destroyed leaving Scurry with no ammunition, food blankets, or other supplies. Chivington returned to Kozlowski's and Slough's reunited command continued in withdrawal toward Ft. Union. Unable to sustain his men in the field Scurry was forced to go back to Santa Fe where Sibley joined him.

Canby had left Ft. Craig early in April and had come north threatening Albuquerque and drawing Sibley's entire force back from Santa Fe. Canby and

Slough united their forces east of the Sandia Mountains and now outnumbered the Texans. Sibley faced with superior numbers and even more destitute than before knew that to stay and fight would mean destruction of his brigade. He decided to retreat from New Mexico. The Confederacy never again seriously threatened the far west.

The hardships endured by men on both sides in New Mexico were unbelievable. Sibley's campaign covered 2000 miles and his men originally equipped as cavalry walked more than half the route. The Colorado Volunteers on their march from Colorado City to Ft. Union set the standard for endurance by troops anywhere. Starvation, thirst, cold heat and disease killed more men on both sides than did bullets. The battles fought in and around Val Verde and Glorietta though tiny by eastern standards were as viciously and brutally contested as Gettysburg. The men who faced the bullets were as brave, hurt as badly and were as mourned as deeply as their comrades elsewhere.

THE GHOSTS

I have been to a number of old military posts in the research for my books. In each I have felt a sense of purpose as if something about those who once served this country still remained. So do does it seem that those who garrisoned Fort Craig and tried to stop the depredations of both marauding Indians as well as the Confederate forces still stand ready to defend their country and the walls of Fort Craig.

Some who have visited Fort Craig late in the evening report, as they approach, seeing figures that appear to be blue clad sentries. However, when they arrive at the site, there is no one to be seen. One individual reported that he was there about dusk and he was absolutely sure that he had heard the faint sounds of taps floating on the breeze.

Figures and glowing orbs have been sighted around the Commander's Quarters and along Officers Row. I am told that one group set up a tape recorder and recorded the sounds of a voice counting cadence as the rhythmic sounds of men marching could be heard in the background. There was also the sound of bits jingling and leather creaking.

Just as I found at Fort Bliss, Texas, apparently there are those who will not leave their posts until the great commander properly relieves them of their duty.

There have been a number of reports that gun shorts have been heard and several have been very adamant that the gunshots came from muskets. Others have reported what sounds like canon fire.

I have also read reports that some witnesses have smelled the distinctive aroma of black powder. When someone fires a black powder pistol or rifle, there is a distinctive smell that is unmistakable.

CHAPTER FIFTY

FORT UNION, NEW MEXICO
Watrous, New Mexico

The general area encompassing Fort Union National Monument has been used historically by travelers along what would become the Santa Fe Trail. They include various American Indian groups of several different tribes, Spanish explorers and settlers, New Mexicans both traveling through the area and using it for grazing for both sheep and cattle, Frenchmen seeking riches in Santa Fe and New Mexico, Americans benefiting from trade with New Mexico, an army of invasion, civilian and military personnel associated with the three Fort Unions and the Santa Fe Trail, and ranchers.

The area around Fort Union has seen a number of settlements over the centuries. The reason for the existence of Fort Union arises from the Santa Fe Trail, whose ruts radiate north and south of the Forts. Indeed the area has long been an area traversed by people. Perhaps the earliest travelers were Pueblo Indians who traveled east over the Sangre de Cristo Mountains and down along the Mora River, out to the plains to hunt buffalo and trade with the plains tribes.

A pueblo type structure has been found along the Mora River near Watrous which dates to circa 1200 indicating that at least one Indian dwelling was nearby. The Jicarilla Apache claimed the Fort Union area as their homeland from about 1525. Within fifty years after Columbus landed in the New World, Francisco Vasquez de Coronado led an expedition to the central plains of the United States. It is probable his expedition on the way out, passed within one hundred miles of Fort Union, and it is generally accepted that on his return to Mexico, he followed close to the future course of the Cimarron branch of the Santa Fe Trail, possibly passing within ten miles of the future site of the fort.

Later Spanish expeditions to the plains in 1696 (Diverges) and 1715 (Hurt ado) crossed the Sangre de Cristo Mountains from Pictures Pueblo, and headed down the Mora River out onto the plains. In 1739, the first recorded group of Frenchmen, led by Paul and Pierre Mallet encountered the people of New Mexico when they arrived at Picuris Pueblo, after a journey across the Great Plains from the present-day site of Kansas City. Their arrival at Picuris indicates a journey up the Mora River valley and over the mountains to Picuris.

William Becknell, the American entrepreneur from Franklin, Missouri, who chanced a journey into the unknown in 1821, passed close to the future site of the fort, was discovered by Captain Don Pedro Ignacio Gallegos and over 400 militia troops just south of Las Vegas and escorted into San Miguel and Santa Fe, where he was welcomed with * great joy.* Thus the American phase of the Santa Fe Trail was born. The junction of two rivers about seven miles south of the site of the fort was well known to New Mexicans and travelers on the trail. The area had been used by New Mexicans to graze cattle and sheep on the extensive grasslands during the summers. The joining of the Mora and Sapello Rivers and surrounding area became known as La Junta, or the junction. This lush area between the rivers provided both wood and grass for grazing of animals, plentiful water, and a meeting place for caravans heading east on the Trail. Perhaps because of these qualities and the surrounding terrain, it also became the juncture, heading west, of the Mountain and Cimarron branches of the Santa Fe Trail.

As trade between New Mexico and the United States matured, nationalistic tendencies of the United States became more evident. The election of President James K. Polk in 1844 assured the annexation of Texas and the Mexican War. Indeed, in May of 1846, war was declared on Mexico and Colonel, soon to be General, Stephen Watts Kearny of the First Dragoons at Fort Leavenworth, was ordered to form the Army of the West and capture New Mexico and California. In August, the Army of the West crossed Raton Pass and marched through New Mexico to the Ocate River crossing about 18 miles north of Fort Union. On the 12th, Kearny and the lead elements of the Army reached a flat table land in the valley of Wolf Creek, where they camped that night. This campsite, called Los Pozos was within a mile of where the first Fort Union would be located.

Although Kearny's occupation of Santa Fe and New Mexico was accomplished without firing a shot, New Mexicans revolted against the occupation in January of 1847, killing Governor Charles Bent and others in Taos and several American traders in Mora. One Officer wrote at the time, that the whole of Northeastern New Mexico was in revolt except for Las Vegas, only because of the military force stationed there. The New Mexican patriots were crushed by the American military forces and an uneasy peace settled over the area with American volunteer forces stationed in Taos, Las Vegas, and Santa Fe among other towns. The attention of the military was then turned to the various tribes of Indians who not only raided New Mexican settlements and their cattle and sheep herds, but also caravans on the Santa Fe Trail. Increasing pressure by westward movement of the United States, in turn, caused dislocation of tribes from their traditional homelands. Hunting grounds and food gathering activities were severely restricted and in order to survive, food was taken from any available sources. Resentment at the loss of their homelands and the long-time practice of capture of Indians for slavery, also added to the motivation of raiding. Active campaigns were conducted against the Ute, Apache, and Navajo Nations without much success. With the end of the Mexican War in 1848 and the Treaty of Guadalupe Hidalgo, New Mexico became an American territory and the Army found that maintaining soldiers in the new territory was expensive.

Fort Union was established in July, 1851, several miles north of the junction of the two main branches of the Santa Fe Trail. Several reasons are commonly given for its establishment including a desire on the part of the new district commander, Colonel Edwin V. Sumner, to remove the troops from the *morally degrading* influences of Santa Fe. The most likely reason was economics, however, and Sumner moved numerous New Mexico garrisons out of leased quarters and directed that self-sufficient operations, such as troop constructed buildings and post farms be initiated. Problems with Comanche, Ute, and Jicarilla Apache tribesmen along the southern-most reaches of the Trail constituted another reason for a post away from the Sangre de Cristos and out on the Great Plains. From such a point, troops could more readily patrol the area and react to trouble in a timelier manner than had been the case.

The one thing the Americans got with the Treaty of Guadalupe Hidalgo that they did not want was the Indian problems of the Southwest. Unfortunately as they were ill prepared to deal with the tribes either militarily or diplomatically, relations with practically every tribe in the area took a decided downhill turn. The sporadic raiding of New Mexican settlements and herds that had characterized the stormy coexistence of Mexicans and Indians prior to Anglo rule swelled to alarming proportions by 1851. Attacks on wagon trains plying the Santa Fe Trail, once considered unusual occurrences, increased as the Southern Plains Tribes grew increasingly resentful. Outrages and depredations became more frequent. Two of the more famous of these incidents took place within the immediate area of where Fort Union was to be built. The *White Massacre* of 1849 and the *Wagon Mound Massacre* of 1850 underscored the need for some sort of military presence.

From their new base of operations, troops stationed or marshaled at Fort Union spent much of the 1850s engaged in active and aggressive campaigning against the Comanche, Jicarilla Apache, Navajo, and Ute people.

But Fort Union, from the beginning, performed another function that would take on increasing importance with time. Sumner had brought with him the district's chief quartermaster and ordnance officer, and established their respective depots at Fort Union. The massive amount of supplies for the army in the Southwest came from eastern depots at Fort Leavenworth and St. Louis, were shipped across the plains on the Santa Fe Trail by contract, and off-loaded and stored at the Fort Union depot facilities. From this point requisitions for the other posts in the Territory were filled and shipped. Except for a brief period in the mid-1850s, the quartermaster and ordinance supply activities would remain at Fort Union until the railroad thrust deep into New Mexico some thirty years later.

The first Fort Union had been constructed by troop labor with indigenous materials. The results, predictably, proved to be false economy, and the extensive post began to disintegrate as soon as it was completed. Troops took to sleeping on the parade ground during fair weather. Ordnance and Quartermaster officers complained of inadequate shelter for their stores. As 1860 approached, it was clear to everyone that improvements had to be made.

The socio-economic atmosphere of the time, however, soon provided the solution to Fort Union's structural ills. Secession and Civil War reached far west. Regular officers discussed, then debated the political issues; finally breaking into rival factions. Suspicion and mistrust permeated the army, far from the momentous activities then taking place. When Southern sympathizers suggested turning Fort Union, its depot supplies, and troops over to the Confederacy, William R. Shoemaker, Ordnance Depot commander, entrenched his storehouses and prepared charges to blow everything into oblivion, issuing an invitation to the would-be rebels to try something.

When war finally broke out in April, 1861, New Mexico provided no safe haven for the rebels. Though numerous officers resigned their commissions to head south, Fort Union and the rest of the Territory remained in Union hands. By late 1861, however, a brigade of Texas Confederates was preparing the southwest expansion of the rebel nation. Their plans included the occupation of the Colorado gold fields and, possibly, expansion to the west coast.

In preparation for a conventional conflict, Fort Union's location, not just the condition of its buildings, became instantly obsolete. If enemy artillery could have been placed on the commanding edge of the mesa just west of the post, even the most inadequate gunners would have had a field day. The Fort Union garrison prepared to move about one mile to the east, across Wolf Creek, to a position less vulnerable to rebel artillery.

New Mexico responded well to Lincoln's call for volunteer troops. During the war years, some 3,500 New Mexicans, mostly Hispanic, served in several regiments of infantry and cavalry raised for Federal service. Fort Union acted as a recruit depot and training camp for many of these troops. Native New Mexicans had always been a common sight around Fort Union, but it was at this point they assumed a major role. Despite extreme ethnic and racial prejudice against them, they formed a major part of the Southwest defense operation, enjoying a number of significant military successes. One of their accomplishments was the hurried construction of the second Fort Union.

To defend against a conventional foe, the second fort better fit the dictionary definition of the word. Rather than the typical frontier fort that consisted of structures distributed around a parade ground, the second fort incorporated earthen walls, gun positions, infantry positions, and bunker like quarters and storehouses. Built for a force of 600 troops, it was deemed sufficient to stop anything the rebels could throw at it. Its frenzied construction, obviously, was done under conditions rife with suspense and anxiety. The work force consisted largely of New Mexico volunteer troops who worked round the clock in four-hour shifts. By the time the Rebels began advancing up the Rio Grande in January of 1862, the second fort earthwork was largely ready.

Colonel E.R.S. Canby, commanding Federal forces in New Mexico, gathered a force of about 3,800 men from the few regular troops remaining in the territory and the New Mexico Volunteer regiments. Defeated at Valverde in February, 1862, Canby pulled his force into Fort Craig while the Rebels sidestepped him and continued their drive north. Albuquerque and Santa Fe fell quickly, the Federal forces and even the Territorial Capital retreating to Fort Union.

The defensive earthwork fort was never used for its anticipated purpose. In March, 1862, a force made up of a regiment of Colorado troops, U.S. Regular infantry and cavalry, departed Fort Union with the intention of meeting the Rebels nearer Santa Fe. A two-day engagement in and around Glorietta Pass resulted in the destruction of the Confederate supply train and forced their abandonment of the campaign. By summer, 1862, Civil War action in New Mexico was over.

Military activity in the Southwest, however, was not over. Almost concurrent with the Rebel defeat came Indian warfare of unprecedented proportions. To the south Apache bands attempted to halt travel on stage and mail routes. To the west, the Navajos aggressively struck at outsider intrusions. And to the north and east the Comanches, Kiowas, and Southern Cheyenne all but halted travel on the Cimarron Route. Military escort or trains consisting of 100 armed men were considered requisites for making the trip, and, for a brief period, regular escort service was instituted by cooperating units from Fort Union and Fort Larned, Kansas. Military activity and military supply grew, and the Fort Union Depot began its zenith years. The earthwork, with its damp subterranean quarters, proved no better than the first fort. Many troops encamped under canvas outside the earthwork. Several structures were also constructed in the immediate area, and some of the buildings at the original post remained in use. Fort Union's importance within the district called for facilities of a more permanent nature and, in 1863, work began on the design and construction of the third, largest, and final facility. Three separate areas were planned: the garrison of Fort Union, the Fort Union Quartermaster's Depot, and the Fort Union Arsenal. Work began first on the depot as hundreds of civilian laborers descended on the site to quarry stone, haul and cut lumber, and make untold numbers of adobe bricks. Not until 1867 was the last building completed in this massive complex, at a cost of over $1,000,000.

During the construction period the various functions at Fort Union operated at unprecedented levels of activity from makeshift facilities. In 1864 the Southern Plains exploded in savage warfare that continued without let-up until 1869. Major campaigns were mounted by district commander Brigadier General James Carleton and Colonel Christopher (Kit) Carson against the Navajo nation to the west and the Comanche/Kiowa coalition to the east. Carson's 1st New Mexico Cavalry, along with California volunteers then stationed in the territory, fought a pitched battle at Adobe Walls in the Texas panhandle, marched the defeated Navahos to Bosque Redondo, and established Camp Nichols on the Cimarron Cutoff, halfway between Forts Union and Larned. The massacre of the Cheyenne winter camp at Sand Creek, Colorado by Glorietta Pass hero John M. Chivington in November, 1864, only served to intensify the resolve of the Plains tribes.

In the midst of all of this the Confederacy crumbled and the huge Federal armies began the mustering out process. The remaining 50,000 man Regular Army responded to Congressional priorities and was doled out to reconstruction duty in the South. Not until 1866 did regular troops return to duty in the Southwest. The arrival of the 3rd Cavalry, 37th Infantry, and 57th U.S. Colored Troops in New Mexico in mid 1866 finally permitted the discharge of the New Mexico troops. The regulars picked up where the volunteers left off, and Fort Union's role as a staging and supply area for campaigning troops continued. Fort Union based units participated in the 1868 winter campaign, attacking a Comanche village at Soldier Spring in present western Oklahoma on Christmas Day. Overshadowed by the better known Washita battle of George A. Custer's 7th Cavalry a month before, Soldier Spring ended the five-year battle for control of the Southern Plains and forced the tribes onto reservations.

The "peace" that followed was a temporary situation. By the early 1870s the Comanches and Kiowas longed for the old life and began to roam. The inevitable clashes, killings, and raiding occurred, and the army was directed to solve the problem. A five pronged campaign was organized to enter the Llano Estacado, the Staked Plains area of the Texas Panhandle, the favorite haunt of the warring bands. One of these columns originated at Fort Union and consisted of three companies of the 8th Cavalry, commanded by Major William R. Price. Having departed Fort Union in August, 1874, the column campaigned into the early months of 1875 before the troops finally returned. The Southern Plains was finally considered free of *Indian threat,* and Fort Union settled into a period of reservation watching its troops held in readiness for future troubles. Not until 1879 did the area witness its final clash with Native Americans.

In 1876 Apache raiding in southern New Mexico and Arizona intensified. The 9th Cavalry moved from Texas to New Mexico, and several companies of the regiment were stationed at Fort Union. The 9th was one of four army regiments (the others being the 10th Cavalry and the 24th and 25th Infantries) made up entirely of black enlisted men. In response to the frequent Apache flare-ups, the Fort Union based companies moved in and out of the post.

The Victorio War of 1880 ended with Victorio's death and the companies of the 9th at Fort Union were re-stationed at New Mexico posts in the immediate vicinity of the Apache reservations. Troopers of the 9th Cavalry won nine medals of Honor for gallantry in New Mexico engagements. When not campaigning against Apaches, these black soldiers often found themselves involved in quelling the civil disturbances and violence of the *Colfax County War* that raged just north of Fort Union during those turbulent late 1870s.

Though Fort Union saw its share of excitement during this period, the principal activity continued to be the operation of the Quartermaster's Depot. By the mid-1860s as many as three thousand wagon loads of military supplies arrived annually over the Santa Fe Trail, to be stored and redistributed. The Fort Union Depot serviced all the garrisons in New Mexico as well as several as far away as Colorado and Arizona.

To receipt, inventory, unload, stock, care for, recrate, invoice, and ship the enormous amount of quartermaster, subsistence, and ordnance stores that passed through the depot took a very large staff. Three sets of offices processed a blizzard of bills of lading, receipts, vouchers, requisitions, abstracts, and other paperwork. Laborers packed and unpacked arriving and departing wagon trains. Transportation officers supervised wagon parks, mule corrals, and up to 200 wagon masters and teamsters. Blacksmiths, wheelwrights, farriers, painters, tinsmiths, carpenters, and plasterers kept buildings, wagons, and draught animals in repair.

The vast majority of depot personnel were civilians, many of them local Hispanics who found government employment advantageous. The depot and the army logistic system in the Southwest, in fact, had a dramatic impact on the New Mexico economy in both direct and indirect ways. Where possible, quartermaster and subsistence needs were procured by local contract. Forage for animals, beef cattle, heating fuel, flour, lumber, and vegetables were all procured locally, providing federal dollars for everyone from the small grower to the large contractor. Government trains and troops stopped at dozens of contractor run forage agencies along main travel routes for meals and rest.

Though not the stuff of Hollywood westerns, the day-in-day-out operation of supplying the military had a far greater impact on the territory than any Indian battle. Even the Wheeler Expedition, one of the Great Surveys of the 1860s and 70s, was supplied from Fort Union Depot while it worked the surrounding area. The Santa Fe Trail, of course, was one of the main reasons for Fort Union's existence. Though some users traveled the Mountain route during its early years, the main route was always the shorter Cimarron route, from the Trail's acknowledged start in 1821 up into the 1860s. The Cimarron route passed the site of Fort Union only five miles to the east, converging with the Mountain Branch in the Mora Valley at La Junta de los Rios Sapello y Mora (present day

Watrous), with cutoffs to Fort Union both north and south of the Turkey Mountains. Here Samuel B. Watrous arrived in 1849 and established a store and trading post little more than a mile from the competing operation of Alexander Barclay. This area witnessed the passage of practically all Santa Fe Trail traffic, both east and west bound, up to Fort Union's establishment in 1851. It served as a campground and gathering point for east-bound trains as it was one of the last areas that offered wood, water, and grass in abundance before crossing the dry Cimarron route.

The nature of the Santa Fe Trail began to change again about 1865. Several factors caused the shift. First among these was the Southern Plains war that swept the area and threatened to halt traffic on the Cimarron Cutoff, a situation that greatly discouraged travel on that route. Secondly were the improvements made to the road through Raton Pass by Richard L. Wooton, which removed the Mountain Branch's most objectionable feature. And third was the post-Civil War railroad construction frenzy that ultimately replaced the Santa Fe Trail. All of these factors combined to almost eliminate the Cimarron route from use by 1869.

The Kansas Pacific Railroad built rapidly west, reaching Hays, Kansas by 1867. Each rail laid marked a new eastern terminus for wagon traffic. By 1869, Kit Carson, Colorado, was the point at which rail freight was loaded into wagons for the remainder of the trip to New Mexico. From Kit Carson the wagons headed southwest over the eastern Colorado plains, in the process blazing a new branch of the Santa Fe Trail. The Atchison, Topeka and Santa Fe Railroad entered Colorado in 1873, and the railhead towns of Granada and West Las Animas became the shipping points, and the wagons still struck south on what was known as the Fort Union þ Granada Road. This route, generally ignored by Trail historians, was the Santa Fe Trail for a number of years, carrying massive amounts of freight, both civilian and military.

The railhead shipping points also spelled the end for the overland freight firms. The reduced distances into New Mexico no longer produced a profit. In their stead came *forwarding and commission houses,* an operation that resembled what would happen today if UPS branched off into the hardware and grocery wholesale business. Many such firms appeared, setting up their mobile warehouses wherever the end-of-track happened to be. Chick, Browne & Company and Otero, Sellars, & Company were the giants among them. With regard to military shipments, the Quartermaster's Department continued to contract the shipping out to civilians. The contractors then subcontracted with the forwarding and commission houses, who, in turn, further hired out the actual transportation, first to the railroad and then to small freighters and even individuals. Far and away the majority of the teamsters and freighters were Hispanic New Mexicans, who had always been heavily represented on the Santa Fe Trail, but, for its final decade, had nearly total domination of the Trails actual operation.

The proximity of the rails after 1873 also caused a decline in the magnitude of the Fort Union Depot operation. The army found it cheaper and less complicated to send supplies directly from the railhead to the posts for which they were bound. The transportation contract for the 1876-77 Fiscal Year reverted to routing all military shipments through the Fort Union Depot, but this proved to be the last gasp of glory for the operation. Use of the depot dropped dramatically thereafter.

From West Las Animas, Colorado the railhead moved to La Junta and Pueblo in 1876 and El Moro (near Trinidad) in 1877. The Mountain route then carried virtually all wagon traffic to and from the railroad. Though the eastern-most seven hundred miles of the Santa Fe Trail lay abandoned across Missouri, Kansas, and parts of Colorado and New Mexico, the two hundred mile stretch still in use was as active as ever. Rushing the railroad over Raton Pass prolonged the Trail's life, but when the rails reached the New Mexico plains at Raton in 1879, the end came rapidly. On July 4th, the first regularly scheduled passenger train steamed into Las Vegas, and in February, 1880 reached Lamy, near Santa Fe. The Santa Fe Trail was no more.

Slowly the Fort Union depot operation was dismantled, and in 1883 ceased operations altogether, along with the Arsenal. The garrison at Fort Union stood alone. The post spread its elbows and assimilated the former depot structures.

Virtually every historian has dated Fort Union's death warrant as 1879, the year the railroad passed by at Watrous, yet the post remained active for an additional eleven years. What happened during that voided decade that contains 25% of Fort Union's history? One of the current museum exhibits claims the post was "reduced to caretaker status." The official National Park Service handbook marks the era with the brief statement "Fort Union had outlived its usefulness." In actuality, Fort Union remained active until 1891 because it had not "outlived its usefulness." To be sure, the strategic and logistical considerations that had thrust importance upon it were gone. Indian raiding was a thing of the past on the Great Plains. Wagons no longer plied the old overland routes. What Fort Union did offer, however, was an established point near the railroad at which to house and garrison troops. With the complete implementation of the reservation system, the army's frontier mission became one of *watch and wait,* maintaining troops in the region in anticipation of just the sort of outbreaks that occurred in southwestern New Mexico and Arizona in the mid-1880s. The policy was only part of the reason so many posts like Fort Union survived the decade, though. Simple economics dictated that they remain in use.

The army desired the consolidation of the small, former frontier garrisons into larger ones that would be strategically positioned around the big reservations and convenient to rapid rail transportation. The dollars, however, simply weren't there. Only toward the end of the century did the army successfully obtain funding for construction of the designated permanent posts.

When that became reality posts like Fort Union had truly "outlived" their usefulness.

The sprawling physical complex at Fort Union offered housing and facilities for six full companies. Though most of 1881 saw one lone company of the 15th Infantry as the entire garrison, the arrival of the field staff, band, and four companies of the 23rd Infantry in October swelled the complement to over 200 troops. By 1886 five companies of the 10th Infantry and one of the 6th Cavalry brought the military population to over 300, and qualified Fort Union again as one of the larger posts in the trans-Mississippi west. Not until 1888 did the strength begin to shrink. When notified of abandonment plans late in 1890, Fort Union still maintained three companies, and all three would probably have marched away together but for the hurried departure of Troop G, 6th Cavalry on December 1st, 1890, to the Pine Ridge country of South Dakota, there to participate in the final drama of the Sioux ghost dance crisis.

The 1880s gave the army a chance to pause and implement some badly needed reforms. Schools of instruction for the professional development of officers and sergeants were begun. Individual marksmanship became something of a craze. Practice marches and tactical exercises were initiated. Such activities were common sights at Fort Union throughout the 1880s. The post also served as something of a holding area for a large number of Apaches thought to be of the hard-core brand. Under the direct observation of the military, they camped in the Wolf Creek Valley below the post, lending color, if not a sense of purpose, at a time when Indian wars were still considered a distinct possibility. These Indians would travel with Companies C & H, 10th Infantry, when they departed Fort Union forever in February, 1891, for their new station at Fort Wingate.

Just 2 1/2 months short of forty years service, Fort Union breathed its last on May 15th, 1891, as Lieutenant John H. Schollenberger and his twenty-man detail lowered the colors for the last time and marched away.

In 1893 the former military reservation reverted to control of the legal owner, the Union Land and Grazing Company. Benjamin Butler, the owner, died that same year, passing the operation to his heirs. The company, over the years, took no particular interest in the physical remains of Fort Union, and locals stripped the structures of useable building materials. The resultant exposure of the adobe walls to the whims of Northern New Mexico weather soon had its effects. By the time the first effort was made in 1930 to provide protection for the fort little remained. The following quarter of a century saw further deterioration, much of it intentional.

Sixty-three years of neglect ended in 1954 with the establishment of Fort Union National Monument. The main 640 acre section includes the site of the Second Fort (earthworks), with perimeter ditches still visible, and over sixty-five adobe buildings of the Third Fort. An 80 acre detached section a mile to the west encompasses the site of the First Fort (including foundations) and ruins of the Arsenal.

Numerous Santa Fe Trail ruts abound throughout the Monument. In 1987 the trail received increased attention and status when Public Law 100-35 designated the Santa Fe Trail as the newest component of the National Historic Trail System.

Fort Union and the Santa Fe Trail is a story of Apaches, Comanches, Kiowas, Navajos, and Ute Indians. Spain, Mexico, and the United States. Hispanics. Indians. Blacks. Anglos. Economics. War and Peace. The Railroad. The Civil War. Politics. Women. Land grants. Land wars.

The ruins of the third Fort Union (1863-91) constitute the largest number of surviving remains. Over sixty-five structures from the post, quartermaster depot, and hospital provide the visual impact of the scene. Exposed to wind, rain, and other erosion elements, these structures have weathered to mere representations of their former stature. Except for the hospital, the most imposing structures are within the quartermaster depot where they inspire significant feelings of space, size, and architectural validity. Some of the walls rise more than 12 feet and carry original brick copings, which uniquely characterize the territorial architectural style.

Susceptible to early erosion activity, however, was the second Fort Union, an earthworks fort (1861-1862). The earthworks once consisted of partially underground, unventilated rooms of unpeeled pine logs and unsodded parapets. Heavy rains quickly turned the roofs and dirt floors to mud. The soldiers moved into tents, and the second fort eroded to its present configuration, which can be recognized as an eight-pointed star from aerial photos or aircraft.

Across the valley on the detached unit of the monument are the structures associated with the third fort's arsenal (ordnance depot) constructed between 1866 and 1882. The structures, although protected through the enabling legislation, have only limited accessibility and visitation.

Largely within the grounds of the arsenal lie the foundations and chimney ruins of first fort structures (1851-1861). Unmarked and difficult to discern, the unstabilized remains continue to erode and wear away. The foundations for the commanding officer's quarters and office, the quartermaster corrals and shops, and other structures fall outside the monument boundaries. These structures, especially the commanding officer's quarters and office, were some of the most significant structures of the first fort.

THE GHOSTS

Due to the large amount of ruins and the many centuries of occupation, it seems that Fort Union has more than its share of hauntings.

I have been told of sightings of misty figures at the Old Quartermaster's Quarters as well as the Commissary Building. Sounds of marching have been heard though no one has been seen that would account for this activity. There have also been unexplained voices heard, though it was not possible to understand exactly what was being said. I have had reports of figures being seen around the old building that contained the Post Stockade (Jail).

Witnesses have also told of seeing parties, dances, etc., going on in the recreation building after it was torn down. It frightened them and they quickly made their way back to the barracks, and usually didn't mention it until something got one of the men to talking, which led others to confess to the same experience. Reports of the ghostly parties are rare today, but there have been reports of sightings of Gen. U.S. Grant fairly often.

Reports were uniformly casual - a caretaker, visitor, whatever, asks about the tall man in the Civil War period uniform who walks from the parade ground to the hospital, walks through the door space, and simply cannot be located when followed.

The Union Land Grant and Grazing Company had charge of the Fort Union acreage for some time after the Fort was closed, as it was no longer necessary to protect travelers and act as a supply depot for other forts in the state. Captain E.B. Wheeler was agent in charge for the Cattle Company. He had earned his Captain's bars at the Fort before it closed.

Wheeler loved the old Fort site and protected the ruins as best he could. His officers were in the upstairs portion of People's Saving Bank in Las Vegas but he kept men patrolling the Fort Union acreage. His men had told him about the heavily bearded man walking to the old hospital but he dismissed the story as inconsequential until he saw him himself. "It can't be, of course, but it was General (later President) Grant so I just don't talk about it. People would say I was getting senile," he told me.

CHAPTER FIFTY-ONE

FORT BAYARD
Silver City, New Mexico

The military post that has become the Fort Bayard Medical Center has been around since the 1800's. It was originally a cavalry outpost where the Buffalo Soldiers (first African American soldiers in the U.S. cavalry) were first introduced in New Mexico.

After military use, a medical center was constructed on the old post and used as a TB center. It is now a long term care facility, and veteran's hospital. Fort Bayard Medical Center is licensed and certified as a 250 bed Long Term Care Nursing Facility, including an Adult Day Health Care program.

Yucca Lodge, a Chemical Dependency Treatment Center is also located on the Fort Bayard campus. Services include in-patient and out-patient programs.

Additional in-house services include Nursing and Medical care, Social Services, Recreational Activities, Pharmacy, Dental, Laboratory and Radiology services, Physical, Occupational and Speech Therapy and an Adult Wellness program. The Medical Center also provides Case Management Services to eligible elderly and physically handicapped individuals living in their own homes through the Community Coordinated In-Home Care Waiver Program.

Fort Bayard is now owned and managed by the State of New Mexico, Department of Health. The Fort Bayard Medical Center is located in a captivating region of southwestern New Mexico where culture, history and climate coalesce. Near alpine forests and high desert plains, the climate is mild and dry. Near the rugged wilderness of the Gila National Forest, the Center has a beautiful campus of old military buildings that harks back to the early days of the last century. Within a few minutes' drive of Silver City, the Center is a historic jewel containing over 400 acres of unspoiled beauty.

THE GHOSTS

In the basement (where the dungeon for the original base was) there have been sighting of wheelchairs rolling down the hall, door opening and closing, sounds of shackles and chains, moaning, crying, conversations, laughing, voices, people touching your shoulder, and apparition sightings, throughout the whole hospital on all 6 floors, esp. 2 west.

In the housing area there are reports of hauntings, footsteps, late at night when everyone is asleep, apparitions, knocking on the doors and no one there, covers being torn off you.

CHAPTER FIFTY-TWO

GLORIETTA BATTLEFIELD
Glorietta, New Mexico

The trans-Mississippi West, New Mexico Territory in particular, was far removed from many of the passions and issues that defined the Civil War for people east of the Mississippi River. For large areas of the West that were recently won from Mexico or still organized under territorial government--where people were still struggling to survive in hostile environments--arguments over secession and states rights may have seemed rarified. Nonetheless, men answered the call to join eastern armies, so the frontier armies were drastically reduced. Indian raids began to increase as some tribes seized the chance to regain lost territory while others turned to raiding for subsistence, their U.S. treaty allotments having been disrupted by the war. Yet, the Civil War was not strictly an eastern war, and in 1862 Confederate forces invaded New Mexico Territory.

Henry Sibley, who resigned his commission in the U.S. Army to join the Confederate Army, realized that the void created in the West could be an opportunity for the South. After raising a brigade of mounted Texas riflemen during the summer of 1861, Sibley led his 2,500 men to Fort Bliss and launched a winter invasion up the Rio Grande Valley.

Colonel Edward Canby, who had been appointed the Union Commander of the Department of New Mexico in June 1861, anticipated the invasion and had already begun to consolidate his 2,500 regular army troops. By early 1862, Canby had almost 4,000 soldiers he could put into the field.

Sibley's Brigade approached Canby's Union forces near Fort Craig in south-central New Mexico. Threatening to cut off the fort by controlling a nearby ford, Sibley drew Canby's soldiers out from the fort and engaged them in a closely contested battle at Valverde on February 21, 1862. The smaller Confederate force prevailed against Canby's troops, who retreated to the security of nearby Fort Craig.

Sibley believed the U.S. forces had been defeated too soundly to present a rear-guard threat, so he advanced north. The Confederates occupied Albuquerque on March 2. Sibley then sent the Fifth Texas Regiment, commanded by Major Charles Pyron, to the unprotected territorial capital of Santa Fe. The few Union troops retreated to Fort Union, destroying ammunition and supplies.

The only thing that appeared to be standing between Sibley's Confederate Brigade and Colorado was Fort Union, the major army depot on the Santa Fe Trail. By seizing the supplies and weapons kept at Fort Union, the Confederates would be able to continue their march north through Raton Pass to Denver, the territorial capital of Colorado.

The First Colorado Volunteers, an infantry brigade of 950 miners, were quickly organized under the command of Colonel John P. Slough. They marched the 400 miles from Denver through the deep snow of Raton Pass to Fort Union in only 13 days, arriving at the fort on March 10. After a brief rest and re-supply, Slough defied orders to remain at Fort Union. Joined by some regular army troops and New Mexico volunteers, Slough's 1,350 soldiers departed Fort Union on March 22, and they followed the Santa Fe Trail westward to meet the enemy. By March 25, the Union advance troops, under the command of Major John M. Chivington, set up Camp Lewis at Kozlowski's Stage Stop east of Glorietta Pass, a gap in the Sangre de Cristo Mountains.

Meanwhile, Pyron's Fifth Texas Regiment had left Santa Fe, following the Santa Fe Trail eastward, marching on Fort Union. After following a southward swing through Glorietta Pass, he intended to join with other Confederate troops. Pyron's Texans camped at Johnson's Ranch in Apache Canyon, just west of Glorietta Pass, unaware of the Union troops only nine miles away.

On the morning of March 26, 1862, a scouting party of Colorado Volunteers led by Chivington left Camp Lewis to locate the Texans. They discovered and captured a Confederate scouting party in Glorietta Pass, then ran into the main body of the Confederate force in Apache Canyon, about 16 miles east of Santa Fe. A two-hour scrimmage, known as the Battle of Apache Canyon, ensued. Although Chivington captured 70 Confederate soldiers, he fell back to Pigeon's Ranch. By evening, both sides called a truce to tend to their wounded.

The following day, when Union spies notified Colonel Slough that the Confederates had been reinforced, Slough decided to divide his forces. Slough's 900 soldiers would proceed west along the Santa Fe Trail and block Glorietta Pass, while Chivington and Lieutenant Colonel Manuel Chavez of the New Mexico Volunteers would take 450 men over Glorietta Mesa to attack the Confederate right flank or rearguard. Colonel Scurry decided to leave his supply train at Johnson's Ranch and march his 900 men eastward along the Santa Fe Trail the next morning to force the battle where he wanted it.

On the morning of March 28, Slough's men broke ranks near Pigeon's Ranch to fill their canteens at Glorietta Creek. Scurry's quickly advancing Confederates came upon the Union troops and opened fire on them. The Union soldiers quickly formed a defensive line along Windmill Hill, but an hour later, fell back to Pigeon's Ranch.

Scurry's Confederate soldiers faced the Union artillery at Pigeon's Ranch and Artillery Hill for three hours, and finally outflanked the Union right. From Sharpshooter's Ridge they could fire down on the Union troops, so Slough ordered another retreat, setting up a third battle line a short distance east of Pigeon's Ranch. The Texans charged the line shortly before sunset. Slough ordered his soldiers back to Camp Lewis leaving the Confederates in possession of the field. Both sides were exhausted after six hours of fighting, each having sustained more than 30 killed and 80 wounded or missing.

Believing he had won the battle, Scurry soon received devastating news. After a 16-mile march through the mountains, the Union force led by Major Chivington had come upon the Confederate supply train at Johnson's Ranch. They had driven off the few guards, slaughtered 30 horses and mules, spiked an artillery piece, taken 17 prisoners, and burned 80 wagons containing ammunition, food, clothing, and forage. Scurry was forced to ask for a cease-fire.

Lacking vital supplies, Scurry could no longer continue his march on Fort Union so he retreated to Santa Fe. Two weeks later, General Sibley ordered his army to retreat from Santa Fe and relinquished control of Albuquerque. There was no further Confederate attempt to invade the western territories. The Battle of Glorietta Pass had decided conclusively that the West would remain with the Union.

THE GHOSTS

There have been reports o shots echoing in the clear desert air as well as clouds of dust as if an army was advancing through the area. Others report seeing figures carrying old style weapons standing what appear to be guard mount.

CHAPTER FIFTY-THREE

FORT STANTON, NEW MEXICO
Ft. Stanton, New Mexico

Fort Stanton is another military post in New Mexico that has a long and eventful history. In 1855, Hispanic settlers entered the sheltered valley that lies in the shadow of Sierra Blanca. Little did they know that the dreaded Mescalero Apache lived in the area. The settlers built small villages called Las Placitas complete with tall round towers where the villagers could gather in to fight and hide from the Apache.

Soon Anglos began coming into the area with their cattle after finding that there was good grazing and abundant water in the Rio Bonita Valley. Behind them came the miners looking for the yellow metal.

Wanting to stop this flood of invaders, Apache raids became more aggressive and as a result, plans were made to build a fort. The fort would be built on the order of the western forts without a stockade and around a quadrangle. Nestled in the foothills of the Sacramento Mountains, the Rio Bonita River provided water for the fort and the horses accompanying it while the area had accessible roads, abundant grazing for the animals, wood and building timber.

Forts of this type became small communities and provided more than just protection to the surrounding villages and ranches. They also provided markets for farm produce, crops, cattle and medical facilities, jails and much of the social life of the area.

Fort Stanton was established on March 19, 1855 by Col. John Garland, 8th U.S. Infantry. It was named after Capt. Henry W. Stanton, 1st U.S. Dragoons who lost his life near the post in a battle against the Apache.

On August 2, 1861 after learning of the fall of Fort Fillmore and the surrender of Major Issac Lynde, Brevet Lieutenant Colonel Benjamin S. Roberts ordered the abandonment of Fort Stanton. Officers all over New Mexico were resigning their posts and their commissions in order to serve with the Confederacy. Roberts set fire to the fort and ordered that all supplies that could not be moved be destroyed. Unfortunately for LTC Roberts' plans, a strong summer rainstorm put out the fires and the Confederates marched into a fort with a good share of its commissary and quartermaster stores intact. They also recovered a working battery.

In fact, the Confederates recovered so much in the way of supplies that they were forced to bring a train from Fort Bliss to carry off the bulk of the supplies to be used by BG Sibley's force. During the months of August and September, 1861, the Confederacy maintained Fort Stanton, with an eye toward permanently garrisoning the post. However, in early September Apache raids began again and after losing three out of four men detailed to watch the roads the Confederates abandoned the fort and returned to the Mesilla Valley.

Following the abandonment of Fort Stanton by the Confederacy it was again reclaimed by the Union. Under the legendary Gen. Kit Carson, five companies of New Mexico Volunteers took possession of the fort. Gen. Carson was well known to New Mexicans as a mountain man, guide and Indian Agent. While he found Ft. Stanton in a state of near collapse with only the stone walls still standing, he did a quick fix and again

Fort Stanton was operational to continue defense of the surrounding ranches, towns and settlers against the raiding Apache. Carson had orders to exterminate all warriors and hold the women and children captive. He did not believe in the extremity of this order and tried a more humane approach. Eventually the Mescalero were subdued and approximately 500 chose to surrender to Carson at Fort Stanton.

In 1865, the Mescalero Apache fed up with broken promises, a lack of understanding and Indian Agents who were bent on profit instead of care left the reservation and once again Fort Stanton was on the alert. In October, 1865 Brevet Lieutenant Colonel Emil Fritz, Company B, First Cavalry, California Volunteers took over as post commandant. He served until March, 1866 when he turned over command to Brevet Major Lawrence G. Murphy, Company C, First New Mexico Calvary. After mustering out in the fall of 1866 Fritz and Murphy formed a partnership and became post sutlers.

In 1869 Lincoln County was formed with Las Placitas becoming the county seat. It was because of this Las Placitas changed its' name to Lincoln to honor the late President. J.J. Dolan was mustered out of the army at Ft. Stanton and went to work for L.G. Murphy. Rebuilding work at Fort Stanton was suspended with only the guardhouse being completed. September the 6th saw the first full election in Lincoln County. William Brady a past commander at Fort Stanton and a good friend of L. G. Murphy's was elected sheriff. In November the Apache again began raiding running off 115 head of cattle from the ranch of Robert Casey. Lts. Cushing and Yeager leave the fort with 32 Buffalo Soldiers and attack an Indian "rancheria" in the Guadalupe Mountains recovering most of Casey's stock. In December Cushing and Yeager again lead a force of 35 buffalo soldiers and 28 civilians against the Apache in the Guadalupe Mountains.

In 1878, during the infamous siege at the McSween House when the Regulators and the Dolan (old Murphy faction) came head to head, the tide of battle was said to have been turned with the entrance of Col. Nathan A. Dudley, a column of troops, a gattling gun and a mountain howitzer. The army at Fort Stanton had orders not to interfere in civilian matters but Dudley took it upon himself to override the order for the safety of the women and children in Lincoln. In effect he was the posse commitas for Sheriff Peppin and the Dolan faction, many of whom had served at Fort Stanton earlier in their careers.

Although Dudley said he was there for the protection of women and children he refused protection to Susan McSween, Elizabeth Shields and her children since they chose to stay in the house with Alexander McSween, Susan's husband and the regulators. Warrants were out for the arrest of McSween and some of the regulators, one of which was William Bonney, alias Billy the Kid. In effect, the regulators held warrants for the arrest of members of the Dolan faction. Susan McSween saw her husband killed and her home burned to the ground while the military looked on. She would later file charges against Col. Dudley that resulted in a court martial hearing. Dudley was found not guilty of any charges including arson but remained a controversial character in Lincoln County history.

During the turbulent 1880s, the famed Buffalo soldiers from Fort Stanton were again called upon to stand duty in the continued Apache raiding. Literally running the Apache to ground they were successful in bringing in the remains of Victorio's band and Geronimo's. Governor Lew Wallace visited at Fort Stanton to take advantage of the peace of the valley while writing his epic Ben Hur. Billy the Kid was brought to the fort to await his hanging but using a trick he had applied before, he escaped by climbing the chimney.

In August of 1887 John J. Pershing arrived at Fort Stanton to begin his first of two tours of duty. Pershing was so impressed with the performance of the Buffalo Soldiers he earned himself the nickname of "Black Jack." While he was at Fort Stanton he had the distinction of participating in a new War Department program called "War Games". Pershing's troops were the "pursuers". Black Jack Pershing would go on to distinguish himself as the commander of the American Expeditionary Force in WWI.

With the ending of the Indian Wars, Fort Stanton was no longer a major player on the frontier. By 1893 the occupancy of the fort was down to fifteen. In August 1896 the fort was officially decommissioned.

On April 27, 1899, Fort Stanton entered a new phrase of operation. Taken over by the United States Public Health Office, it became a hospital for tubercular patients. It was a made to order sanatorium with a constant water supply, peaceful environment and temperate climate. Dr. Francis Creeson, medical officer in command at Fort Stanton in 1900, stated it thus: "This vast and salubrious stretch of country, which is sometimes sneeringly alluded to as 'a land of sand, sagebrush and cacti,' possesses in an almost illimitable degree those very elements which observation and experience have proven to be of the utmost value in the treatment of tuberculosis." (Gomey 1969: 56-58). In April 1899 when Fort Stanton was transferred to the Public Health Service, it had a total of 38 buildings. These were in various states of repair. It took approximately six months to get the fort hospital ready.

During 1900 and 1902, with the patient load increasing every advantage was taken to make the fort a self-sufficient operation. During this time an ice and cold storage plant were installed. This was followed by a laundry, patient wards and electric power plant and new office buildings. The establishment of a dairy farm, truck farm and the addition of poultry made the fort not only self-sustaining but allowed therapy for some of the patients. The regimen for tubercular patients was very specific: fresh air, good diet, and rest. A set of rules was given to each patient and he could only be considered for a "tent house" after he had passed a test on the rules. "Tent houses" were a coveted privilege over living in the wards.

Given the nature of sailors, the rules also warned against liquor, cigarettes, and card games. A patient could be dismissed for use of alcohol and card playing was not permitted if a patient was running a fever. However, because of the number of patients treated at this facility and the need to feed them Fort Stanton still played a major role in the economy of Lincoln County. Working at the hospital was considered a "plum" job. Room and board was furnished. Pay was a dollar a day but you had commissary privileges, free wood and electricity and two Sundays off a month. Fort Stanton also continued to play its part in the social life of Lincoln County. Patients held, paid for and sometimes participated in an annual rodeo. As the fort had a theater it provided entertainment for patients and staff.

In 1939, Captain Wilhelm Daehne the commander of the German luxury liner, the Columbus, scuttled her off the coast of Cuba rather than have her captured by British warships. Captain Daehne after investigating a number of different sites settled on Fort Stanton as an internment site. As we were not at war with Germany at the time the sailors were considered "distressed seaman.

In the spring of 1941 Captain Daehne and 410 German sailors occupied a former CCC Camp across from Ft. Stanton. They promptly began to convert it into a quality resort for POW's. They furnished themselves with a recreation hall complete with a basketball court, reading room, and a music room where they listened to the ship's orchestra. They also built a swimming pool. When the United States went to war with Germany a barbed wire fence was added.

The Germans established their own gardens growing corn, beans, squash, cabbage, potatoes and other vegetables which they stored, dried, or froze for later use. In 1942 a small contingent of Japanese farmers were transported here from California and interned in a separate camp. German workers were taken by truck to the gardens each morning and occasion prisoners escaped. The Border Patrol employed expert Apache trackers to search out these escapees. However, the Germans had seen a number of wild west movies and upon their capture by the Apache scouts, they pleaded not to be scalped.

In 1953 Marine hospital supervision was suspended with the availability of drugs to treat tuberculosis. The hospital was transferred to the state of New Mexico for a treatment facility. The curiosity of this transfer came with the first patients. Many were Navajos, one of the tribes the fort had originally been designed to subdue. The hospital maintained a patient load of 200 to 300 for the next ten years. This necessitated the building of a new bed wing and the establishment of occupational and rehabilitation programs. A school was added for child patients.

In 1966, following a tubercular patient decline, Fort Stanton again underwent change. This time it became a branch of the Los Lunas Hospital and Training School for the mentally handicapped.

In 1996, when Los Lunas no longer found it feasible to operate a facility the state turned the fort over to the State Corrections Facility. It was used to house minimum security prisoners until 1999. At this time part of the fort was leased to Amity, International who currently operates a rehab center on the premises.

THE GHOSTS

With a history as long and as violent as that of Fort Stanton, there should be little surprise that there are a number of spirits that seem to feel that this location is their permanent home.

INDEX

Printed in the United States
25844LVS00002B/106-111